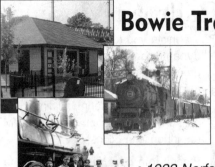

WESTERN MASS. EXCURSION TRIPS

20 mile round trips along the Housatonic River over former New York New Haven & Hartford track in the beautiful Berkshire Hills between restored stations in Lenox and Stockbridge, Massachusetts. Diesel hauled trips in former DL&W 1920s coaches. Alco and EMD power. 90 and 45 minute trips Saturdays, Sundays and holidays only, June through October. HO train layout, train, trolley and Gilded Age exhibit. For schedules and pricing see www.berkshirescenicrailroad.com Just 5 miles from MassPike Exit 2 follow US Rte. 20 west, go right on Housatonic St. (413) 637-2210
10 Willow Creek Road, Lenox, MA 01240

Berkshire Scenic Railway MUSEUM

Crossroads Huckleberry
Village & Railroad

Always Family Friendly

Railfans Weekend!

For one special weekend in August, the spotlight is on the Huckleberry Railroad and America's romance with the rails. Shop tours and special photo runs. Visitors may view model railroad displays and exhibits throughout theVillage. Spotlight on special entertainers singing songs of the rail.

North of Flint – I-475 to Saginaw Street (exit 13) – Follow the signs.

Just 15 minutes south of Frankenmuth
Order your Village & Train tickets online at
www.GeneseeCountyParks.org
or call **1.800.648.PARK (7275)**

A facility of the Genesee County Parks and Recreation Commission
6140 Bray Road, Flint, MI 48505

Genesee County Parks and Recreation Commission

Advertising Index

TOURIST TRAINS GUIDEBOOK

KALMBACH
BOOKS

Printed in Canada

11 10 09 08 07   1 2 3 4 5

Visit our Web site at
http://kalmbachbooks.com
Secure online ordering available

Publisher's Cataloging-In-Publication Data
(Prepared by The Donohue Group, Inc.)

Tourist trains guidebook / [from the publishers of *Trains* magazine].

     p. : ill. ; cm.

  "150 reviews of great train rides & museums."
  Includes index.
  ISBN: 978-0-87116-237-3

1. Railroad museums--United States--Guidebooks. 2. Railroad museums--United States--Directories. 3. Railroad museums--Canada--Guidebooks. 4. Railroad museums--Canada--Directories. I. Kalmbach Publishing Company

TF6.N75 T68 2007
625.1/0074/013

Contents

Introduction

American railroads have always been great tools for exploration. And that's no different today. Scores of scenic railroads will transport you into some of the most rugged wilderness left in North America. What's more, many museums in the United States and Canada are a great way to explore railroad history. They're all found within the pages of this guide.

Tourist Trains Guidebook is essentially a passport into the exciting world of heritage railroading, examples of which you'll find across the continent. If you want to view spectacular sights, enjoy a meal while you pass through incredible vistas, or marvel at some of the magnificent machines that made America and Canada great, we're here to point out some of the finest examples.

You'll learn where to find real operating steam locomotives from the classic era of railroading. You'll discover some trains that run literally within sight of, or right through, some of our land's greatest national parks. You'll find out about trains that will take you to see examples of wildlife close up.

But that's not all. We'll also put you in touch with the places that hold railroading's most treasured artifacts as well as some of its most common items, all preserved to keep that part of our heritage alive for future generations. You'll find out where you can step inside a genuine roundhouse, learn about narrow gauge trains that once climbed the Rockies, and discover more than one place that tells the story of man and machine vs. the mountains. Some museums even have programs that allow you to run a locomotive.

So don't sit back and relax with this guidebook. I encourage you to let it steer you to the nearest set of railroad tracks, where adventure and excitement are just around the bend.

Jim Wrinn

Jim Wrinn, Editor
Trains

Using the Guidebook

Tourist Trains Guidebook is a new publication that provides detailed information to more than 150 excursion trains and museums across the United States and Canada. It also provides concise directory listings to almost 300 additional train rides, rail museums, and historical depots. All the sites offer a unique experience while preserving a piece of railroading history, focusing primarily on standard and narrow gauge trains.

The editorial staff and contributors of *Trains* magazine reviewed the 150 top tourist train attractions. Their reviews provide a description of each site and offer choices for your visit. They give you an idea of when to go for the best experience and provide other information that is good to know about the site or the area. They point out activities that are worth doing and what you shouldn't miss to make your trip enjoyable.

Directory listings include a variety of other rail-related sites. Each listing offers a brief description of the site as well as current contact information.

We have used the most up-to-date information possible for every attraction. Due to the nature of the tourist train industry, we recommend that you contact any site before planning your visit. Steam engines may not be running, hours and prices may change, and museums may be under renovation.

You can use the enclosed discount card at more than 40 different attractions found in the book.

To make future editions of the guidebook better, we would like to hear from you. Let us know about the sites you visited, your experiences, and if our descriptions were accurate. We want the *Tourist Trains Guidebook* to help you enjoy the best railroading has to offer. Please send your comments to Tourist Trains editor, Kalmbach Books, 21027 Crossroads Circle, Waukesha, WI 53187-1612. You can also enter your comments at www.kalmbach.com/books.

ALABAMA

Calera   *Museum, Train ride*
Heart of Dixie Railroad Museum

The museum features two restored depots and displays railroad artifacts,
memorabilia, locomotives, and rolling stock. It operates a standard gauge, diesel-
powered, nine-mile excursion and a two-foot narrow gauge ride as well. The museum
is open Monday through Saturday, and trains run Saturdays from March through mid-
December.

ADDRESS: 1919 Ninth St., Calera, AL 35040
TELEPHONE: 800-943-4490 or 205-668-3435
E-MAIL: mgarner@hodrrm.org
WEB SITE: www.hodrrm.org

Foley   *Museum*
Foley Railway Museum

The Foley Railway Museum houses Louisville & Nashville Railroad artifacts, as well as
those representing the history of Foley and Baldwin County. It displays an L&N diesel
switch engine, several boxcars, and a caboose. The museum is open Monday through
Friday.

ADDRESS: 125 E. Laurel Ave., Foley, AL 36536
TELEPHONE: 251-943-1818
WEB SITE: www.cityoffoley.org/html/depot_museum.php

Fort Payne   *Museum*
Fort Payne Depot Museum

Located in northeast Alabama, the museum is a former train depot from the late 1800s and displays railroad artifacts, memorabilia, and a caboose. It also includes historical items from every war since the Civil War and 95 dioramas. The depot is open Monday, Wednesday, Friday, Saturday, and Sunday.

ADDRESS: 105 Fifth St. NE, Fort Payne, AL 35968
TELEPHONE: 256-845-5714
E-MAIL: info@fortpaynedepotmuseum.org
WEB SITE: www.fortpaynedepotmuseum.org

Huntsville   *Museum, Depot*
Huntsville Depot & Museum

Built in 1860, the depot is one of the nation's oldest remaining railroad structures and is listed on the National Register of Historic Places. You can read graffiti left by Civil War soldiers and climb aboard several steam locomotives for an up-close look. The museum is open Wednesday through Saturday March through December.

ADDRESS: 320 Church St., Huntsville, AL 35801
TELEPHONE: 256-564-8100
E-MAIL: info@earlyworks.com
WEB SITE: www.earlyworks.com

Huntsville   *Museum, Train ride*
North Alabama Railroad Museum

The museum runs a diesel-powered, 10-mile excursion on select days April through December. The museum offers guided tours on these train days. Otherwise, you can view 30 pieces of rolling stock, the restored Chase depot, and other rail exhibits on a self-guided walking tour seven days a week.

ADDRESS: 694 Chase Rd., Huntsville, AL 35815
TELEPHONE: 256-851-6276
E-MAIL: narm-mail@comcast.net
WEB SITE: www.northalabamarailroadmuseum.com

ALASKA

Fairbanks *Train ride*

Tanana Valley Railroad

The railroad operates a restored 1899 Porter 0-4-0 steam locomotive on a 36-inch narrow gauge track. The locomotive was used to bring residents and supplies to Fairbanks. Train rides take place at Pioneer Park on select weekends during summer and for special events.

ADDRESS: 2300 Airport Way, Fairbanks, AK 99708
TELEPHONE: 907-459-7421
E-MAIL: ftvrr_inc@hotmail.com
WEB SITE: www.ftvrr.org

Wasilla *Museum*

Museum of Alaska Transportation & Industry

The museum is home to the trains and other machines that helped develop the state. It features a train yard with locomotives and cars, a renovated section house, and a short train ride. The museum is open Tuesday through Sunday during the summer months.

ADDRESS: 3800 W. Neuser Dr., Wasilla, AK 99687
TELEPHONE: 907-376-1211
WEB SITE: www.museumofalaska.org

Anchorage

Alaska Railroad

Train ride

ALASKA

ADDRESS: 411 W. First Ave., Anchorage, AK 99501
TELEPHONE: 800-544-0552
E-MAIL: reservation@akrr.com
WEB SITE: www.akrr.com

Completed in 1923, the Alaska Railroad was built to link the Pacific seaport of Seward with Anchorage, Fairbanks, and the natural resource-rich interior long before there were highways. Passenger service offers breathtaking excursions into rugged back-country terrain that is often inaccessible by car.

CHOICES: The *Denali Star* operates daily between Anchorage and Fairbanks with stops at Talkeetna and Denali National Park. The train features a fascinating combination of refurbished "lower 48" heritage domes, Korean-built coaches, new Gold Star dome cars sporting open-air viewing decks, and cruise line double-decker domes. Other offerings include the *Coastal Classic* south to Seward and the *Glacier Discovery* to remote Spencer Glacier, and Whittier. The *Hurricane Turn* operates with 1950s-era Budd railcars on a four-day round-trip out of Talkeetna.

WHEN TO GO: Trains operate mid-May to mid-September when the weather is warm and the days are long. Early in the season is best when there is still snow on the mountains and little rain. The *Hurricane Turn* operates the first Thursday of every month but starts the winter trip in Anchorage. Colorful September or snowy March offer more light than the short days of December and January, yet winter's Northern Lights deliver a bonus.

GOOD TO KNOW: There are all-inclusive hotel packages to Denali, Seward, and Talkeetna from Anchorage featuring winter excursions that include Anchorage-Fairbanks airfare. With its variety of equipment and room to roam, the *Denali Star* is a better bet than the more deluxe but confined-to-one-car atmosphere of the cruise line domes.

WORTH DOING: The *Hurricane Turn* provides a welcome escape from sightseeing and tourism overload and a chance to visit with friendly Alaskans on their way to remote cabins. The town of Talkeetna is off the main road, has plenty of accommodations, and is reminiscent of the television series *Northern Exposure*.

DON'T MISS: Try either the *Coastal Classic* or *Glacier Discovery* trains. The scenery south of Anchorage is more varied and breathtaking than most of the Denali route, and the *Glacier Discovery* can be arranged to include a rafting tour along Spencer Glacier.

GETTING THERE: Alaska Airlines has the most flights to and from Anchorage, but Anchorage is also served by other carriers. Cruise ships from Vancouver and Seattle docking at Seward or Whittier are another option.

Skagway *Train ride*

White Pass & Yukon Route

ADDRESS: 231 Second Ave., Skagway, AK 99840
TELEPHONE: 800-343-7373
E-MAIL: info@whitepass.net
WEB SITE: www.wpyr.com

With the reopening for scheduled service in 2007 of the line from Bennett to Carcross, the White Pass & Yukon's 67.5 route miles make it once again the longest operating narrow gauge railroad in North America. More importantly, virtually every one of those miles is knock-out beautiful, a potpourri of lakes, rivers, and snow-capped mountains. Completed in 1900, the railroad was built to link the Yukon and other booming gold-mining districts with tidewater at Skagway.

CHOICES: There are many options for riding. The most popular is the half-day, 40-mile round trip to White Pass Summit. Other possibilities include going seven miles further to Fraser. Even better are the summer-only, all-day round trips to Bennett station at the southern tip of Lake Bennett, 41 miles from Skagway.

WHEN TO GO: The White Pass & Yukon operates from mid-May to mid-October, and any time in that window is fine for a visit – though it is likely to be bracingly chilly early and late. In compensation, there will be more snow in the mountains.

GOOD TO KNOW: The few hotels and handful of B&Bs in Skagway are best booked in advance. As you might expect of a tourist town, there's an ample variety of restaurants.

WORTH DOING: Either of the railroad's two steam locomotives, Mikado no. 73 or Consolidation no. 69, operates on summer weekends. Alternatively, the unique and colorful diesels – shovel-nose General Electric units dating from 1954 to 1966 and newer chopnose road switchers built by Alco and then MLW – handle all the other trains.

DON'T MISS: Though the entire line is spectacular, pay particular attention to the first 20 miles to White Pass Summit. Here the railroad uses grades of up to 3.9 percent to climb 2,885 feet. For the best views, grab seats on the left side of the train.

GETTING THERE: Most passengers arrive at Skagway by cruise ship, but the railroad successfully caters to independent travelers as well. They can get to Skagway from Bellingham, Wash., or Prince Rupert aboard the comfortable ferries of the Alaska Marine Highway. For motorists, Skagway is 110 miles south of the Alaska Highway, via the South Klondike Highway. A commuter airline serves Skagway directly from Juneau.

ARIZONA

Chandler

Arizona Railway Museum

Museum

The museum focuses on restoring and displaying railroad equipment and artifacts of the Southwest and has more than 30 pieces of equipment including locomotives, freight cars, and passenger cars. It is open weekends September through May, with work sessions taking place on many Saturday mornings.

ADDRESS: 330 E. Ryan Rd., Chandler, AZ 85224
TELEPHONE: 480-821-1108
WEB SITE: www.azrymuseum.org

Tucson

Sierra Madre Express

Train ride

For a different vacation, try a weeklong rail adventure to Mexico's Copper Canyon aboard classic sleepers and railcars. During the trip, the train travels through 80 tunnels, crosses nearly 40 bridges, and climbs rugged landscapes through almost every climate zone.

ADDRESS: 4415 S. Contractors Way, Tucson, AZ 85726
TELEPHONE: 800-666-0346 or 520-757-0346
E-MAIL: adventure@sierramadreexpress.com
WEB SITE: www.sierramadreexpress.com

Tucson

Southern Arizona Transportation Museum

Museum

The centerpiece of the museum is locomotive no. 1673, which was built in 1900, converted to an oil burner in 1906, and is listed on the National Register of Historic Places. You can tour the former Southern Pacific Railroad depot Tuesday through Sunday. Guided tours are available by appointment.

ADDRESS: 414 N. Toole Ave., Tucson, AZ 85701
TELEPHONE: 520-623-2223
E-MAIL: contactus@tucsonhistoricdepot.org
WEB SITE: www.tucsonhistoricdepot.org

Clarkdale *Train ride, Dinner train*

Verde Canyon Railroad

ADDRESS: 300 N. Broadway, Clarkdale, AZ 86324
TELEPHONE: 800-320-0718
E-MAIL: info@verdecanyonrr.com
WEB SITE: www.verdecanyonrr.com

On the Verde Canyon Railroad, you'll ride a former copper mining spur down a lush green valley where eagles often soar. Ride across bridges, around rock formations, and through a 680-foot tunnel.

CHOICES: The four-hour, historic route from Clarkdale to the deserted Perkinsville Ranch travels between two national forests and into Verde Canyon, which is accessible only by rail. Narration describes the history, archaeology, geology, and wildlife of the area. Open cars offer canopies to protect riders from the intense sun, and air-conditioned cars are also an option for the heat. Special events on the Verde Canyon are too numerous to mention. Among our favorites are the Grape Train Escape, a wine tasting train, and Throw Mama on the Train, a Mother's Day special.

WHEN TO GO: Trains run year-round, but summer can be exceptionally hot. In winter, you can view nesting bald eagles in their natural habitat.

GOOD TO KNOW: The railroad's pair of streamlined diesel locomotives from the 1950s features a special eagle paint scheme. Located in Clarkdale, the Verde Canyon Railroad depot opened in 1997 on the site of two previous depots.

WORTH DOING: Watch for the railroad trestle over a 175-foot-deep gorge and the Perkinsville covered bridge.

DON'T MISS: Visit the Tuzigoot National Monument, where an ancient Sinagua pueblo was built. The 42-acre site includes guided tours of the pueblo ruins and hiking trails.

GETTING THERE: The railroad is about 40 minutes from Sedona and two hours from Phoenix. From Sedona, go southwest toward Cottonwood on Hwy. 89A to Cornville Road/Mingus Avenue. Turn right on Mingus Avenue and to Main Street. Turn right and travel through Old Town Cottonwood on Historic 89A. Look for the sign and turn right on Broadway. From Phoenix, take I-17 north to Exit 287. Turn left on Hwy. 260. Then turn left at Hwy. 89A to Clarkdale/Jerome and travel through Old Town Cottonwood. Look for the sign and turn right on Broadway.

Williams

Grand Canyon Railway

Train ride

ADDRESS: 233 N. Grand Canyon Blvd., Williams, AZ 86046
TELEPHONE: 800-843-8724
E-MAIL: info@thetrain.com
WEB SITE: www.thetrain.com

This train doesn't take passengers into the canyon, or even along the rim, except for a short distance, but what it does do is provide a unique way to reach one of the great scenic wonders of North America in style. Steam- and diesel-powered trains take riders from Williams on a 65-mile journey to South Rim through high desert and pine forests to the Grand Canyon. An exceptional ride, the trip is also a great value in that it saves you time in trying to find a parking space at the ever-popular South Rim.

CHOICES: Grand Canyon offers five levels of service: coach, club, first-class, dome, and parlor. Service and attention are hallmarks of this railroad. Coach passengers won't be disappointed with the strolling musicians and complimentary soft drinks, while those in cars with higher levels of service will be pampered with extra room, private bars, and exceptional views. Ride the parlor car for the ultimate experience: the chance to stand on the back platform of your private car for the day.

WHEN TO GO: Traveling this area anytime of the year is fascinating. The only two days the railroad doesn't run are December 24 and 25. Steam trains operate Memorial Day through Labor Day and diesel-powered trains the rest of the year. The summer's heat is foiled by air-conditioned cars.

GOOD TO KNOW: You can ride from Williams, spend the night at South Rim, and return on the next day's train. Packages are available from the railroad. Also, the railroad has its own hotel, restaurant, RV park, and pet-sitting services available at Williams. Williams itself is a charming western town with plenty of shops and restaurants worth checking out. The Williams depot, built in 1908, was originally home to a Harvey Hotel and is listed on the National Register of Historic Places.

WORTH DOING: Steam locomotive no. 4960, built for the Chicago Burlington & Quincy Railroad in 1923 as a 2-8-2 or Mikado type engine, is one of the largest steam locomotives in daily use and also one of the highest mileage engines.

DON'T MISS: At South Rim, the train arrives at the old Santa Fe Railway depot. Walk up the hill to El Tovar, the historic railroad hotel, and you'll stand in awe of nature at its finest.

GETTING THERE: Williams is about 50 miles west of Flagstaff. Take I-40 to Exit 163 and follow Grand Canyon Boulevard to the depot.

ARKANSAS

Eureka Springs   *Train ride, Dinner train*

Eureka Springs & North Arkansas Railway

This railway takes you on a 4.5-mile round trip through the Ozarks, complete with narration. You can chat with the conductor and crew as the train is switched. Dinner trains offer the chance for a relaxed meal. Around the depot, you can inspect a turntable, rolling stock, and other equipment. The railway is open Tuesday through Saturday April through October.

ADDRESS: 299 N. Main St., Eureka Springs, AR 72632
TELEPHONE: 479-253-9623
E-MAIL: depot@esnarailway.com
WEB SITE: www.esnarailway.com

Fort Smith   *Museum, Trolley ride*

Fort Smith Trolley Museum

Visit this working museum and you can see restoration work in progress as well as railroad and streetcar exhibits. You can ride on no. 224, a restored Fort Smith streetcar. The museum is open weekends, and trolleys run daily May through October and on weekends the rest of the year.

ADDRESS: 100 S. Fourth St., Fort Smith, AR 72901
TELEPHONE: 479-783-0205
E-MAIL: info@fstm.org
WEB SITE: www.fstm.org

Arkansas & Missouri Railroad

ADDRESS: 306 E. Emma St., Springdale, AR 72764
TELEPHONE: 800-687-8600 or 479-750-7291
WEB SITE: www.arkansasmissouri-rr.com

From the highest point to down in the hollers, the Arkansas & Missouri operates excursion trains powered by its all-Alco roster of diesels from April to December. Rebuilt air-conditioned coaches transport riders over 100-foot trestles and through a 1,702-foot tunnel across some of the most rugged terrain between the Appalachians and the Rockies. The A&M operates 139 miles of former St. Louis San Francisco trackage from Monett, Mo., to Fort Smith, Ark., through the Boston Mountains of northwest Arkansas.

CHOICES: The longest ride is a 134-mile round trip from Springdale to Van Buren with a stop in Van Buren, where passengers can shop or dine near the 1901 Frisco depot. Another ride is a 70-mile round trip from Van Buren to Winslow with a ride through the Winslow tunnel. As an occasional special run, the Slots of Fun train takes casino goers from Springdale to Fort Smith, where they meet buses bound for the casinos in Pocola, Okla., for a few hours of gambling.

WHEN TO GO: Fall offers the best scenery and fall trips sell out quickly, but spring is also popular because everything is blooming.

GOOD TO KNOW: Fares increase for all trips during the fall foliage season and members in the A&M fan club receive a 10 percent discount. Three classes – first-class, upgraded coach, and coach – are offered on all trips, with lunch or snacks offered for first-class and upgraded coach but not coach. The A&M's oldest car starred in the film *Biloxi Blues* and was built in the late 1910s and used by the Delaware, Lackawanna & Western.

WORTH DOING: Groups can arrange a shop tour of the railroad's all-Alco fleet.

DON'T MISS: The A&M excursion fits in nicely with a trip to Branson or to the William J. Clinton Presidential Library in Little Rock. Eureka Springs offers shopping, and the nearby Buffalo and Mulberry Rivers provide camping, canoeing, and hiking opportunities. Two Civil War battlefields are also nearby.

GETTING THERE: American, Delta, Northwest and United offer flights into Northwest Arkansas Regional Airport. Travel over I-540 and I-40 gives the area quick access, making the A&M easily accessible for a day of fun.

DISCOUNT: For coach seating, buy one and get one free (excluding October).

ARKANSAS

Mammoth Spring   *Museum, Depot*
Frisco Depot Museum

This restored Victorian depot was built in 1886 and operated by the Frisco Railroad. Take a self-guided tour and hear the stories of 14 figures representing passengers, station workers, and train crew. You can also take a guided tour, view several short films, and examine a caboose. Now located in Mammoth Spring State Park, the depot is closed on Mondays.

ADDRESS: Hwys. 9 and 63, Mammoth Spring, AR 72554
TELEPHONE: 870-625-7364
E-MAIL: mammothspring@arkansas.com
WEB SITE: www.arkansasstateparks.com/mammothspring

Pine Bluff   *Museum*
Arkansas Railroad Museum

This museum, located in the former Cotton Belt locomotive shops, contains the last two Cotton Belt steam engines, several Alco diesel locomotives, and various railcars. On display are SSW 4-8-4 no. 819 and 2-6-0 no. 36. The museum is open Monday through Saturday.

ADDRESS: 1700 Port Rd., Pine Bluff, AR 71613
TELEPHONE: 870-535-8819
WEB SITE: www.geocities.com/thetropics/8199/cb819

CALIFORNIA

Barstow   *Depot*
Western America Railroad Museum

Housed in the restored Casa Del Desierto, a 1911 Harvey House, the museum features railroad art, artifacts, and memorabilia. Its outdoor displays include locomotives, rolling stock, and other equipment, highlighted by a Santa Fe 95 in classic Warbonnet scheme and a Santa Fe horse car. It is open Fridays, Saturdays, and Sundays.

ADDRESS: 685 N. First. St., Barstow, CA 92311
TELEPHONE: 760-256-9276
E-MAIL: warm95@verizon.net
WEB SITE: www.barstowrailmuseum.org

Colma   *Depot*
Colma Depot

This former Southern Pacific depot was built in 1865 and is part of the Colma Historical Association's museum, which also includes a blacksmith shop and freight shed. The second stop between San Francisco and San Jose, the depot was built to shelter passengers at Colma, where farmers and teamsters stopped on the way to San Francisco.

ADDRESS: 1500 Hillside Blvd., Colma, CA 94014
TELEPHONE: 650-757-1676
E-MAIL: colmahist@sbcglobal.net
WEB SITE: www.colmahistory.org

Eureka   *Museum*
Fort Humboldt State Historic Park

The park includes a logging museum that displays historic, steam-powered redwood-logging equipment, including two 0-4-0 locomotives and a steam donkey. On select days, the Timber Heritage Association steams up the equipment, and short train rides are provided. The park also includes a historical museum on the site where Ulysses S. Grant briefly served.

ADDRESS: 3431 Fort Ave., Eureka, CA 95502
TELEPHONE: 707-445-6567
WEB SITE: www.parks.ca.gov or www.timberheritage.org

CALIFORNIA

Bishop

Laws Railroad Museum

Museum

ADDRESS: Silver Canyon Rd., Bishop, CA 93515
TELEPHONE: 760-873-5950
E-MAIL: lawsmuseum@aol.com
WEB SITE: www.lawsmuseum.org

The 11-acre Laws Railroad Museum is home to the largest collection of equipment that operated on Southern Pacific's narrow gauge empire. At one time, the line's narrow gauge rails stretched almost 300 miles from Nevada, near Carson City, to Keeler, Calif., in the Lone Pine area of the Owens Valley. About 70 miles of track, from Keeler north to Laws, operated until 1960.

CHOICES: Museum displays include SP 4-6-0 no. 9, one of the last three steam engines to operate on the line, various freight cars, a caboose, a turntable, and the original station. By the time the railroad was abandoned, Laws, four miles east of Bishop, existed pretty much in name only with the station being the only major building still standing. The museum has built a number of structures to show what Laws looked like in its heyday. Volunteers have restored a former Death Valley Railroad gas-electric doodlebug to operating status.

WHEN TO GO: Weather permitting, the museum is open daily from March to November with all buildings open to visitors. Some buildings are closed during the winter.

GOOD TO KNOW: The nearest city with restaurants and accommodations is Bishop. If you are driving up from the south on Hwy. 395, there are numerous towns with hotels and eateries, starting with Lone Pine, Independence, and Big Pine. During the ski season, Hwy. 395 is the main route to and from the various resorts north of Bishop, so you might consider making reservations to the area well in advance.

WORTH DOING: The area from Keeler on the south to Laws on the north is littered with narrow gauge artifacts, ranging from the remains of trestles and buildings to 4-6-0 no. 18 in Independence. The former SP standard gauge Lone Pine depot is intact as a private residence. The remains of the Manzanar Relocation Center, one of the places where Japanese-Americans were interned during World War II is now part of the National Park Service and open to the public.

DON'T MISS: Owens Valley is known for the many motion pictures, mostly westerns, that have been filmed there over the years. A number of small nonrail museums dot the area.

GETTING THERE: Laws is truly in the middle of nowhere, and the trip to the museum is truly half the fun. Locate Hwy. 395 on a California map and look about halfway between Reno, Nev., and Barstow, Calif. The highway is well traveled, but consider bringing a cooler of refreshments for the long dry-spots between towns.

Buena Park

Knott's Berry Farm

Train ride

ADDRESS: 8039 Beach Blvd., Buena Park, CA 90620
TELEPHONE: 714-220-5200
WEB SITE: www.knotts.com

Knott's Berry Farm is a Southern California theme park that has morphed from its 1952 western-style operation to a world class attraction with rides and events designed for every age. Part of the theme park is the original three-foot-gauge Ghost Town & Calico Railroad.

CHOICES: The railroad is just one part of this large theme park operation that rivals any other attraction in the United States. Most trains are powered by one of two Denver & Rio Grande Western 2-8-0s, either no. 41, former Rio Grande Southern no. 41 (originally Denver & Rio Grande Western no. 409), and no. 340, also a former D&RGW of the same number. There is also a Rio Grande Southern Galloping Goose and a number of authentic narrow gauge coaches, a parlor car, and a caboose.

WHEN TO GO: Southern California is enjoyable almost any time of the year. Summers can get very hot, so a hat comes in handy.

GOOD TO KNOW: If you're bringing the family, plan to stay all day. Like other theme parks in the area – Universal Studios and Disneyland – this is a kid-friendly destination with everything you need in one giant arena to tucker out even the hardiest person by the end of the day.

WORTH DOING: Be prepared to be overwhelmed by the amount of rides and sheer number of people. The good thing for the railroad fan is that by carefully selecting your photographic spots, you can come away with images that make it look like you snapped them in Colorado 60 years ago.

DON'T MISS: Southern California abounds in attractions. Any local tourist brochure will overwhelm you with possibilities.

GETTING THERE: Buena Park is part of the greater Los Angeles area in Orange County and is near a number of local commercial airports. A vehicle is a must. Freeway exits are clearly marked.

Campo

Museum, Train ride

Pacific Southwest Railway Museum

ADDRESS: 31123-1/2 Hwy. 94, Campo, CA 91906
TELEPHONE: 619-478-9937
WEB SITE: www.psrm.org

The Pacific Southwest Railway Museum operates in two locations near San Diego. The main collection is at Campo, just north of the U.S.-Mexican border. At Campo, visitors can enjoy a number of train-riding options, including one to Tecate, Mexico. The other location is at La Mesa, about 10 miles east of downtown San Diego.

CHOICES: The museum has numerous pieces of equipment at Campo including a dozen diesel locomotives – among them, two rather rare EMD MRS-1 military road switchers – steam locomotives, freight cars, passenger cars, and cabooses. Train rides feature round-trip weekend excursions to Miller Creek or Division, and locomotive cab rides are available on either trip.

WHEN TO GO: The Campo facility is open on weekends and specific major holidays.

GOOD TO KNOW: The museum offers a variety of special events throughout the year, including some tailored to kids such as the *Pumpkin Express* and *North Pole Express*.

WORTH DOING: San Diego is a great tourist destination. Sea World is just north of the city, and the coastline is tourist friendly. Amtrak's *Pacific Surfliner* makes it easy to get up and down the coast to Los Angeles, and the city's efficient light-rail system can take you almost anywhere you wish to go.

DON'T MISS: The greater San Diego area is brimming with places to visit, including Old Town. If you have always wanted to tour a U.S. Navy aircraft carrier, the decommissioned USS *Midway* is open to the public, with many types of aircraft positioned on its flight deck.

GETTING THERE: San Diego is served by many major airlines and Amtrak. Traveling to the Campo museum requires an automobile.

Fremont   *Museum*

Niles Depot Museum

This museum focuses on the early railroads of Fremont, Newark, and Union City, mainly the Southern Pacific and Western Pacific. Exhibits in the 1901 Southern Pacific depot include photographs, track equipment, signals, locomotive artifacts, and uniforms. It is open every Sunday from April to September, and every other Sunday from November through March.

ADDRESS: 36997 Mission Blvd., Fremont, CA 94536
TELEPHONE: 510-797-4449
E-MAIL: nilesdepot@railfan.net
WEB SITE: nilesdepot.railfan.net

Fremont   *Museum*

Society for the Preservation of Carter Railroad Resources

Visit this museum on a work day and you'll see restoration of wooden cars completed using hand tools and 19th century techniques. Most cars the society preserves were built by Carter Brothers in Newark. Belgian draft horses pull cars along a section of track, and special trains run occasionally.

ADDRESS: 34600 Ardenwood Blvd., Fremont, CA 94555
TELEPHONE: 866-417-7277 or 925-373-6884
E-MAIL: curator@spcrr.org
WEB SITE: www.spcrr.org

Goleta   *Museum, Train ride*

South Coast Railroad Museum

The museum's centerpiece is the historic Goleta depot, a Victorian-styled Southern Pacific country station. The museum features hands-on exhibits. Special events are scheduled throughout the year, and handcar rides are offered. In the Gandy Dancer Theater, you can view films on a variety of railroad topics. It is open Wednesday through Sunday.

ADDRESS: 300 N. Los Carneros Rd., Goleta, CA 93117
TELEPHONE: 805-964-3540
E-MAIL: director@goletadepot.org
WEB SITE: www.goletadepot.org

Felton   *Train ride*

Roaring Camp Railroads

ADDRESS: Graham Hill Rd., Felton, CA 95018
TELEPHONE: 831-335-4484
E-MAIL: depot@roaringcamp.com
WEB SITE: www.roaringcamp.com

Located in forested coastal mountains, Roaring Camp Railroads presents two rides that offer the best of California scenery and vintage railroading. Roaring Camp & Big Trees operates small but powerful steam locomotives over a narrow gauge line through redwood forests; the Santa Cruz, Big Trees & Pacific travels the scenic San Lorenzo River Gorge to the Santa Cruz beach.

CHOICES: Each Roaring Camp railroad has its own unique personality. Roaring Camp & Big Trees operates a fleet of 1880s Shay, Heisler, and Climax locomotives on a winding route up Bear Mountain. The 75-minute excursions feature open-air coaches, perfect for viewing the big trees, and at the summit, you can detrain to visit a grove of redwoods. Santa Cruz trains employ 1920s coaches and open-air cars pulled by an ex-Santa Fe CF-7 diesel. The three-hour round trip runs through Henry Cowell Redwoods State Park, down the San Lorenzo River Gorge, and through an 1875 tunnel before arriving at the historic boardwalk. Passengers may board from either Roaring Camp or Santa Cruz.

WHEN TO GO: While crowds may be thick, summer is still the best time to go. The higher altitude and proximity to the ocean deliver moderate temperatures; however, the marine climate can bring chilly, foggy days. Special trains include moonlight dinner trains. Two ghost trains travel through a haunted forest in late October, and a beautiful holiday lights train rolls through the streets of Santa Cruz from late November through December.

GOOD TO KNOW: Santa Cruz is a typical resort town with plenty of lodging and a downtown filled with great dining and shops. The seaside boardwalk is a historic gem and features a 1924 wooden roller coaster.

WORTH DOING: Roaring Camp, home base for both trains, is a re-creation of an 1880s logging town that includes a steam-powered saw mill and period buildings, a general store, depot, engine house, antique cabooses, picnic grounds, and more.

DON'T MISS: While riding the narrow gauge line up Bear Mountain, watch for a large trestle that was once part of the loop that carried trains to the summit. It was destroyed by fire in 1974, so today's trains navigate an old switchback.

GETTING THERE: Roaring Camp is six miles north of Santa Cruz off Hwy. 1. Exit at Mount Hermon Road and drive 3.5 miles to Felton. Mount Hermon Road ends at Graham Hill Road. Turn left on Graham Hill Road and drive a half mile to Roaring Camp.

Train ride, Dinner train

Fillmore & Western Railway

ADDRESS: 351 Santa Clara St., Fillmore, CA 93016
TELEPHONE: 800-773-8724 or 805-524-2546
WEB SITE: www.fwry.com

Operating over a segment of a former Southern Pacific branch line, the Fillmore & Western Railway is a well-run combination of weekend scenic excursion trains, murder mystery dinner trains, and special trains. It is also one of the premier movie location sets. Billing itself as the "Home of the Movie Trains," from wrecks to shootouts, Hollywood has used this scenic little Southern California line to represent Washington D.C., Florida, the Pacific Northwest, and just about every place in between.

CHOICES: On weekend excursion trains, you can ride in an open-air railcar or in restored vintage passenger coaches. For a full afternoon tour, the Museum or Murals Train offers a luncheon tour to Santa Paula with a choice of a walking tour of the city's murals or of the California Oil Museum. Mystery dinner trains offer a wide range of themes from Perry Mason to Cirque de Foul Play and When the West Was Wild.

WHEN TO GO: Anytime is a good time in southern California, with summers obviously being hotter then other seasons. The rainy season, which is spotty at best, is from about November to March. The trains consist of vintage and antique pieces of rolling stock, which are not climate controlled, so wear weather-appropriate clothing.

GOOD TO KNOW: Fillmore is a suburb in a sea of suburbs north of Los Angeles. Lodging and restaurants is found in Fillmore and nearby Santa Paula, Piru, Oxnard, and Ventura.

WORTH DOING: Explore the healthy roster of passenger and freight equipment in various states of repair found on the property.

DON'T MISS: Just down the road from the F&W is a state-run fish hatchery at Piru. You can view the ponds on self-guided tours. Farther north up the California coast is Santa Barbara, San Luis Obispo, and the Hearst Castle, the ultimate in opulence and home of the man who ran the Hearst newspaper and radio empire.

GETTING THERE: Fillmore is about 60 miles northwest of downtown Los Angeles and about 25 east of Ventura. The nearest large-scale commercial airport is the Bob Hope Airport in Burbank. Flights also originate in Santa Barbara.

DISCOUNT: Take $2 off each adult ticket (excludes special or holiday trains).

Fish Camp   *Train ride*

Yosemite Mountain Sugar Pine Railroad

ADDRESS: 56001 Hwy. 41, Fish Camp, CA 93623
TELEPHONE: 559-683-7273
WEB SITE: www.ymsprr.com

The Yosemite Mountain Sugar Pine Railroad is a four-mile railroad excursion at Yosemite National Park's south gate. The ride allows you to see what it was like when steam locomotives hauled massive log trains through the Sierra Nevadas. It is a restored segment of the old narrow gauge Madera Sugar Pine Lumber Company Railroad, with a portion of the original right-of-way reconstructed using the same techniques as 100 years ago.

CHOICES: Two geared Shay steam locomotives, formerly used on the Westside Lumber Company, power the excursion trains. A unique experience is riding a Jenny railcar powered by Model A Ford automobile engines. The *Moonlight Special*, which operates Saturday nights in the spring and fall and Saturday and Wednesday nights during the summer, begins with a steak dinner and includes masked bandits, moonlight, and camp-fire sing-a-longs.

WHEN TO GO: The Yosemite Mountain Sugar Pine Railroad operates daily from mid-March through mid-October and on select days during the winter months. At close to 5,000 feet elevation, it can get chilly at Fish Camp, even in the summertime. The height of tourist season in Yosemite is extremely crowded.

GOOD TO KNOW: Refurbished railcars, once used to transport logging crews, now carry excursion passengers.

WORTH DOING: Other activities in the Fish Camp area include fishing, backpacking, hiking, camping and mountain biking.

DON'T MISS: Enjoy the beauty that is Yosemite and take in the entire experience, enhanced by the inclusion of an active narrow gauge steam railroad. Be prepared to spend an entire day or longer in the area.

GETTING THERE: Fish Camp is 40 miles north of Fresno and 60 miles east of Modesto. The nearest big-time commercial airline services are at Fresno and Sacramento.

Skunk Train

ADDRESS: Laurel and Main Sts., Fort Bragg, CA 95437
TELEPHONE: 800-866-1690 or 707-964-6371
E-MAIL: info@sierrarailroad.com
WEB SITE: www.skunktrain.com

One of the most amazing attributes of the Skunk Train is its ability to make you feel small. Ride the train from the coastal town of Fort Bragg and you'll soon find out. The route travels through a scenic wilderness filled with giant redwoods. As the train takes you through the mountain scenery, the giant trees will make your neck sore unless you move to an open car, where you can stand in wonder.

CHOICES: You can ride from either end of the 40-mile line, boarding at Willits or Fort Bragg. The line features 30 trestles, two tunnels, and a route that snakes its way up the redwood-covered mountainside. At Northspur, the mid-point on the railroad, you can enjoy a picnic lunch and watch the locomotive turn on a wye for the return trip. A shorter 90-minute trip also operates out of Willits to Wolf Tree. A barbecue dinner train is another option.

WHEN TO GO: Trains operate all year, but most excursions to Northspur run April through December. Specials, limited runs, and a motorcar also operate during the year.

GOOD TO KNOW: The railroad got its nickname from the yellow-painted, self-propelled gas-powered cars of the California Western Railway that provided transportation starting in 1925 and prompted local people to say, "You can smell 'em before you can see 'em."

WORTH DOING: Ride the train on days when steam locomotive no. 45 is running. A 2-8-2 Mikado type built by Philadelphia's famous Baldwin Locomotive Works in 1924, the locomotive is among the largest in regular service today. If you're really into the experience, this railroad offers a ride in the cab of the steam locomotive. Join the engineer and fireman for the chance to see how it all works.

DON'T MISS: Along the coast between December and April, you have a good chance to see a California gray whale as they migrate south from Alaska and then return. Whale-watching boats can be chartered out of Fort Bragg for an up-close experience.

GETTING THERE: Just over three hours north of San Francisco, the scenic drive to Fort Bragg starts on Hwy. 101. At Cloverdale, exit onto Hwy. 128 west, which turns into Hwy. 1, and continue north to Fort Bragg. The depot is at the foot of Laurel Street.

La Mesa   *Depot, Museum*

La Mesa Depot Museum

This restored 1894 station includes a train order board, furniture, telegraph and telephone equipment, and a potbellied coal stove. The depot is the only San Diego and Cuyamaca Railway station remaining. Operated by the Pacific Southwest Railway Museum, a steam locomotive and caboose are also displayed. The depot is open on Saturdays.

ADDRESS: 4695 Nebo Dr., La Mesa, CA 91941
TELEPHONE: 619-465-7776
WEB SITE: www.psrm.org/la-mesa

Lomita   *Museum*

Lomita Railroad Museum

This museum is a replica of the Boston & Maine station at Wakefield, Mass. You can climb into the cab of Southern Pacific no. 1765, a 2-6-0 Baldwin built in 1902, and walk inside a 1910 UP caboose. Several freight cars and a wooden water tower are also displayed. The museum exhibits lanterns, china, and other artifacts. It is open Thursday through Sunday.

ADDRESS: 2137 W. 250th St., Lomita, CA 90717
TELEPHONE: 310-326-6255
WEB SITE: www.lomita-rr.org

Millbrae   *Museum*

Millbrae Train Museum

The Millbrae Historical Society operates a museum containing photos, artifacts, and documents related to the railroad history of the Millbrae area. Housed in the former Southern Pacific train station, the museum displays a 1941 Pullman sleeper, with its original configuration and paint scheme, from the *City of San Francisco* streamliner. The museum is open on Saturdays.

ADDRESS: 23 E. Millbrae Ave., Millbrae, CA 94030
TELEPHONE: 650-333-1136
WEB SITE: www.millbraehs.org

National City   *Museum*

National City Depot

Still in its original location, the National City depot, built in 1882, is the oldest railroad-related structure in San Diego County. Operated by the San Diego Electric Railway Association, it exhibits railroad and local historical items. The depot is open weekends and holidays.

ADDRESS: 922 W. 23rd St., National City, CA 91950
TELEPHONE: 619-474-4400
E-MAIL: webmaster@sdera.org
WEB SITE: www.sdera.org/index.html?Info.shtml

Jamestown   _Museum, Train ride_

Railtown 1897 State Historic Park

ADDRESS: Fifth Ave. at Reservoir Rd., Jamestown, CA 95327
TELEPHONE: 209-984-3953
WEB SITE: www.csrmf.org/railtown

The Railtown 1897 State Historic Park is considered by many as the premier place for seeing first-hand California railroad history. It was originally part of the Sierra Railroad, arguably one of the best-known railroads in the world due to its extensive use in movies, television shows, and commercials. The state of California purchased the station, shops, and roundhouse facilities in 1982 to create Railtown 1897.

CHOICES: One of the highlights of any visit is taking the roundhouse tour and experiencing for yourself what a working facility looks, feels, and smells like. The historic shops and roundhouse have been operating as a steam locomotive maintenance facility for more than 100 years. Every Saturday through Sunday, April through October, six-mile, 40-minute round trips take passengers over the Sierra Railroad through California's Gold Country.

WHEN TO GO: The park, including the roundhouse tours, is open year-round, however the train excursions run only during specific months. During the height of the tourist season, make reservations well in advance and look to towns and cities in the surrounding area. California's Gold Country is almost universally seductive, so even if you have to travel a little to enjoy Railtown 1897, you'll enjoy the trip.

GOOD TO KNOW: Railtown is operated by the California State Railroad Museum and is part of California State Parks System. With more than 200 credits, it is one of the most-filmed railroad locations. The first known filming was in 1919 for a silent movie, and scenes for _High Noon_, _Back to the Future Part III_, and _Unforgiven_ were filmed here.

WORTH DOING: This part of the state, up through Sutter's Mill, is where people settled during the gold strikes, so history abounds here. If you like the outdoors, exploring, and learning western history, this is the place.

DON'T MISS: The Sierra Railroad is a full-time operating entity traveling through some of the most gorgeous countryside in the state.

GETTING THERE: From any direction, you have to drive to get to the Jamestown area. The nearest cities with regular airline service are San Francisco, Oakland, Sacramento, and Fresno. But the drive is mostly scenic and pleasant.

CALIFORNIA

Los Angeles

Travel Town Museum

Museum, Train ride

ADDRESS: 5200 Zoo Dr., Los Angeles, CA 90039
TELEPHONE: 323-662-5874
E-MAIL: TravelTown@rap.lacity.org
WEB SITE: www.laparks.org/grifmet/tt/index.htm

Travel Town is a good place to enjoy a couple of hours looking at equipment that has been preserved nowhere else. The museum, part of the Griffith Park complex in Los Angeles County, has a collection of small- to medium-sized steam, diesel, and electric locomotives and rolling stock with a surprisingly diverse roster of equipment.

CHOICES: Operated by the Department of Recreation and Parks, the museum is free and kid-friendly, which sometimes takes its toll on the equipment. Nevertheless, the diversity of the saved equipment makes Travel Town worth stopping at if you're in the area. Steam equipment includes tank locomotives, 0-6-0s, 2-8-0s, a 2-6-2, a 2-8-2, a Shay, and a Heisler. Other equipment worth taking in includes an operating EMD Model 40 diesel, a Baldwin RS-12, a Santa Fe gas-electric, a Pacific Electric freight motor, plus various pieces of rolling stock.

WHEN TO GO: Summertime can get very hot in Southern California so bring a hat or other head covering.

GOOD TO KNOW: A food concession is inside the museum, but eating and picnic areas are located nearby in other parts of Griffith Park.

WORTH DOING: If you want to take a break from walking, a rideable scale train encircles the collection.

DON'T MISS: Explore Griffith Park, a quiet oasis in busy LA, and especially take the time and visit the park's other sites including the famous observatory and world-class Los Angeles Zoo, which is right next to Travel Town.

GETTING THERE: Travel Town is near the confluence of I-5 and the 134 freeways. Freeway exits are clearly marked.

McCloud   *Dinner train*

Shasta Sunset Dinner Train

ADDRESS: 328 Main St., McCloud, CA 96057
TELEPHONE: 800-733-2141 or 530-964-2142
E-MAIL: info@shastasunset.com
WEB SITE: www.shastasunset.com

The Shasta Sunset Dinner Train operates over part of the McCloud Railway in northern California. Ivory linens, fine china, and polished silver accent the four-course dining experience aboard refurbished passenger cars originally built for the Illinois Central Railroad in 1916.

CHOICES: The Shasta Sunset Dinner Train operates year-round and has a number of special events every year. Dinner Train fare includes an elegant, four-course dinner, which changes menu offerings throughout the year. The McCloud Railway also offers a number of open-air excursions.

WHEN TO GO: Operating every month of the year, the dinner train features a warm and festive atmosphere, especially in winter time when it gets chilly in the northern California mountains.

GOOD TO KNOW: The dinner train operates over the historic McCloud Railway, which was built over the southern flank of 14,162-foot Mount Shasta. You'll experience the steep grades, sharp curves, and unique switchback of the original construction.

WORTH DOING: The McCloud area in northern California is ideal for rail enthusiasts and family vacationers alike. The Union Pacific's north-south Los Angeles-Portland main line is nearby as are other short lines. Depending on the time of year, the area is fertile ground for skiers.

DON'T MISS: There is always something doing in the McCloud area, including the Main Street Flea Market, a Lumberjack Fiesta, a Civil War reenactment, Heritage Day, and Christmas celebrations. In the greater McCloud area, there are a number of accommodations and restaurants. The Yreka Western Railroad is north of McCloud on I-5.

GETTING THERE: McCloud is between Redding and Yreka, just off of I-5 on Hwy. 89. The best way to get there is via automobile. Commercial airports are located in Sacramento to the south and Medford, Ore., to the north.

Napa   *Dinner train*

Napa Valley Wine Train

ADDRESS: 1275 McKinstry St., Napa, CA 94559
TELEPHONE: 800-427-4124 or 707-253-2111
WEB SITE: www.winetrain.com

When you think of Napa Valley, you think of wine. And if you want a unique wine experience, take this ride. It is true that it parallels busy Hwy. 29 through one of the world's most famous grape-growing valleys. But the difference is that you ride in elegant style onboard a fashionable train on a three-hour, 36-mile round trip while enjoying gourmet food and a glass of wine while watching the traffic.

CHOICES: Ride in a heavyweight passenger car, open car, or a vista dome, each with a different dining experience. The open-air *Silverado* features casual dining. Dining in the dome offers great views and a four-course meal. Aboard the restored Pullman cars, the menu includes a large selection of gourmet choices. As part of luncheon excursions, the train makes two winery tour stops. Other trips do not include stops. A family fun train allows parents some quiet time together. While they dine, the children eat, play, and watch movies in a separate car.

WHEN TO GO: Any time of the year, but the September grape-harvesting season is among the most popular. Special trains run around select holidays.

GOOD TO KNOW: Attire is generally casual at lunchtime, depending on the time of year or type of special event. Dinner is more dressy and cocktail-party attire is acceptable. Jackets are suggested, but not required. One bit of advice: no blue jeans.

WORTH DOING: Take a peek inside the kitchen to see the tiny space where all the meals are prepared and watch the chefs in action.

DON'T MISS: Enjoy the wine. The railroad offers a selection of more than 100 wines, in addition to beer and cocktails. Wine is included in some, but not all, meals. Napa Valley is filled with hundreds of wineries to visit as well as special events to partake in.

GETTING THERE: From San Francisco, take I-80 east to Exit 19. Follow Hwy. 29 north and exit at Napa/Lake Berryessa. Take Hwy. 221, which becomes Soscol Avenue, into Napa. Turn right on First Street and then turn left on McKinstry Street.

DISCOUNT: Receive 10 percent off train fares.

Nevada City   *Museum*
Nevada County Narrow Gauge Railroad and Transportation Museum

The museum's collection features NCNGRR engine no. 5. The 1875 Baldwin hauled timber, passengers, and freight. Other narrow gauge locomotives and wooden railcars are on display as are a 1901 steam-powered carriage and other historic transportation pieces. Docent-led tours of the museum are available.

ADDRESS: 5 Kidder Ct., Nevada City, CA 95959
TELEPHONE: 530-470-0902
E-MAIL: contact@ncngrrmuseum.org
WEB SITE: www.ncngrrmuseum.org

Nevada City   *Train ride*
Nevada County Traction Company

Discover a 90-minute, three-mile historic excursion in Gold Country. You ride in open-top cars over part of a narrow gauge line that was originally built in the 1870s, now on the grounds of the Northern Queen Inn. Along the way, you can see vintage rolling stock and a mine. A stop at History Hill allows you to visit a Chinese cemetery.

ADDRESS: 402 Railroad Ave., Nevada City, CA 95959
TELEPHONE: 800-226-3090 or 530-265-0896
E-MAIL: depotpeople@nccn.net
WEB SITE: www.northernqueeninn.com

Pomona   *Museum*
Railway & Locomotive Historical Society, Southern California Chapter

Featuring classic gingerbread architecture, a former AT&SF depot was moved to the Los Angeles Fairplex. The museum includes indoor exhibits and outdoor displays of rolling stock and locomotives, including a Union Pacific Big Boy. You can visit the museum during the county fair in September or during open house weekends each month.

ADDRESS: Fairplex Dr., Pomona, CA
TELEPHONE: 909-623-0190
WEB SITE: www.trainweb.org/rlhs

Poway   *Train ride*
Poway-Midland Railroad

You can ride a variety of railroad equipment on this railroad. It operates a 1907 Baldwin 0-4-0 steam locomotive, a trolley car, and a speeder. You'll also see restored historic buildings and rolling stock, a gallows turntable, and an expanded train barn. The railroad is restoring a 1907 San Francisco cable car.

ADDRESS: 14134 Midland Rd., Poway, CA 92074
TELEPHONE: 858-486-4063
E-MAIL: pmrrweb@powaymidlandrr.org
WEB SITE: www.powaymidlandrr.org

Oakdale

Dinner train

Sierra Railroad Dinner Train

ADDRESS: 330 S. Sierra Ave., Oakdale, CA 95361
TELEPHONE: 800-866-1690 or 209-848-2100
E-MAIL: info@sierrarailroad.com
WEB SITE: www.sierrarailroad.com

The Sierra Railroad was formed in 1897 to connect the San Joaquin Valley to Gold Country. As the third oldest railroad in North America, the Sierra continues to haul freight, carry passengers, and make Hollywood movies. The Sierra Railroad Dinner Train, launched in 1999, provides visitors an opportunity to travel on the historic Sierra Railroad while dining and enjoying the passing countryside.

CHOICES: There are more than 20 different types of trips to choose from, including a rail and raft trip. Every week of the year, the Sierra offers romantic dinners, murder mysteries, lunches, Sunday brunches, Wild West shows and wine tastings.

WHEN TO GO: Almost any time is a good to go into California's historic and fascinating Gold Country.

GOOD TO KNOW: The Sierra offers a variety of packages and services, even assisting with overnight accommodations that can include a bottle of wine with souvenir Sierra Railroad wine glasses.

WORTH DOING: Love chocolate? Oakdale is home to the only Hershey chocolate factory in the country that still gives tours to the public. Next to the Hershey plant is the Cowboy Museum, which is housed in a historic Southern Pacific depot.

DON'T MISS: The Sierra Railroad is also a functioning freight operation, so railfans can see more then just passenger cars. Also visit Railtown 1897 Historic Park in nearby Jamestown to see a historic steam locomotive maintenance facility.

Orange Empire Railway Museum

ADDRESS: 2201 S. A St., Perris, CA 92572-0548
TELEPHONE: 951-943-3020
E-MAIL: oerm@juno.com
WEB SITE: www.oerm.org

The Orange Empire Railway Museum was organized in 1956 by trolley and electric railway enthusiasts to preserve a fast disappearing way of transportation. Visitors can ride on classic trolleys, passenger trains, and other railroad equipment from Southern California's past.

CHOICES: Two trolleys run on a half-mile loop line, and one is usually an early Los Angeles streetcar. Another train, pulling freight or passenger cars, operates on the 1.5-mile standard gauge main line, provides rides in either a caboose or open gondola on the freight train. The cars and locomotives are rotated from the museum's collection, which contains more than 180 vintage pieces. There is also the opportunity to learn how to run a locomotive.

WHEN TO GO: The museum is located in Southern California's Inland Empire. The weather is usually bearable during most of the year, however summertime temperatures can reach triple digits. Winter weather can be mild, but there is an occasional cold snap.

GOOD TO KNOW: The museum, situated on 100 acres of land, is about 20 miles south of Riverside. It has preserved, and is restoring, an eclectic mix of more than 225 pieces of railroad equipment, which includes electric, steam, and diesel power as well as a variety of freight and passenger rolling stock.

WORTH DOING: The surrounding area, from Riverside to Temecula, is well developed with all the amenities a traveler would expect. For military aircraft fans, the March Air Field Museum has an extensive collection of aircraft adjacent to March Air Reserve Base in Riverside.

DON'T MISS: The museum can be part of a family vacation to Southern California that might also include such world-renowned attractions as Disneyland, Universal Studios, and Sea World.

GETTING THERE: Besides Los Angeles International Airport, there are a variety of commercial airports, including Ontario International Airport, 35 miles from the museum, and Palm Springs International Airport, 50 miles away.

CALIFORNIA

Portola   *Museum, Train ride*

Western Pacific Railroad Museum

ADDRESS: 700 Western Pacific Way, Portola, CA 96122
TELEPHONE: 530-832-4131
WEB SITE: www.wplives.org

Here at one of the Western Pacific's last diesel locomotive shops is a great collection of rolling stock. The focus is on one of the West's most beloved railroads, which traveled through beautiful mountain scenery and hosted the legendary *California Zephyr*. The setting couldn't be more appropriate.

CHOICES: This 37-acre site displays more than 150 pieces of equipment. Three former Western Pacific streamlined diesels call the museum home, as do locomotives from the Union Pacific and Southern Pacific. Western Pacific 0-6-0 no. 165, a steam switcher, now under restoration, is the only steam locomotive in the collection. Rolling stock includes passenger cars, boxcars, cabooses, and maintenance-of-way equipment.

WHEN TO GO: The museum is open year-round, weather permitting. On weekends, caboose rides through a pine forest on a one-mile loop of track make a great activity. In December, Santa trains run.

GOOD TO KNOW: Check in August for the annual Portola Railroad Days festival, which includes train rides, food, music, and a parade.

WORTH DOING: Run a locomotive in the museum's program that puts you in the engineer's seat.

DON'T MISS: Close by is Lassen Volcanic National Park, where you can see hydrothermal features such as boiling mud pots, steaming ground, and roaring fumaroles.

GETTING THERE: Portola is located in the Feather River Canyon between Sacramento and Reno. From the west, take I-80 to Hwy. 89 and go north to Hwy. 70, which runs into Portola. From the east, take I-80 to Hwy. 395 to Hwy. 70.

DISCOUNT: Receive 10 percent off a locomotive rental.

Sacramento

Museum, Train ride

California State Railroad Museum

ADDRESS: 111 I St., Sacramento, CA 95814
TELEPHONE: 916-445-6645
WEB SITE: www.csrmf.org

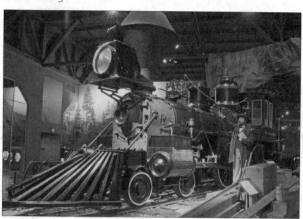

This is among the best interpretive museums about railroading. The museum mixes a magnificent large-artifact collection with plenty of details and a sense of drama that bring them to life. Displays, hands-on exhibits, and human interaction all combine to produce an excellent experience for everyone, from those with a passing interest in railroads to those with a deep appreciation for railroading. And if you want the real thing, the museum operates its Sacramento Southern Railroad, a short train ride, in season.

CHOICES: Made up of several buildings, the museum features a library, screens films, and offers guided tours. The Railroad History Museum, at 100,000 square feet, is the largest exhibit space and contains 21 restored cars and locomotives. Be sure to climb the stairs that take you into the cab of one of the largest preserved steam locomotives, a rare Cab Forward with its crew compartment in front of the boiler.

WHEN TO GO: Weekends, April through September, is when the museum offers Sacramento Southern Railroad train rides behind Granite Rock no. 10, a rebuilt 1943 tank engine. The 40-minute, six-mile round trip travels over the levees of the Sacramento River.

GOOD TO KNOW: Situated in the Old Sacramento district of the state capital near where the first transcontinental railroad was launched eastward in the 1800s, the museum has hosted three Railfairs (1981, 1991, and 1999). These multi-day events include visiting locomotives and cars from around the world. Another may occur when the former Southern Pacific Sacramento Shops complex is restored and added to the museum.

WORTH DOING: Walk through the *St. Hyacinthe*, a 1929 heavyweight sleeper car. But this is no walk through a lifeless artifact. Inside the beautifully restored Canadian National Pullman car, sound, light, and motion combine to provide the sense that you are speeding through the night on this hotel on wheels.

DON'T MISS: The California State Railroad Museum is located within Old Sacramento State Historic Park. The park operates a number of original and reconstructed historic buildings including the Central Pacific passenger station and Central Pacific freight depot.

GETTING THERE: When driving to Sacramento, take I-80 from San Francisco or I-5 from Reno. If you want the full rail experience, take an Amtrak train. The station is adjacent to Old Sacramento. The museum is at the corner of Second and I Streets.

San Francisco   *Museum*

San Francisco Cable Car Museum

Visit this historic cable car barn and powerhouse for a unique opportunity. You can watch the huge engines and winding wheels pull the cables and view the sheaves and cables entering the building from under the street. The museum also contains historic cable cars, photographs, and displays. It is open year-round.

ADDRESS: 1201 Mason St., San Francisco, CA 94108
TELEPHONE: 415-474-1887
WEB SITE: www.cablecarmuseum.org

San Francisco   *Trolley ride*

San Francisco Municipal Railway

The San Francisco Municipal Railway operates city transit services, historic streetcars, and cable cars. Cable cars run on three lines: Powell & Hyde, Powell & Mason, and California. Streetcars run regularly on the F-Market and Wharves line that connects the downtown area with Fisherman's Wharf.

ADDRESS: 1145 Market St., San Francisco, CA 94103
TELEPHONE: 415-673-6864
WEB SITE: www.sfmuni.com

San Jose   *Museum, Trolley ride*

Trolley Barn

The replica trolley barn recaptures the form of early California barns. Located in History Park, the structure houses the trolley restoration projects of the California Trolley and Railroad Corporation. The barn contains trolleys and other historic vehicles including a horse-drawn streetcar. Trolley rides take place on park grounds on weekends and during special events.

ADDRESS: 1650 Senter Rd., San Jose, CA 95112
TELEPHONE: 408-287-2290
WEB SITE: www.historysanjose.org or www.ctrc.org

San Pedro   *Trolley ride*

Waterfront Red Car Line

The Red Car line runs along the Port of Los Angeles waterfront as it did in the 1900s. It operates a restored car, no. 1058, as well as several replicas. You can board at World Cruise Center, Downtown, Ports O' Call, and Marina Stations. Cars run Friday through Monday and on select weekdays when cruise ships are in port.

ADDRESS: Sixth St. at Harbor Blvd., San Pedro, CA 90731
TELEPHONE: 310-732-3473
WEB SITE: www.portoflosangeles.org/recreation_redcar.htm

Santa Clara *Train ride*
Rail Journeys West

Take a luxurious rail vacation aboard the *Silver Solarium*, an original dome sleeper from the *California Zephyr*. Riding in a private railcar over Amtrak or VIA Rail routes, you can take a day trip from the San Francisco area or longer trips to major destinations in the United States and Canada.

ADDRESS: 3770 Flora Vista Ave., Santa Clara, CA 95051
TELEPHONE: 408-241-7807
E-MAIL: info@railjourneyswest.com
WEB SITE: www.railjourneyswest.com

Santa Clara *Museum, Depot*
Santa Clara Depot

This restored former Southern Pacific Santa Clara Depot houses a collection of artifacts and memorabilia that highlights western railroads, with a focus on signaling, and local railroaders. Along with the depot, which dates to 1863, the site features a restored 1926 tower, a section tool house, and a speeder shed. The museum is operated by the South Bay Historical Railroad Society.

ADDRESS: 1005 Railroad Ave., Santa Clara, CA 95050
TELEPHONE: 408-243-3969
E-MAIL: information@sbhrs.org
WEB SITE: www.sbhrs.org

Woodland *Dinner train, Train ride*
Sacramento RiverTrain

Leaving from Woodland, the train offers dining and entertainment options on a three-hour round trip. Operated by the Sierra Railroad, the RiverTrain follows the Sacramento River, crosses the long Fremont trestle, and travels through a wildlife refuge. Open-air cars offer an enjoyable experience for lunch, brunch, or dinner.

ADDRESS: E. and Main Sts., Woodland, CA 95776
TELEPHONE: 800-866-1690
E-MAIL: info@sierrarailroad.com
WEB SITE: www.sacramentorivertrain.com

Yreka *Train ride*
Yreka Western Railroad

The *Blue Goose* excursion train takes you on a 15-mile, three-hour round trip over a railway that was first established in 1889. Providing scenic views of Mount Shasta, the train goes through Shasta Valley, crosses the Shasta River, and travels to the old cattle town of Montague. The depot includes some rail exhibits.

ADDRESS: 300 E. Miner St., Yreka, CA 96097
TELEPHONE: 800-973-5277 or 530-842-4146
E-MAIL: yrekawesternrr@aol.com
WEB SITE: www.yrekawesternrr.com

CALIFORNIA

Suisun City

Western Railway Museum

Museum, Train ride

ADDRESS: 5848 Hwy. 12, Suisun City, CA 94585
TELEPHONE: 707-374-2978
E-MAIL: info@wrm.org
WEB SITE: www.wrm.org

The Western Railway Museum gives visitors the opportunity to ride historic streetcars and interurban electric trains that once served California and other western states. There are more than 50 historic cars on display.

CHOICES: A trip to the Western Railway Museum begins in the mission-revival inspired visitor center. After purchasing admission tickets, explore Cameron Hall, a large display and exhibit hall designed in the grand railroad station style. The building contains many exhibits of historic interest including a permanent exhibit on the transportation history of Solano County. The museum offers 15-minute, one-mile-long streetcar rides around the grounds and a 50-minute interurban ride over the re-electrified portion of the former Sacramento Northern Railway main line to Gum Grove.

WHEN TO GO: The Western Railway Museum is open Saturdays and Sundays from September to May. From Memorial Day through Labor Day, the museum expands its schedule and is open Wednesday through Sunday.

GOOD TO KNOW: The admission ticket to the museum is good all day, and you can ride as often as you wish. Although the Depot Café offers hot dogs, ice cream, beverages, and snacks on weekends, the museum features a 1.5-acre shaded picnic area that is well suited for family or group outings.

WORTH DOING: Visitors can stroll through the museum's large car house that houses historic electric-powered rail vehicles.

DON'T MISS: During October, special Pumpkin Patch Trains take visitors on a scenic five-mile journey to a pumpkin patch, complete with a hay-bale fort, hay rides, live music, animals, and pumpkins.

GETTING THERE: The museum is about 45 miles northeast of San Francisco, 12 miles east of I-80 on Hwy. 12. Gas, restaurants, and lodging are available in nearby Suisun City, Fairfield, and Rio Vista.

Niles Canyon Railway

ADDRESS: 6 Kilkare Rd., Sunol, CA 94586
TELEPHONE: 925-862-9063
E-MAIL: pla_ncry@ncry.org
WEB SITE: www.ncry.org

This museum railroad, a project of the Pacific Locomotive Society, provides a magnificent ride through a dramatic canyon at the edge of the San Francisco Bay area. An outstanding collection of equipment and beautiful scenery make this an excellent day trip in central California.

CHOICES: The railway runs 70-minute round trips through scenic Niles Canyon between Sunol and Niles. Departures are scheduled at both stations. The railroad operates most Sundays during the year except in December, when holiday trains are the rule. On all trains, you can select from open cars, covered cars, or enclosed coaches. Trains are powered by either a diesel or a steam locomotive, when available, from the railway's impressive collection that also includes a variety of passenger cars, freight cars, and cabooses.

WHEN TO GO: Spring and fall can be most pleasant. During April and May, the trains run more often for wild-flower excursions. After Thanksgiving, there is a holiday schedule for the nighttime *Train of Lights*.

GOOD TO KNOW: Unlike other trips, the last daily train out of Niles is a one-way ride to Sunol, so make sure you have a ride back to Niles if needed. The line through Niles Canyon was the last completed link of the transcontinental railroad.

WORTH DOING: Visit the shops at Brightside, which is open on Saturdays, for a behind-the-scenes look at the railroad when the trains aren't running.

DON'T MISS: The restored Sunol depot was originally built in the 1880s, and the Niles depot in 1901. The Niles depot features colonnade-style architecture and houses railroad exhibits.

GETTING THERE: The Niles Canyon Railway is situated between Oakland and San Jose. From San Jose, you can take I-880 to Fremont and exit on Hwy. 84 east. Turn left onto Mission Boulevard and continue three blocks west to Sullivan Street, and Niles station is on the left. To reach the Sunol depot from San Jose, just take I-680 to Hwy. 84. Travel west on Hwy. 84 one mile and turn right onto Main Street to Kilkare Road. From Oakland, take I-880 to Hwy. 84 east to get to either location.

COLORADO

Alamosa   *Train ride*
Rio Grande Scenic Railroad

The Rio Grande Scenic Railroad operates two excursions. The *San Luis Express* crosses scenic La Veta Pass over the Sangre de Cristo Mountains to La Veta. The T*oltec Gorge Limited* takes you through the San Luis Valley to Antonito, where you can connect with the Cumbres & Toltec Scenic Railroad. The trains, made up of vintage equipment, operate May through October.

ADDRESS: 601 State St., Alamosa, CO 81101
TELEPHONE: 877-726-7245
E-MAIL: agent@iowapacific.com
WEB SITE: www.alamosatrain.com
DISCOUNT: Receive $5 off each adult ticket.

Craig   *Museum*
Moffat Railway Car

Tours of this 1906 Pullman car are available through the Moffat County Visitors Center, where it is on display. The car originally belonged to rail magnate David Moffat and was named for his daughter Marcia. It contains solid mahogany woodwork and sleeping quarters for 12.

ADDRESS: 360 E. Victory Way, Craig, CO 81625
TELEPHONE: 800-864-4405 or 970-824-5689
E-MAIL: craigcoc@craig-chamber.com
WEB SITE: www.craig-chamber.com

Cripple Creek   *Train ride*
Cripple Creek & Victor Narrow Gauge Railroad

The four-mile, round trip tour lasts 45 minutes and covers a portion of the old Midland Terminal Railroad. The train runs south from Cripple Creek, passes the old MT wye over a reconstructed trestle and many historic mines near the deserted mining town of Anaconda.

ADDRESS: Fifth and Bennett Aves., Cripple Creek, CO 80813
TELEPHONE: 719-689-2640
E-MAIL: ccvngrr@aol.com
WEB SITE: www.cripplecreekrailroad.com

Train ride, Dinner train

Royal Gorge Route Railroad

ADDRESS: 410 Water St., Cañon City, CO 81212
TELEPHONE: 888-724-5748 or 303-569-1000
WEB SITE: www.royalgorgeroute.com

Nowhere else in America can you ride a train through a very narrow mountain gorge with a fast-flowing river and look straight up at one thousand feet of cliff. Originally part of the historic Denver & Rio Grande Western Railroad, passenger service through the magnificent Royal Gorge ended in 1967 and was resumed in 1999 by the Royal Gorge Railroad.

CHOICES: The railroad offers six types of service on its two-hour, 24-mile round trip, beginning with coach class in air-conditioned cars. First-class features larger seats, big windows, a cash bar, and a food menu. You can also step into open-air cars made from full-length passenger cars. Observation-dome class provides panoramic views under glass, food service, and a full service bar. The Lunch Train offers a three-course lunch, while the three-hour Dinner Train has a four-course gourmet dinner. Becoming more popular is the Murder Mystery Train, which presents an entertaining whodunit while you enjoy dinner.

WHEN TO GO: Summer offers more schedule options and more dinner trains, sometimes running up to 13 cars in push-pull fashion with a locomotive on each end. While the scenery is gorgeous year-round, Colorado is known for its brilliant yellow Aspen trees in September.

GOOD TO KNOW: Cañon City has a generous array of motels and restaurants, and the railroad offers overnight packages with area hotels and B&Bs.

WORTH DOING: In summer, raft-and-rail packages include a nine-mile raft trip down the Arkansas River in Bighorn Canyon. Also available for would-be engineers is a cab ride in the F7 locomotive.

DON'T MISS: Riding through the Royal Gorge in one of the former Milwaukee Road or AT&SF full-length dome cars, where the visitor can also enjoy lunch or dinner, is the best way to see the world's highest suspension bridge, which spans the gorge 1,053 feet above the river.

GETTING THERE: Cañon City is 115 miles from Denver and 45 minutes from Colorado Springs via Hwy. 115. Colorado Springs has the nearest airport.

Colorado Springs   *Museum, Trolley ride*

Pikes Peak Historical Street Railway

ADDRESS: 2333 Steel Dr., Colorado Springs, CO 80907
TELEPHONE: 719-475-9508
E-MAIL: cstrolleys@comcast.net
WEB SITE: www.coloradospringstrolleys.org

Located in an 1888 Rock Island Railroad roundhouse, the Pikes Peak Historical Street Railway Foundation is working on plans to run trolleys in the Colorado Springs area and has acquired a fleet of cars for that purpose. In the meantime, a ride can be taken on a short demonstration line.

CHOICES: Inside the roundhouse is a trolley museum with model displays and a restoration shop where work can be seen taking place on Fort Collins Birney car 22 and Colorado Springs Laclede car 59. A Southern Pacific baggage car holds a museum of Rock Island Railroad artifacts and models. The museum and grounds are normally open to the public on Saturdays, but by calling ahead, visitors can arrange for a tour on Tuesday through Friday.

WHEN TO GO: Any Saturday is a good time to visit, but Rock Island Days in October offer three days of operation and additional activities on site.

GOOD TO KNOW: Colorado Springs is a major city and popular tourist destination with full amenities. The natural beauty of nearby Garden of the Gods Park was used by the railroads to entice visitors to Colorado. Take an extended stroll around the many red sandstone formations.

WORTH DOING: Enjoy a meal at Giuseppe's Old Depot Restaurant in the former Denver and Rio Grande Western/Rock Island station in downtown Colorado Springs. Be sure to ask for a window seat for close-up trackside viewing of the busy joint BNSF/UP line. Don't forget to take a look at narrow gauge Denver and Rio Grande 10-wheeler no. 168 in the park across the street.

DON'T MISS: Directly behind the Pikes Peak Historical Street Railway is the freight corridor used by the BNSF and the UP between Denver and Pueblo. You can enjoy a picnic lunch and view the trains from the deck attached to the Rock Island Museum baggage car.

GETTING THERE: Exit I-25 on Fillmore Street heading east. Turn south at the second right on Steel Drive. Follow Steel Drive to the museum entrance.

Ski Train

ADDRESS: 17th St. at Wynkoop St., Denver, CO 80202
TELEPHONE: 303-296-4754
E-MAIL: askskitrain@skitrain.com
WEB SITE: www.skitrain.com

Climbing up almost 4,000 feet through the Rocky Mountains, the Ski Train is one of the most scenic rides in North America. It traverses 28 tunnels in 17 miles, including the 6.2-mile-long Moffat Tunnel, which is the third-longest tunnel in the United States and sixth-longest in the world.

CHOICES: The Ski Train sells out quickly, especially the limited club seats, so reservations are recommended. Both coach and club classes offer reserved seating and group rates. Club features a continental breakfast buffet in the morning and snacks and beverages on the trip home. Coach passengers may purchase those items in the lounge cars. A full train can carry more than 750 passengers. Even if you don't ski, there is plenty to do in Winter Park including snowshoeing, snowboarding, and daily Snowcat tours. Summer ski trains are popular for family fun such as hiking and biking (you can bring your own bike aboard the train), and the alpine slide is a must-do activity.

WHEN TO GO: The train starts running on its 56-mile trip just after the Christmas holidays and usually operates Saturdays and Sundays until the first weekend in April. It also operates on Fridays beginning in February and on Thursdays beginning in March. In summer, it runs Saturdays from mid-July to the end of August.

GOOD TO KNOW: The ski train operates even in bad weather, often being the only transportation that makes it to the ski slopes. There are free shuttle buses to the nearby towns of Winter Park and Fraser. All fares are based on same-day, round-trip travel, so if you are planning to stay overnight, you will have to purchase two round-trip tickets.

WORTH DOING: Observe some of the most beautiful Rocky Mountain scenery not accessible by a highway, particularly on snowy days. Local citizens know the train as a good way to get out of town for the day and yet be back home in time for dinner.

DON'T MISS: Sit on the right side to watch the train climb the Front Range around the famous Big 10 curves and look back at the Denver skyline on the plain. After negotiating curved Tunnel 8, the train enters dramatic South Boulder Canyon.

GETTING THERE: Denver International Airport is 20 miles from Union Station. Amtrak also serves Denver. I-25 and I-70 intersect about a mile from the depot.

Denver   *Museum*
Forney Museum of Transportation

This museum features more than 500 exhibits relating to historical transportation. It includes a Forney tank-type locomotive, which was used on elevated railways, a Union Pacific Big Boy locomotive, cable cars, and other pieces. The museum is open Monday through Saturday.

ADDRESS: 4303 Brighton Blvd., Denver, CO 80216
TELEPHONE: 303-297-1113
E-MAIL: museum@forneymuseum.com
WEB SITE: www.forneymuseum.com

Denver   *Trolley ride*
Platte Valley Trolley

Located by the Children's Museum of Denver, the Platte Valley Trolley offers the Riverfront ride, a 25-minute sightseeing trip, and the Route 84 excursion, which is five miles longer and crosses many trestles. It also shuttles fans to Bronco games. It is open April through October.

ADDRESS: Children's Museum Dr. and Water St., Denver, CO 80211
TELEPHONE: 303-458-6255
E-MAIL: mail@denvertrolley.org
WEB SITE: www.denvertrolley.org

Dolores   *Museum*
Rio Grande Southern Railroad Museum

The Rio Grande Southern Railroad Museum is located in a replica of the original Dolores depot. It is home to the restored Galloping Goose no. 5, one of the most unique rail vehicles ever built.

ADDRESS: 421 Railroad Ave., Dolores, CO 81323
TELEPHONE: 970-882-7082

Durango   *Train ride, Museum*

Durango & Silverton Narrow Gauge Railroad

ADDRESS: 479 Main Ave., Durango, CO 81301
TELEPHONE: 877-872-4607 or 970-247-2733
E-MAIL: info@durangotrain.com
WEB SITE: www.durangotrain.com

The Durango & Silverton is one of the most spectacular narrow gauge steam train rides in North America. Traveling through the Rockies, coal-fired locomotives pull trains through the rugged Animas River Gorge on a railroad built in the 1880s to reach southwest Colorado silver mines.

CHOICES: The Durango & Silverton offers several options for passengers. If you like the great outdoors, ride in an open car but come prepared with jackets and slickers in case of snow or cold in the Rockies. Coaches with windows are also available, but on the day-long trip, the seats may be uncomfortable for those taller than six feet. If you want to splurge, book space on one of the line's three private cars, which are available on at least two trains during the busy summer months; do so and you'll live like a robber baron for a few hours, complete with a glass of champagne.

WHEN TO GO: Winter provides incredible snowy vistas. Summer provides the excitement of up to four trains running each way, but it is also a busy time of the year for visitors who also come here for whitewater rafting, hiking, and visits to Mesa Verde National Park. The month of September provides the best nature show when Aspen trees turn a brilliant yellow and quiver in the autumn breeze.

GOOD TO KNOW: Durango is a well-developed city with every amenity available to tourists, including at least two historic hotels. Several restaurants in Silverton cater to passengers, providing a quick meal and a taste of the old West.

WORTH DOING: Take the shop tour to see how the locomotives are maintained and restored in a working roundhouse, a C-shaped structure whose form was once found in rail yards coast-to-coast but now only in a few spots. There is a two-hour layover in Silverton, which gives you time to visit the freight yard museum in the depot.

DON'T MISS: If you can, when outbound from Durango, ride the right side of the train. It provides the best view of the Animas River Gorge from the high line, 350-feet above the water.

GETTING THERE: The station is located in downtown Durango. The drive to the Four Corners area on Hwy. 550, dubbed the "Million Dollar Highway" because of the great expense it took to build in the Rockies, is a scenic delight, as long as you don't mind heights.

COLORADO

Georgetown   *Train ride*

Georgetown Loop Railroad

ADDRESS: Loop Dr., Georgetown, CO 80444
TELEPHONE: 888-456-6777
E-MAIL: info@railstarusa.com
WEB SITE: www.georgetownlooprr.com

This railroad shows how engineering overcame mountains when it came to reaching precious minerals in the Colorado Rockies. As the name states, the highlight is a full loop, where the tracks cross over themselves to gain elevation. The reconstructed Devil's Gate viaduct stands no less spectacular than when it was built in the late 1800s. Abandoned in 1938, the route was rebuilt in 1984.

CHOICES: You can board at the Devil's Gate station in Georgetown or at Silver Plume. Either way, you experience the same trip, but riding up grade first is always the better show. As you ride the train, scan the mountain slopes for bighorn sheep. Be sure to spot the grade of the abandoned Argentine Central Railroad, which went even higher than Silver Plume.

WHEN TO GO: Because of the climate and elevation the season is short – Memorial Day through mid-October. Interstate traffic from Denver over the July 4th holiday can be a major headache when everyone heads to Grand Lake, at the west entrance of Rocky Mountain National Park, for its dazzling fireworks display.

GOOD TO KNOW: The town of Georgetown is quaint and quiet with little influences of the modern world – with the exception of nearby I-70. Its National Historic Landmark District features unique shops, restaurants, and small museums in restored Victorian buildings.

WORTH DOING: After riding the train, travel on I-70 between Georgetown and Silver Plume and watch another train tackle the mountain, with not only the loop but also with a series of zigzags.

DON'T MISS: Inspect Colorado & Southern Mogul type steam locomotive no. 9. Built in 1884, she plied this route for many years until the line was abandoned. At Silver Plume, you can take a guided walking tour through the 1870s Lebanon Silver Mine.

GETTING THERE: The railroad is about 50 miles west of Denver off I-70. Exit 226 takes you to both Georgetown and Silver Plume, which are only a few miles apart.

DISCOUNT: Receive a 10 percent discount at Silver Plume or Devil's Gate depot gift shops.

Colorado Railroad Museum

ADDRESS: 17155 W. 44th Ave., Golden, CO 80402
TELEPHONE: 800-365-6263 or 303-279-4591
E-MAIL: info@crrm.org
WEB SITE: www.crrm.org

When you think of Colorado railroading, you think of mountain-climbing, narrow gauge trains of the Denver & Rio Grande Western. And that is exactly what you'll see at this museum just outside of Denver in Golden. But that's not all – the museum features 100 pieces of equipment from many other Colorado railroads.

CHOICES: The museum features narrow gauge and standard equipment, from a steam locomotive once used on the Pikes Peak Cog Railway to a 317-ton Burlington Route steam locomotive and even a set of streamlined 1950s passenger diesels from the Rio Grande. You'll see examples of the famous Galloping Goose self-propelled rail buses that ran on the narrow gauge Rio Grande Southern in southwestern Colorado and the only preserved standard gauge Rio Grande steam locomotive, no. 687, a 2-8-0 or Consolidation type built in 1890 and retired in 1955.

WHEN TO GO: The museum is open year-round, except for several holidays. Go on "steam up" days when a vintage steam locomotive or diesel engine powers passenger trains on a short ride around the 15-acre property.

GOOD TO KNOW: Be sure to see the monument that once stood along the Rio Grande tracks to commemorate the creation of the dome car – a bubble-top passenger car that became famous in the 1950s and 1960s for its superb views.

WORTH DOING: Visit the five-stall roundhouse that houses the museum's restoration shop. A viewing gallery gives you a peek at the work it takes to maintain the collection.

DON'T MISS: The Coors Brewery is adjacent to the museum and offers tours Monday through Saturday.

GETTING THERE: The Colorado Railroad Museum is located 12 miles west of downtown Denver and is easily reached from I-70. Take Exit 265 westbound or Exit 266 eastbound and it is just off Hwy. 58 between I-70 and Golden.

DISCOUNT: Take $1 off the regular admission for each member of your party.

Evergreen *Train ride*

GrandLuxe Rail Journeys

GrandLuxe Rail Journeys offers deluxe rail journeys on a private train throughout North America. Itineraries cover seven to nine nights, and accommodations range from vintage Pullman to a grand suite. Destinations include Mexico City, the Northwest, the Rocky Mountains, Napa Valley, and many national parks of the West.

ADDRESS: 35715 Hwy. 40, Evergreen , CO 80439
TELEPHONE: 800-320-4206 or 303-962-5400
E-MAIL: info@americanorientexpress.com
WEB SITE: www.americanorientexpress.com

Fort Collins *Trolley ride*

Fort Collins Municipal Railway

The three-mile, round trip trolley ride travels in a peaceful residential setting on its original right-of-way. The restored Fort Collins Birney safety car no. 21 was one of four cars purchased by the city in 1919. It now operates along the rebuilt line on West Mountain Avenue May through September.

ADDRESS: Roosevelt and Oak Sts., Fort Collins, CO 80522
TELEPHONE: 970-224-5372
E-MAIL: fcmrs@netzero.net
WEB SITE: www.fortnet.org/trolley

Limon *Museum*

Limon Heritage Museum & Railroad Park

This museum focuses on local history and the Union Pacific and Rock Island Railroads. Located in a restored 1910 depot, it includes a restored office and a lunch-counter diner. On display are several railcars including a saddle boxcar, a dining car, and a caboose.

ADDRESS: 899 First St., Limon, CO 80828
TELEPHONE: 719-775-8605
WEB SITE: www.townoflimon.com/culture/museum.htm

Pueblo   *Museum, Train ride*
Pueblo Railway Museum

Concentrating on the golden age of railroading, the museum displays steam and diesel locomotives, including AT&SF no. 2912, and rolling stock in the yard behind Union Depot. Artifacts and rotating displays are in the Southeastern Colorado Heritage Center located across from the depot. Locomotive cab, caboose, and coach rides are offered during special events.

ADDRESS: 132 W. B St., Pueblo, CO 81003
TELEPHONE: 719-251-5024
E-MAIL: info@pueblorailway.org
WEB SITE: www.pueblorailway.org

Ridgway   *Museum*
Ridgway Railroad Museum

Known as the birthplace of the Rio Grande Southern Railroad, Ridgway is home to a museum that focuses on the history of railroading in the surrounding area. It displays an assortment of railcars, and its indoor collection includes artifacts, photos, and tools. The museum holds special events and work sessions throughout the year.

ADDRESS: 150 Racecourse Rd., Ridgway, CO 81432
TELEPHONE: 970-626-5181
WEB SITE: www.ridgwayrailroadmuseum.org

Windsor   *Museum*
Windsor Museum

Located in Boardwalk Park, this 1880s Colorado & Southern depot houses an exhibit of steam-era railroading history with an emphasis on local operations of the Colorado & Southern and the Great Western Railway. You can view an REA platform baggage truck, artifacts, signals, photos, and an operating telegraph display.

ADDRESS: 116 N. Fifth St., Windsor, CO 80550
TELEPHONE: 970-674-2439

Leadville   *Train ride*

Leadville, Colorado & Southern Railroad

ADDRESS: 326 E. Seventh St., Leadville, CO 80461
TELEPHONE: 866-386-3936 or 719-486-3936
WEB SITE: www.leadville-train.com

In a state with so many spectacular scenic railroads, this line doesn't disappoint. Leaving from the charming mining town of Leadville, the LC&S marches up the side of the Rockies near the tree line. Upon departure from the 1893 brick depot, the train leaves the 10,200-foot elevation for a 900-foot climb along the southern side of the upper Arkansas River Valley to a point close to Climax at Fremont Pass. The train passes through forests of lodgepole pine, spruce, aspen, and fir.

CHOICES: On the 22-mile train trip, you can ride in an open car or a car with a roof. Especially for train fans, there are several seats available in the locomotive or in the caboose. If it's a beautiful day in Colorado, as it often is, stick to the open cars for unobstructed views. Along the way, the conductor provides narration and answers questions. The line also offers a special train for those interested in photography and another for history buffs. Packages are also available for raft trips on the Arkansas River.

WHEN TO GO: The trains run late May through late September when the aspen trees put on a magnificent show of yellow. In mid-summer, the *Wildflower Special* lets you view alpine flowers at their peak.

GOOD TO KNOW: Incorporated in 1878, Leadville is the highest incorporated city in the continental United States at 10,152 feet above sea level. Downtown Leadville is home to many shops, galleries, restaurants, and lodging establishments and makes an easy base camp from which to explore the central Rockies.

WORTH DOING: On the return trip, the train pauses for a break at French Gulch, where a wooden water tank that once supplied steam locomotives with water still stands. The break is a great chance to walk forward to the locomotive, where you can inspect the cab, meet the crew, and get a snapshot. Stick to the right side of the train for spectacular views of the mountains and the molybdenum mine at the end of the line.

DON'T MISS: Be sure to explore Leadville's National Historic Landmark District, which includes many buildings built between 1880 and 1905.

GETTING THERE: From Denver, take I-70 west and then Hwy. 91 south to Leadville. From Vail, take I-70 west to Hwy. 24 and then Hwy. 24 south to Leadville.

DISCOUNT: Receive $1 off each adult ticket.

Pikes Peak Cog Railway

ADDRESS: 515 Ruxton Ave., Manitou Springs, CO 80829
TELEPHONE: 719-685-5401
E-MAIL: info@cograilway.com
WEB SITE: www.cograilway.com

The Pikes Peak Cog Railway offers a unique Swiss Alpine experience on rails. Diesel-powered, self-propelled passenger cars navigate unbelievably steep grades with the help of a cog to ascend the 14,110-foot high peak. The view at the top is beautiful, but the journey is awe inspiring as well with trains going beyond the timberline, passing herds of bighorn sheep, and arriving at a station that includes a high-altitude research center.

CHOICES: The railroad offers three-hour round trips several times each day that include 30-40 minutes at the summit. However, it also provides a one-way trip to the top for anyone who would like to hike back down (about six hours) or ride a mountain bike with an outfitter service. During the first part of the trip, the train travels through boulder fields, where you may see some interesting "faces" in the giant boulders. And about five miles out of the station, you'll see a bristlecone pine forest with trees believed to be about 2,000 years old and among the oldest living things on earth.

WHEN TO GO: The railroad, unbelievably, operates year-round, thanks to a homemade snow plow that operates like a giant snow blower on rails. During the summer the railroad offers up to eight trains a day with departures every 80 minutes. During winter, November through March, the railway runs a limited schedule that is subject to a minimum number of passengers and may run at different times.

GOOD TO KNOW: The railroad uses modern Swiss-built trains of a type used in the Alps. The first of these modern cars came to the Pikes Peak line in the 1960s and the most recent in the late 1980s. These units tackle grades of up to 25 percent – which mean the track rises 25 feet for every 100 feet of forward travel.

WORTH DOING: At the peak, make sure to walk around the summit and look for Denver. Just be careful. On the north side is a drop-off called the Bottomless Pit.

DON'T MISS: At the base of Pikes Peak, about an hour's drive away, lie the two historic gold-mining towns of Cripple Creek and Victor. You may still find gold in Cripple Creek – at the town's casinos – and ride the Cripple Creek & Victor Narrow Gauge Railroad.

GETTING THERE: Manitou Springs is six miles from Colorado Springs. Take Exit 141 off I-25 and go west (toward the mountains) on Hwy. 24 four miles to the Manitou Avenue (Manitou Springs) Exit. Go west on Manitou Avenue for 1.5 miles to Ruxton Avenue. Turn left and go to the top of Ruxton Avenue.

DISCOUNT: Receive 15 percent off any gift shop purchase over $5.

CONNECTICUT

Danbury   *Museum, Train ride*
Danbury Railway Museum

This museum contains 50 pieces of equipment representing 11 different northeastern railroads and includes unique pieces such as a New Haven Railroad Mack FCD railbus. Vintage train rides in the yard go to the only operating turntable in Connecticut. The 1903 station houses displays and a model layout of the Danbury yard.

ADDRESS: 120 White St., Danbury, CT 06810
TELEPHONE: 203-778-8337
E-MAIL: info@danburyrail.com
WEB SITE: www.danbury.org/drm
DISCOUNT: Take $1 off each regular admission.

East Haven   *Museum, Trolley ride*
Shore Line Trolley Museum

A visit to the museum is a unique sensory journey into the past as you hear trolley motors growl, smell the electric arc, and feel rattan seats. The museum operates a three-mile round trip along the scenic shore over the last remaining portion of Branford Electric Railway. It boasts a collection of almost 100 vintage vehicles.

ADDRESS: 17 River St., East Haven, CT 06512
TELEPHONE: 203-467-6927
WEB SITE: www.bera.org

East Windsor   *Museum, Trolley ride*
Connecticut Trolley Museum

Founded in 1940, this museum offers a narrated three-mile, round-trip trolley ride. Its collection contains passenger and freight streetcars, interurban cars, elevated railway cars, service cars, and other rail equipment. The 17-acre site includes a power substation, a restoration shop, and storage barns.

ADDRESS: 58 North Rd., East Windsor, CT 06088
TELEPHONE: 860-627-6540
E-MAIL: office@ceraweb.org
WEB SITE: www.ceraonline.org

Train ride, Dinner train

Essex Steam Train & Riverboat

ADDRESS: 1 Railroad Ave., Essex, CT 06426
TELEPHONE: 800-377-3987
E-MAIL: valley.railroad@snet.net
WEB SITE: www.essexsteamtrain.com

Operated by the Valley Railroad Company, the Essex Steam Train is unusual in offering a direct boat connection, providing views of the scenic Connecticut River from both rail and water. While the train portion is authentic steam – hauled by either 2-8-2 no. 40 or 2-8-0 no. 97, both built by Alco – riverboat *Becky Thatcher* is a replica. The 12-mile rail round trip from Essex to Deep River takes about an hour while the rail-water package lasts more than two hours.

CHOICES: Beyond basic train and train-and-riverboat tours, the railroad offers a number of special events, including a Gillette Castle outing. On some weekends, a caboose is available for riding. For the ultimate rail experience, the Your-Hand-on-the-Throttle program lets fans actually run a locomotive.

WHEN TO GO: : The railroad operates May through October, with Day Out with Thomas weekends in November and the *North Pole Express* – with Santa, holiday stories, and caroling – weekends during the Christmas season. Spring and fall are fine times to visit, with the leaves either a new green or in brilliant autumn colors.

GOOD TO KNOW: Essex is a historic seaport village, with lots of white-clapboard New England charm. The Griswold Inn, which traces its heritage back to 1776, is located there. The "Gris" is noted for its Sunday Hunt Breakfast (a brunch, really), offered in a discount package with the steam train and riverboat.

WORTH DOING: The diesel-hauled *Essex Clipper* dinner train, which operates seasonally and offers a four-course dinner, actually makes the longest run of any of the trains, going beyond Deep River and up to Haddam. One of its two dining cars is a special treat: the heavyweight Pullman parlor car *Wallingford*, built in 1927 for the New York, New Haven & Hartford Railroad.

DON'T MISS: Nearby Gillette Castle is a whimsical faux-medieval mountaintop estate built of local fieldstone and completed in 1919 for actor and playwright William Gillette, most famous for his portrayal of Sherlock Holmes. Visit it on your own or as a train-ferry-hiking package offered by the railroad. The charmingly Victorian Goodspeed Opera House in nearby East Haddam presents excellent productions of classic musical comedies.

GETTING THERE: Essex is located on Hwy. 9 just three miles from I-95. The nearest major airports are in New Haven and Hartford, roughly equidistant.

Thomaston   *Train ride, Museum*

Naugatuck Railroad

ADDRESS: 242 E. Main St., Thomaston, CT 06787
TELEPHONE: 860-283-7245
E-MAIL: naugatuck.railroad@snet.net
WEB SITE: www.rmne.org

Today's Naugatuck Railroad runs over 19.6 miles of former New Haven Railroad, between Waterbury and Torrington, a line built by the original Naugatuck in 1849. The tracks follow the railroad's namesake river for the entire route. The Naugatuck Railroad, part of the Railroad Museum of New England, offers excursions over an eight-mile portion of its line.

CHOICES: Trains depart the 1881 Thomaston station on Saturdays, Sundays, and Tuesdays from Memorial Day until late October. Operating locomotives include U23B 2203 (the last domestic "U-Boat" built by General Electric), and Alco RS3s New Haven 529 and Naugatuck 1508. Riding in 1920s heavyweight coaches built for Canadian National, you cross two trestles over the Naugatuck River, see century-old New England brass mills, and roll high across the face of giant Thomaston Dam. The Thomaston station features a display track of historic New England railroad rolling stock that is undergoing restoration. Santa specials run weekends in December, a Day Out With Thomas provides family fun, and early evening music and wine-tasting trains are also scheduled.

WHEN TO GO: Fall foliage in early to mid-October is the most popular time to ride Naugatuck's trains.

GOOD TO KNOW: Built in 1881 by the original Naugatuck Railroad, the Thomaston station is being restored as are several outbuildings and an operating control tower.

WORTH DOING: Naugatuck's Engineer-for-an-Hour program provides the opportunity to run one of the railroad's diesels over the challenging north portion of the railroad with its many curves and grades.

DON'T MISS: Thomaston offers a pleasant New England downtown with historic mills, a picturesque opera house, and other buildings. Waterbury's Mattatuck Museum shows visitors the history of Connecticut's brass industry.

GETTING THERE: Take I-84 to Waterbury, then take Exit 20 to Hwy. 8, and follow Hwy. 8 north to Exit 38.

DISCOUNT: Take $1 off each adult ticket.

Connecticut Antique Machinery Association

The association features an operating three-foot-gauge railroad that is powered by a 1925 Baldwin locomotive that was used in the sugar cane fields of Hawaii. A variety of other locomotives and rolling stock fill out this exhibit. The site contains six other exhibits dedicated to antique industrial and agricultural machinery.

ADDRESS: Hwy. 7, Kent, CT 06757
TELEPHONE: 860-927-0050
E-MAIL: camainfo@ctamachinery.com
WEB SITE: www.ctamachinery.com

South Norwalk *Museum*

SoNo Switch Tower Museum

This 1896 New Haven Railroad switch tower has been restored, complete with an original 68 Armstrong lever mechanical machine. Located next to the Northeast Corridor main line, the unique museum is open Saturdays and Sundays May through October.

ADDRESS: 77 Washington St., South Norwalk, CT 06854
TELEPHONE: 203-246-6958
E-MAIL: info@westctnrhs.org
WEB SITE: www.sonotower.org

Willimantic *Museum*

Connecticut Eastern Railroad Museum

Located at the Columbia Junction freight yard, the collection includes several diesel locomotives and railcars. Buildings include a restored station and freight house and a reconstructed six-stall roundhouse. The museum conducts ongoing restoration projects and special events, and you can operate a replica pump car. It is open weekends May through October.

ADDRESS: 55 Bridge St., Willimantic, CT 06226
TELEPHONE: 860-456-9999
E-MAIL: info@cteastrrmuseum.org
WEB SITE: www.cteastrrmuseum.org

DELAWARE

Train ride, Dinner train

Wilmington & Western Railroad

ADDRESS: 2201 Newport-Gap Pike, Wilmington, DE 19808
TELEPHONE: 302-998-1930
E-MAIL: schedule@wwrr.com
WEB SITE: www.wwrr.com

The Wilmington & Western is one of the premier tourist railroads on the East Coast. Attractive equipment, historic steam locomotives, and a scenic route through Delaware's Red Clay Valley make this line a must-see when visiting the mid-Atlantic.

CHOICES: Since 2003, when a flood destroyed all six of the railroad's wooden bridges, trains have been running only from Greenbank. By spring of 2007, during its 41st year, the W&W expects to be fully operational over its entire 10-mile line, with departures again leaving from Hockessin. The train is composed of vintage steel coaches with adjustable windows, and an open-air car is available during the warmer months. Special trains offer on-board dining, tours of an early 20th century amusement park, and full-moon hayrides.

WHEN TO GO: The W&W is open from March through December, but steam trains operate on only select dates for much of the season. Fall foliage and winter holidays see steam excursions nearly every weekend. Mid-October through early November is prime season for autumn leaves in the Red Clay Valley. December is *Santa Claus Express* time, with the focus on families and fun.

GOOD TO KNOW: The W&W offers cab rides in the line's steam and diesel locomotives by advance reservation; the cab rider must be at least 18 years of age and must sign a liability release. Guided tours through the engine shop are offered on select dates throughout the season.

WORTH DOING: Built by the American Locomotive Company in 1909 for the Mississippi Central, 4-4-0 American no. 98 returned to service after extensive restoration in 2004. Today, it's one of the few American Standard types operating anywhere.

DON'T MISS: Nearby attractions include the Hagley Museum & Library, a museum of American industrial history, and Winterthur, a magnificent estate showcasing rare collections of antiques and Americana amidst a 979-acre private garden.

GETTING THERE: Greenbank station is about four miles southwest of downtown Wilmington on Hwy. 41, close to I-95. Amtrak's Northeast Corridor provides frequent service to downtown Wilmington. Worldwide air connections are available 35 miles away at Philadelphia International Airport.

DISTRICT OF COLUMBIA

Smithsonian National Museum of American History

The National Museum of American History includes an exhibit of railroad objects ranging from tools, tracks, and models to the massive 1401, a 280-ton locomotive built in 1926. Currently, the museum is closed for major renovations and is scheduled to reopen by summer 2008.

ADDRESS: 14th St. and Constitution Ave., Washington, DC 20013-7012
TELEPHONE: 202-633-1000
E-MAIL: info@si.edu
WEB SITE: www.americanhistory.si.edu

FLORIDA

Train ride, Dinner train
Seminole Gulf Railway

Two-hour, narrated excursions run Wednesday, Saturday, and Sunday across the Caloosahatchee bridge system to Bayshore. A murder mystery takes place Wednesday through Sunday on the dinner train, which serves five-course meals on its way toward Punta Gorda.

ADDRESS: 2805 Colonial Blvd., Fort Myers, FL 33912
TELEPHONE: 800-736-4853 or 239-275-8487
WEB SITE: www.semgulf.com

Fort Myers *Museum*
Southwest Florida Museum of History

Housed in the former Atlantic Coast Line Railroad depot, the museum displays a 1929 Pullman railcar. You can tour the *Esperanza* and get a glimpse of travel aboard a private car. The museum features exhibits from prehistoric times to modern day showcasing southwest Florida. It is open Tuesday through Saturday.

ADDRESS: 2300 Peck St., Fort Myers, FL 33901
TELEPHONE: 239-332-5955
E-MAIL: museuminfo@cityftmyers.com
WEB SITE: www.cityftmyers.com/attractions/historical.htm

Miami   *Museum, Train ride*

Gold Coast Railroad Museum

ADDRESS: 12450 SW 152 St., Miami, FL 33177
TELEPHONE: 305-253-0063
E-MAIL: webmaster@goldcoast-railroad.org
WEB SITE: www.goldcoast-railroad.org

With its impressive collection of rolling stock and locomotives – featuring the *Ferdinand Magellan*, a Pullman office car used by Presidents Roosevelt, Truman, Eisenhower, and Reagan – and its historic location at the site of a World War II airship base, the Gold Coast Railroad Museum is a fascinating place to visit.

CHOICES: Interested in former Florida East Coast Railway or *California Zephyr* passenger equipment? You'll find it here, along with diesels and steam locomotives from various railroads. But the museum isn't just a display of restored or preserved equipment. On weekends, the Gold Coast offers a 20-minute standard gauge train ride, using a diesel-electric (sometimes an EMD E8 or E9) and the *Belle Glade*, a former Florida East Coast stainless coach. Also on weekends, it operates a two-foot-gauge children's railroad.

WHEN TO GO: The Gold Coast Railroad Museum operates year-round, seven days a week. Keep in mind that mid-December through Easter is when the Sunshine State is most popular with tourists. Florida summers are typically hot, but the reward for travelers willing to deal with the heat is shorter lines at attractions and better hotel rates.

GOOD TO KNOW: It's no secret that the greater Miami area is a tourist mecca, with its beaches, tony shopping, deep-sea fishing and nightclubs. But it's also a railroad buff's paradise, with extensive West Palm Beach-Fort Lauderdale-Miami commuter rail service offered by Tri-Rail, vibrant freight operations by both the Florida East Coast and CSX, and significant Amtrak service (including a maintenance facility at Hialeah).

WORTH DOING: The Gold Coast offers cab rides on its weekend diesel-hauled passenger trains for an additional fee. Make sure, however, you call ahead for reservations. And consider combining your trip to the Gold Coast with a visit to the Miami Metrozoo, which is located next to the railroad museum.

DON'T MISS: Florida East Coast Railway 4-6-2 steam locomotive no. 153, built by the American Locomotive Company in 1922, like the *Ferdinand Magellan*, is a National Historic Landmark. Used on "the railroad that died at sea," Florida East Coast's line between Miami and Key West, the 153 pulled a rescue train that delivered evacuees safely to Miami just before a hurricane destroyed the Key West line in 1935.

GETTING THERE: Miami is served by all major airlines, Amtrak, and major highways. The museum is located between Miami and Homestead, off the Florida Turnpike.

Parrish

Florida Railroad Museum

ADDRESS: 12210 83rd St. E, Parrish, FL 34219
TELEPHONE: 877-869-0800
E-MAIL: traininfo@frrm.org
WEB SITE: www.frrm.org

The Florida Railroad Museum (formerly the Florida Gulf Coast Railroad Museum) operates diesel-powered trains on a 13-mile round trip over former Seaboard Air Line trackage in southwest Florida. Leisurely rides on air-conditioned and open-air coaches through farmland, piney woods, and palmetto flats give you a glimpse of Florida before Disney and interstate highways.

CHOICES: Variety is the order for the day with the Florida Railroad Museum's equipment. Passenger equipment ranges from railroads such as the Lackawanna to the Union Pacific and the Louisville & Nashville. Regardless of the time of year, you'll want to opt for the air-conditioned rolling stock instead of open-air – after all, air-conditioning was invented by Florida physician John Gorrie in 1851 for good reason! Get there well before train time to get a cool seat.

WHEN TO GO: The Florida Railroad Museum operates weekends only, year-round. Mid-December through Easter is Florida's high season. The Florida Railroad Museum is at its busiest then, but the high season also boasts Florida's mildest weather, making it the perfect time to combine a ride on the railroad with a canoe trip or a picnic at nearby Little Manatee River State Park.

GOOD TO KNOW: The museum is located in the small town of Parrish, population 5,800, located on Hwy. 301. Parrish is quiet, but it's hardly remote, sited between Tampa and the Sarasota-Bradenton area, not far from the Gulf of Mexico and its beaches. Packing a lunch for the museum's picnic area makes an enjoyable break.

WORTH DOING: The Florida Railroad Museum's Rent-a-Locomotive program allows you to operate one of three diesel-electrics from the 1950s (Alco, EMD, and GE) for a fee. You'll need to make a reservation in advance.

DON'T MISS: Number 12, a Porter 0-6-0T steam locomotive is on display at the museum's own picnic grove in Parrish. The engine was built in 1916 for the Brooklyn Navy Yard and later served with the Brooklyn Eastern District Terminal.

GETTING THERE: You have plenty of choices. Tampa International Airport and Sarasota Bradenton International Airport are each fairly close by. Amtrak serves Tampa by train and Sarasota and Bradenton by dedicated connecting motor coach. By car, take I-75 for speed or Hwy. 301 to see more of the real Florida.

Palm Beach   *Museum*
Flagler Museum

The home of Henry Flagler, who developed the Florida East Coast Railway, is now a
museum of the Gilded Age. Docent-led tours are offered, or you can tour the 55-room
Whitehall on your own. The Flagler Kenan Pavilion, designed in the style of a 19th
century Beaux Arts railway palace, houses Henry Flagler's private railcar.

ADDRESS: 1 Whitehall Way, Palm Beach, FL 33480
TELEPHONE: 561-655-2833
E-MAIL: mail@flaglermuseum.us
WEB SITE: www.flaglermuseum.us

Tampa   *Trolley ride*
TECO Line Streetcar System

Tampa once again enjoys the nostalgic charm of the streetcar. Replicas of the original
Birney safety cars connect downtown, Channelside, and historic Ybor City along a
2.4-mile section of track. With 10 stops along the way, convenient and fun
transportation is available to major destinations.

ADDRESS: St. Pete Times Forum Dr., Tampa, FL 33619
TELEPHONE: 813-254-4278
E-MAIL: riveral@hartline.org
WEB SITE: www.tecolinestreetcar.org

Winter Garden   *Museum*
Central Florida Railroad Museum

Located in a former 1913 Tavares & Gulf Railroad station, the museum features a
Clinchfield caboose and a 1938 Fairmont motorcar. Exhibits focus on central Florida
railroads including the "Tug and Grunt." The museum is operated by the Winter
Garden Heritage Foundation. That organization also operates the nearby Heritage
Museum, which is housed in an Atlantic Coast Line depot and contains some railroad
memorabilia and a Chessie caboose.

ADDRESS: 101 S. Boyd St., Winter Garden, FL 32803
TELEPHONE: 407-656-0559
WEB SITE: www.wghf.org

GEORGIA

Albany   *Museum*
Thronateeska Heritage Center

The Thronateeska Heritage Center contains several historic railroad buildings. Its
history museum is located in the 1912 Union Depot. The original 1857 freight depot
and the Railway Express Agency building house a planetarium and science center.
Its transportation annex displays a variety of rail cars and Georgia Northern Railway
steam locomotive no. 107.

ADDRESS: 100 W. Roosevelt Ave., Albany, GA 31701
TELEPHONE: 229-432-6955
E-MAIL: info@heritagecenter.org
WEB SITE: www.heritagecenter.org

Stone Mountain   *Train ride*
Stone Mountain Scenic Railroad

A 1950s locomotive with open-air cars takes you on a five-mile, 30-minute excursion
around Stone Mountain. Narration provides a look at rail history, beginning in the
mid-1800s when the rail line was first built, and interesting facts about the mountain.
And tune up your singing voice, as sing-alongs take place during the ride. Special
Halloween and Christmas trains also run.

ADDRESS: Hwy. 78 E, Stone Mountain, GA 30086
TELEPHONE: 800-401-2407 or 770-498-5690
WEB SITE: www.stonemountainpark.com

Tifton   *Museum, Train ride*
Agrirama Museum of Culture & Historic Village

At Agrirama, Georgia's Museum of Agriculture, you can tour 35 buildings that
represent the state's past, including a railroad depot and sawmill. A ride aboard a
logging train takes you around the historic site. The living museum is open Tuesday
through Saturday year-round. Special events are scheduled throughout the year.

ADDRESS: 1392 Whiddon Mill Rd., Tifton, GA 31793
TELEPHONE: 800-767-1875 or 229-386-3344
E-MAIL: market@agrirama.com
WEB SITE: www.agrirama.com

Blue Ridge   *Train ride*

Blue Ridge Scenic Railway

ADDRESS: 241 Depot St., Blue Ridge, GA 30513
TELEPHONE: 800-934-1898 or 706-632-9833
E-MAIL: info@brscenic.com
WEB SITE: www.brscenic.com

The Louisville & Nashville's original route from Knoxville to Atlanta covered some rugged territory, and today it makes for a scenic ride into the wilderness. Following the unspoiled Toccoa River, this 26-mile round trip takes riders between the 1905 depot at Blue Ridge and McCaysville near the Tennessee border.

CHOICES: Trains depart downtown Blue Ridge from the depot, which was constructed in 1906 and is listed on the National Register of Historic Places. You can ride in either a closed-window car or an open-air car. As the diesel-powered train climbs through the north Georgia mountains, commentary is piped into the cars, and a conductor may add his own perspective to the trip.

WHEN TO GO: Trains run April through December, and spring and fall are great seasons for travel in the Southeast. The region's lush vegetation has a tendency to create a tunnel effect. But during spring and autumn you have the chance to see into the forest as well as take in the scenery. The *Christmas Express* offers family fun in late November and December.

GOOD TO KNOW: This railroad started out as a narrow gauge line in the late 1880s with the tracks being three feet wide. Later investors changed it to standard gauge. The railway is the only mainline railroad excursion service based in Georgia.

WORTH DOING: The railroad offers a combination rail-and-raft package that is good for the Toccoa River, which the railroad crisscrosses, or for the nearby Ocoee River. The Toccoa is a slow run, while the Ocoee is a wild whitewater ride. Both options include return transportation to Blue Ridge.

DON'T MISS: During your layover, take the opportunity to walk around McCaysville, have lunch, and visit some of the town's antique shops.

GETTING THERE: Blue Ridge is about 90 miles north of Atlanta and about 80 miles from Chattanooga, Tenn. From Atlanta, take I-75 north to I-575, which turns into Hwy. 515, and continue on Hwy. 515 to Blue Ridge. The depot is on the left side of Depot Street.

Cordele

Train ride

SAM Shortline

ADDRESS: 105 E. Ninth Ave., Cordele, GA 31015
TELEPHONE: 877-427-2457 or 229-276-0755
WEB SITE: www.samshortline.com

The SAM Shortline offers a relaxing trip through the small towns of southwest Georgia. The train leaves from Cordele, and the main objective is to reach Archery. Along the way, you travel through Georgia Veterans State Park and the towns of Leslie, Americus, and Plains, the home of President Jimmy Carter.

CHOICES: There are six different excursion trains, each one laying over in different towns on the route. If you would like to explore the location longer, you may be able to catch the train on its return trip. Both coach and lounge cars are available, and you can board at any of the depots along the route.

WHEN TO GO: Trains run Fridays and Saturdays as well as on select Mondays and Thursdays March through December. Special excursions operate throughout the season.

GOOD TO KNOW: Why SAM? The original railroad was the Savannah, Americus and Montgomery Railroad built during the 1880s and headed by Col. Samuel Hugh Hawkins of Americus.

WORTH DOING: Many of the excursions, such as the *Peanut Express*, stop in Plains and Archery, where you can visit Jimmy Carter's childhood home. In Plains, the Seaboard Coast Line depot was his campaign headquarters during the 1976 election. While you're there, make sure to buy a bag of peanuts.

DON'T MISS: In Americus, you can visit Habitat for Humanity's Global Village, and if you want to make a longer trip, the Andersonville National Historic Site and National POW Museum is 11 miles northeast.

GETTING THERE: Cordele is about 140 miles south of Atlanta. From I-75, take Exit 101 and go west on Hwy. 280. At Hwy. 41 turn north to Cordele.

Southeastern Railway Museum

GEORGIA

ADDRESS: 3966 Buford Hwy., Duluth, GA 30096
TELEPHONE: 770-476-2013
E-MAIL: admin@srmduluth.org
WEB SITE: www.srmduluth.org

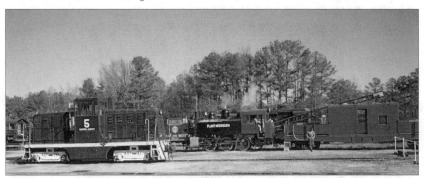

The museum showcases railroading in Georgia and the Southeast with displays and more than 90 pieces of rolling stock. Among the highlights are a business car used to help convince leaders to bring the 1996 Olympics to Atlanta, a private car once used by President Warren G. Harding, and one of the famous green and gold Southern Crescent passenger diesels. It also offers short train rides.

CHOICES: The 34-acre museum features a variety of buildings and displays. Building One, the main exhibit hall, contains Southern Railway E8 passenger diesel-electric no. 6901 and the 1911 Pullman private car *Superb*, which was used by President Harding and is on the National Register of Historic Places. The museum's collection includes passenger coaches, private cars, trolleys, baggage cars, freight cars, cabooses, and maintenance-of-way equipment. The diesel-powered train rides take you around the museum's site aboard vintage cabooses.

WHEN TO GO: The museum is open Thursdays, Fridays, and Saturdays April through early December. It is also open Saturdays during January, February, and March. Train rides are offered in season, and a special railroad festival takes place each September.

GOOD TO KNOW: Housed here are famous excursion engines Savannah & Atlanta Pacific type no. 750 and Atlanta & West Point Pacific type no. 290, the latter known for appearing in the movie *Fried Green Tomatoes*.

WORTH DOING: On select Saturdays during summer and fall, when available, steam locomotive no. 97 pulls the on-site train.

DON'T MISS: Take a few days and see all that the Atlanta area has to offer.

GETTING THERE: The museum is located in Duluth, a northeast suburb of Atlanta. It is just south of downtown Duluth. From Atlanta, take I-85 to Exit 104 and take Pleasant Hill Road to Buford Highway. Turn right on Buford Highway and then left onto Peachtree Road to the museum.

Southern Museum of Civil War and Locomotive History

ADDRESS: 2829 Cherokee St., Kennesaw, GA 30144
TELEPHONE: 770-427-2117
WEB SITE: www.southernmuseum.org

A museum of high-caliber exhibits and static displays, the Southern Museum of Civil War and Locomotive History traces its roots back to 1972, when the City of Kennesaw acquired the famed steam locomotive *General*. The *General*, a Western & Atlantic Railroad 4-4-0 built in 1855, was the star in one of the Civil War's greatest acts of intrigue – the Great Locomotive Chase. The museum (part of which is located in a former cotton gin) has widened its collections and focus, making it a must-see attraction for visitors to the Atlanta area.

CHOICES: While the story of Andrews Raid and the *General* is still the biggest offering at the museum, more comprehensive Civil War history and the story of Georgia locomotive manufacturer Glover Machine Works are also now chronicled here. The Glover Machine Works manufactured steam locomotives, locomotive parts, and other industrial products from 1902 until the 1930s. Patterns from the casting shop are artfully displayed in the museum, and extensive exhibits cover the story of the locomotive manufacturer. The facility is also home to the Southern Railway Historical Association's archival collection.

WHEN TO GO: The museum is open daily year-round, and the weather is generally mild. The Atlanta area has lots of modern railroad action, and other museums, such as the Atlanta History Center, help tell the story of the Civil War and railroading in Atlanta.

GOOD TO KNOW: The story of the Andrews Raid was thrilling and unique enough to attract the attention of the Walt Disney Company, which released the film *The Great Locomotive Chase* in 1956.

WORTH DOING: Take a walking tour of historic Kennesaw (once known as Big Shanty) after exiting the front door of the museum and view a 1908 Western & Atlantic Railroad depot, numerous 19th century residences, and an 1887 grocery store.

DON'T MISS: The Atlanta Cyclorama, located in Atlanta's Grant Park, houses the *Texas*, the Western & Atlantic Railroad locomotive used by Confederates to hunt down Andrews Raiders. Andrews – tried as a spy and hanged by the Confederacy – several of his men, and other Civil War figures are buried in nearby Oakland Cemetery.

GETTING THERE: Kennesaw is located off of I-75 and Hwy. 41. Hartsfield-Jackson Atlanta International Airport is the world's busiest, with flights to anywhere in the world daily. Amtrak's *Crescent* also serves the city twice daily.

Savannah

Roundhouse Railroad Museum

Museum

GEORGIA

ADDRESS: 601 W. Harris St., Savannah, GA 31401
TELEPHONE: 912-651-6823
E-MAIL: roundhouse@chsgeorgia.org
WEB SITE: www.chsgeorgia.org/roundhouse

Part of the five-site Coastal Heritage Society museum complex, Savannah's Roundhouse Railroad Museum is a must-see for students of early American railroading technology. Located on the edge of Savannah's renowned historic district, the museum encompasses 13 structures from the original Central of Georgia shops complex, several of which date back to the early 1850s.

CHOICES: The 1926 roundhouse houses a collection of Georgia steam locomotives, passenger cars, and freight cars, including the 1886 0-6-0T shop switcher no. 8 and a rare 1878 wooden business car. The docent-led history/technology tour provides general information about the history and technology of the site and the impact of the railroad on the local economy.

WHEN TO GO: The museum is open year-round. Savannah's near-tropical climate offers a welcome relief from northern cold throughout the winter months.

GOOD TO KNOW: The Savannah Historic District, a National Historic Landmark, is one of America's premier urban historic neighborhoods. Fine examples of buildings in the Georgian, Greek Revival, and Gothic styles abound. Nearby, Hilton Head, S.C., offers world-class golf and water sports.

WORTH DOING: The underground smoke-management system made the Central of Georgia shops one of the cleanest coal-fired industrial complexes in the 19th century. Buildings throughout the complex are connected to the central smokestack by hidden ducts. Smoke from the main boiler and dozens of individual forges and furnaces was sucked through the ducts, routed to the stack, and discharged away from the workers 125 feet in the air.

DON'T MISS: Expand your tour with a visit to the Savannah Visitors Center and History Museum, housed in the 1850s Central of Georgia passenger station and train shed one block north of the roundhouse.

GETTING THERE: Amtrak's *Palmetto*, *Silver Meteor*, and *Silver Star* all call at Savannah's suburban station. Seven major airlines or their regional affiliates serve Savannah International Airport.

69

HAWAII

Lahaina Kaanapali Railroad

ADDRESS: 975 Limahana Pl., Lahaina, HI 96761
TELEPHONE: 800-499-2307 or 808-667-6851
WEB SITE: www.sugarcanetrain.com

The Sugar Cane Train travels between the historical whaling town of Lahaina to the lush Kaanapali Resort on the Hawaiian island of Maui. Narrow gauge steam engines transport visitors through the Kaanapali golf courses, along the ocean, and across a scenic railroad trestle. A narrating conductor entertains everyone with fun Hawaiian facts, the history of the train, and the sugar cane industry.

CHOICES: Steam trains operate daily, all year round. On Thursday evenings, a special train departs from the Puukolii station at sunset and travels to Kaanapali station. There, guests enjoy a Hawaiian-style BBQ and entertainment featuring Hawaiian music and dancing. The meal includes Maui minted pineapple and Huli Huli chicken made with brown sugar cane.

WHEN TO GO: While the most popular time is summer, if you visit Maui between December and April, you just might see a humpback whale from the train. During this time, many whales can be seen leaping out of the ocean off the west Maui coast.

GOOD TO KNOW: The Sugar Cane Train is one of many exciting adventures for the Maui visitor including glass bottom boat cruises, snorkeling assorted water sports, plus five-star hotels and exquisite dining and shopping experiences. While few Hawaiian railroads remain today, for more than 100 years, they hauled sugar cane to the mills and transported workers.

WORTH DOING: By sitting in the same seat, you will be able to experience both an ocean view and a mountain view. The views alternate depending on the direction of the train. West Maui is a premier Hawaii tourist destination.

DON'T MISS: Don't miss the beautiful views of the Pacific Ocean and of the neighboring islands Molokai and Lanai from the 325-foot curved wooden trestle.

GETTING THERE: The Sugar Cane Train runs between the town of Lahaina and Kaanapali on the western coast of Maui. Many large airlines offer direct to Maui flights from most mainland, West Coast cities. Once on Maui, both of the railroad's stations are located off of Hwy. 30, the coast's main and only highway.

Ewa

Hawaiian Railway

Train ride, Museum

HAWAII

ADDRESS: 91-1001 Renton Rd., Ewa, HI 96706
TELEPHONE: 808-681-5461
E-MAIL: info@hawaiianrailway.com
WEB SITE: www.hawaiianrailway.com

The Hawaiian Railway is the only active railroad on Oahu. As the operating arm of the Hawaiian Railway Society, it runs on 6.5 miles of track, and the society is working to restore more.

CHOICES: The Hawaiian Railway offers two regularly scheduled 90-minute, fully narrated rides each Sunday. One Sunday a month, the famous Dillingham parlor car *Ambassador* is added to the regular train of open cars. Reservations are suggested for riding in the *Ambassador*. Three side-rod diesel locomotives have been restored to operation, and several steam locomotives have been cosmetically restored. Wear comfortable shoes and wander through the museum's vast collection of locomotives, cars, and other equipment.

WHEN TO GO: The museum is open year-round except for certain major holidays. Regularly scheduled train rides are on the weekends, however, charters can be arranged for weekday excursions.

GOOD TO KNOW: The Oahu Model Railroad Society is also located at the museum.

WORTH DOING: At one time or another, seven common carrier railroads ran on four of the islands – trains did not operate on Nihau and Kahoolaw – and 47 sugar plantations had private railway. The military also had its own railway system, primarily hauling ammunition. Pieces of Hawaii's railroading past can be spotted all over the islands. Drive around the industrial area of Honolulu and you may still find short stretches of three-foot-gauge rail in the streets.

DON'T MISS: The museum, which is situated on what was part of the Oahu Railway & Land Company main line, is north of Pearl Harbor. The scenery is incredible.

GETTING THERE: From Honolulu, take H1 west, exit on 5A Ewa. Stay on Hwy. 76 south for 2.5 miles. Turn right at the Tesoro Gas Station (Renton Road) and continue for 1.5 miles. Turn left onto small lane with a cul-de-sac. Entrance to the Hawaiian Railway is on your right through the chain link fence. City bus service is also available.

IDAHO

Museum
Canyon County Historical Museum

Built in 1903, the building served as the Oregon Short Line depot until 1925, when it was used as offices for the Union Pacific. The building now houses displays of Union Pacific and local historical photos and memorabilia. Outside, you can tour a UP caboose. The museum is open year-round Tuesday through Saturday.

ADDRESS: 1200 Front St., Nampa, ID 83651
TELEPHONE: 208-467-7611
E-MAIL: info@canyoncountyhistory.com
WEB SITE: www.canyoncountyhistory.com

Wallace   *Museum, Depot*
Northern Pacific Depot Railroad Museum

Listed on the National Register of Historic Places, this building served as a station until the 1980s. The elegant chateau-style depot was built at the turn of the 20th century from brick transported from China and concrete panels made from mine tailings. It now serves as a railroad museum that features exhibits on railroading in the area's mining district.

ADDRESS: 219 Sixth St., Wallace, ID 83873
TELEPHONE: 208-752-0111
WEB SITE: wallace-id.com/business.html#tourist

Thunder Mountain Line Railroad

ADDRESS: 120 Mill Rd., Horseshoe Bend, ID 83629
TELEPHONE: 877-432-7245 or 208-793-4425
WEB SITE: www.thundermountainline.com

This is one of the most scenic trips in the northern part of the Rocky Mountains. The train parallels the Payette River for most of the journey through sagebrush-covered hills, fir trees, and mountain meadows. Often visible are fox, deer, elk, blue heron, osprey, and bald eagles. Much of the river is good for whitewater rafting, so you not only get entertainment from the scenery but from the rafters as well.

CHOICES: Three different trips are possible. The *Horseshoe Bend Express* makes a two-hour round trip between Horseshoe Bend and Banks and travels along an old wagon road. The *Cabarton Flyer* leaves from the mountain town of Cascade and follows the Payette River. The *Cascade Limited* is a five-hour, one-way trip from Horseshoe Bend to Cascade that passes through Boise National Forest, which includes lunch and a return bus trip. The railroad also operates theme trains that allow you to experience a reenacted train robbery, murder mystery, or elegant dinner.

WHEN TO GO: The countryside is rugged and beautiful to travel through any time of the year. The *Horseshoe Bend Express* operates March through December, and the *Cabarton Flyer* and *Cascade Limited* run May through October. Themed train rides and special events take place throughout the year.

GOOD TO KNOW: The *Cabarton Flyer* boards at the Ashley Inn in Cascade.

WORTH DOING: Ride the *Cabarton Flyer* through what is believed to be the world's shortest railroad tunnel at 38 feet in length.

DON'T MISS: You can raft or kayak through Class IV rapids or just float along the scenic Payette River.

GETTING THERE: The Horseshoe Bend depot is located about 25 minutes north of Boise. Take Hwy. 55 from Boise to Horseshoe Bend and once there turn right on Mill Road. Cascade is about another 40 miles north of Horseshoe Bend on Hwy. 55, and the Ashley Inn is on Main Street (Hwy. 55).

ILLINOIS

Amboy   *Museum, Depot*
Amboy Depot Museum

Built in 1876, this former Illinois Central division headquarters building has been
restored, inside and out. It is now a local museum that presents the history of Amboy
and its relationship to the Illinois Central Railroad. The museum also contains a freight
house with additional artifacts, a retired steam engine, and a caboose. It is open year-
round.

ADDRESS: Main St., Amboy, IL 61310
TELEPHONE: 815-857-4700
E-MAIL: comments@amboydepotmuseum.org
WEB SITE: www.amboydepotmuseum.org

Chicago   *Museum*
Historic Pullman Foundation

The Historic Pullman Foundation operates the Pullman Visitor Center, which features
artifacts, photos and a video that informs visitors about George Pullman, the Pullman
Company, and Pullman's 1880s model industrial town. Guided walking tours of the
historic area are offered the first Sunday of the month from May through October.

ADDRESS: 11141 S. Cottage Grove Ave., Chicago, IL 60628
TELEPHONE: 773-785-8901
E-MAIL: foundation@pullmanil.org
WEB SITE: www.pullmanil.org

Chicago   *Museum*
Museum of Science and Industry

Board the *Silver Streak* and step into history. The showpiece of the museum's rail
collection, the *Pioneer Zephyr* completed a record-setting run in 1934 by traveling
from Denver to Chicago in just over 13 hours at an average speed of 77.5 mph. The
museum's 3,500-square-foot layout shows a train's journey from Chicago to Seattle.
Touring the German submarine *U-505* and the coal mine are a must.

ADDRESS: 57th St. and Lake Shore Dr., Chicago, IL 60637
TELEPHONE: 800-468-6674 or 773-684-1414
E-MAIL: msi@msichicago.org
WEB SITE: www.msichicago.org

Elizabeth

Elizabeth Train Depot Museum

Museum

This depot museum displays artifacts of the Chicago Great Western and other railroads. The depot serviced the nearby Winston Tunnel, the longest railroad tunnel in Illinois. The museum features a Milwaukee Road caboose, a working telegraph, and operating model railroads. It is open weekends May through October.

ADDRESS: 111 E. Myrtle St., Elizabeth, IL 61028
TELEPHONE: 815-858-2343
E-MAIL: elizabethhistoricalsociety@yahoo.com
WEB SITE: www.elizabeth-il.com

Galesburg

Galesburg Railroad Museum

Museum

The Galesburg Railroad Museum's display of artifacts and memorabilia includes a 1930 Burlington Route Hudson steam locomotive, a Railway Post Office/Railway Express Agency Car, a 1930 caboose, and two inspection cars. The museum is open April through November.

ADDRESS: 211 S. Seminary St., Galesburg, IL 61401
TELEPHONE: 309-342-9400
WEB SITE: www.visitgalesburg.com/attractions.html

Greenup

Historic Greenup Depot

Museum, Depot

Historic Greenup depot is a museum that displays artifacts of railroad and telegraph history. The preserved 1870 Vandalia Line depot also maintains a collection of audio, visual, and written materials related to these subjects. It is open year-round.

ADDRESS: 204 W. Cumberland St., Greenup, IL 62428
TELEPHONE: 217-923-9306
E-MAIL: historic@rr1.net
WEB SITE: www.greenupdepot.org

Kankakee

Kankakee Railroad Museum

Museum

Kankakee's restored train depot displays railroad memorabilia and a model train layout of Kankakee in the 1950s. A 1947 Pullman coach is displayed outside the depot. The museum is open weekends.

ADDRESS: 197 S. East Ave., Kankakee, IL 60901
TELEPHONE: 815-929-9320
WEB SITE: www.kankakeerrmuseum.us

Freeport   *Museum, Train ride*

Silver Creek & Stephenson Railroad

ADDRESS: 2954 S. Walnut Rd., Freeport, IL 61032
TELEPHONE: 815-232-2306
WEB SITE: www.thefreeportshow.com

This railroad offers a four-mile ride behind a 1912 geared Heisler steam engine. Trains leave from a reproduction of the original Illinois Central depot in Elroy, and the building houses a large collection of railroad memorabilia.

CHOICES: A Heisler steam locomotive pulls several cabooses and an open-car through farmlands and across the Yellow Creek on a 30-foot-high cement and stone pier bridge. The Silver Creek depot houses the ticket office and the railroad displays.

WHEN TO GO: The train ride operates on various weekends and holidays between Memorial Day and the end of October.

GOOD TO KNOW: Volunteers created this railroad on the abandoned right-of-way of the Chicago, Milwaukee, St. Paul & Pacific Railroad. Because rails and ties were removed prior to purchase, members had to haul rail in from as far away as Minnesota, and ties were salvaged from across Illinois. Members of the Stephenson County Antique Engine Club laid their first tracks in May 1985.

WORTH DOING: Ride the train on one trip and photograph the engine at work on a following outing.

DON'T MISS: Give the 36-ton Heisler a close inspection. Unlike most steam locomotives, it is driven with a V-2 arrangement of the cylinders on either side of the boiler; they run a crankshaft that moves a gearbox and wheels. Fewer than 1,200 of these locomotives were built and only a handful remain in operation today.

GETTING THERE: Freeport is about 20 miles west of Rockford on Hwy. 20, and the museum is on the corner of Walnut and Lamm Roads.

Monticello   *Museum, Train ride*

Monticello Railway Museum

ADDRESS: 993 Iron Horse Pl., Monticello, IL 61856
TELEPHONE: 877-762-9011 or 217-762-9011
E-MAIL: info@mrym.org
WEB SITE: www.mrym.org

In the midsection of Illinois, this museum offers one of the best collections of rolling stock and a good train ride to boot over former Illinois Central and Illinois Terminal trackage. Two streamlined diesel locomotives of the 1950s – one from the Canadian National and the other from the Wabash Railroad all decked out in their original attire – are among the most popular locomotives.

CHOICES: Although the museum has several steam engines, with a Milwaukee Road SWX and a former Illinois Central RS3, it has one of the Midwest's premier diesel locomotive collections. More than 80 pieces of rolling stock are on display. You can board the eight-mile round trip at one of two historic depots. At the museum, there is an Illinois Central depot, built in 1919 at Deland, and in downtown Monticello, an 1899 Wabash depot. You can make a layover at either location for further exploration and catch a later return trip.

WHEN TO GO: The museum is open on weekends and holidays May through October, with special events scheduled throughout the year, including a spring photo outing with its an extravaganza of operating equipment.

GOOD TO KNOW: The museum commissioned an entirely new boiler for Southern Railway Consolidation steam locomotive no. 401. The engine rebuild is expected to be completed in 2007.

WORTH DOING: For a fee, you can operate a locomotive for 30 minutes under the supervision of a regular member of the train crew during throttle time in spring and fall.

DON'T MISS: If you've ever dreamed of riding in a caboose, visit the museum in August when its annual Caboose Train is running. You could have a choice of up to seven different cabooses to ride in.

GETTING THERE: The museum is located between Champaign and Decatur, just off I-72. At Exit 166, take Market Street to Iron Horse Place and follow the frontage road to the end. The town of Monticello is just a few miles away via Hwy. 105.

Rochelle

Rochelle Railroad Park

ADDRESS: 124 N. Ninth St., Rochelle, IL 61068
TELEPHONE: 815-562-7031
E-MAIL: tourism@rochelle.net
WEB SITE: www.rochellerailroadpark.org

With more than 80 trains passing through daily, Rochelle Railroad Park is one of the most popular railroad-watching destinations in North America thanks to a perfect blend of heavy railroad action and a safe, well-appointed place to watch the passing trains.

CHOICES: BNSF Railway and Union Pacific double-track main lines cross right in the middle of Rochelle. Recognizing the popularity of their city to railfans, the city of Rochelle built a railroad park adjacent to the tracks that features picnic tables and a scanner tuned to the railroad radio frequencies. The park is an excellent place to watch trains around the clock. However, if you're interested in shooting photos or videos, the sun can be troublesome at times. At those times, you can venture out to other railroad hot spots in the area like the BNSF Mendota Subdivision in Mendota or the heavily trafficked BNSF Trancon at Toluca. Regardless of where your day takes you, the park is a great place to relax and watch trains.

WHEN TO GO: Since the park is always open, you can visit at any time of the day or any time of the year. Braving the cold winter months provides special viewing opportunities.

GOOD TO KNOW: There are a handful of hotels to choose from in the Rochelle area. Also, if you'd like a preview of the action in Rochelle, visit *Trains* magazine's Web site and watch from a live Web cam perched above the park's pavilion. Go to www.trainsmag.com and click on Web cams link. (The site requires registration, which is free.)

WORTH DOING: The Illinois Railroad Museum in Union has one of the greatest collections of railroad equipment in United States, and at only an hour's drive, it's well worth the trip.

DON'T MISS: For photographers looking for a unique old-meets-new vantage point, a drive west to Nelson is a must. There, a steam-era coal tower still straddles the very active Union Pacific double-track main line.

GETTING THERE: Rochelle is conveniently located at the junction of I-88 and I-39 in north central Illinois, a little over an hour from Chicago's O'Hare International Airport. Regional airports include Rockford, (30 minutes away) or Moline (90 minutes away).

Union   *Museum, Train ride, Trolley ride*

Illinois Railway Museum

ADDRESS: 7000 Olson Rd., Union, IL 60180
TELEPHONE: 800-244-7245 or 815-923-4000
WEB SITE: www.irm.org

Just 90 minutes northwest from downtown Chicago – and about half an hour from Union Pacific's Geneva Subdivision – lies the Illinois Railway Museum, which prides itself on running more diesel trains than other comparable museums. The museum also pays homage to its beginnings as an electric railway museum by operating streetcars and interurbans daily.

CHOICES: As an operating museum, there are many choices of trains to ride, including Chicago streetcars, North Shore and Chicago, Aurora & Elgin interurbans, and other commuter cars pulled by vintage diesels. You can even ride a trolley or electric bus from one equipment barn to another. When you're not riding trains, explore the nearly 80 acres of land and 400 pieces of equipment, plus signals, tools, signage, and other railroad artifacts. Six barns contain rail equipment; another has bus equipment. Admission includes unlimited rides.

WHEN TO GO: The museum is open weekends in April and October and daily from May through September. During July and August, remember that not all the cars and none of the barns are air-conditioned.

GOOD TO KNOW: Union is centrally located between Rockford and suburban Chicago and also offers tourists Donley's Wild West Town with gunslinger shows, pony rides, and gold panning. Nearby Marengo has several restaurants, including Main Street Pizza on Hwy. 23. About a dozen hotels are within a half-hour drive from the museum.

WORTH DOING: Diesel Days in July and Museum Showcase Weekend in September are great times to see a lot of equipment running. Typically, 14 vintage locomotives are put to work pulling freight and commuter trains on Diesel Days. On Museum Showcase Weekend, the staff operates less-frequently run equipment.

DON'T MISS: In addition to its extensive collection of locomotives and transit and passenger rail cars, the museum boasts 87 freight cars, a Little Joe, and even Chicago freight tunnel equipment. And for train watching, the Rochelle Railroad Park is 45 minutes away.

GETTING THERE: If driving from Chicago, take I-90 to Hwy. 20, the Marengo exit. Drive northwest about 4.5 miles to Union Road and take Union Road north.

Mendota   *Museum*
Union Depot Railroad Museum

The railroad museum is housed in the remaining portion of the 1888 depot. Fully restored, it contains materials related to the CB&Q, Illinois Central, and Milwaukee Road. You can tour a 1923 Mikado type 2-8-2 steam locomotive and a Milwaukee Road combine car. Grab a bite at the Freight House Grill in the newly renovated Illinois Central freight house.

ADDRESS: 683 Main St., Mendota, IL 61342
TELEPHONE: 815-538-3800
E-MAIL: mendotamuseums@tsf.net
WEB SITE: www.mendotamuseums.org/UDRR.htm

Rockford   *Trolley ride*
Trolley Car 36

Departing from downtown's Riverview Park, a 45-minute trolley ride transports you along Rockford's historic riverfront, with a 10-minute stopover at Sinnissippi Gardens and Lagoon. Excursions take place during the summer.

ADDRESS: 324 N. Madison St., Rockford, IL 61107
TELEPHONE: 815-987-8894
WEB SITE: www.rockfordparkdistrict.org/facilities.html

South Elgin   *Museum, Trolley ride*
Fox River Trolley Museum

Passengers ride the historic remnant of an 1896 interurban railroad on a four-mile trip along the banks of the Fox River and the Blackhawk Forest Preserve. The museum operates a variety of antique Chicago-area trolleys. The museum is open May through early November, and a number of special events are also scheduled.

ADDRESS: 361 S. LaFox St., South Elgin, IL 60177
TELEPHONE: 847-697-4676
E-MAIL: info@foxtrolley.org
WEB SITE: www.foxtrolley.org

INDIANA

Elkhart   *Museum*
National New York Central Railroad Museum

At this museum, you begin your journey through the history of the New York Central by entering through a 1915 passenger coach. In the main gallery, a 100-year-old freight house, hands-on exhibits let you construct track and operate a steam locomotive. Outside, the museum features a collection of locomotives and rolling stock including an NYC Mohawk 4-8-2.

ADDRESS: 721 S. Main St., Elkhart, IN 46515
TELEPHONE: 574-294-3001
E-MAIL: info@nycrrmuseum.org
WEB SITE: www.nycrrmuseum.org
DISCOUNT: Receive $1 off regular admission.

Knightstown   *Train ride*
Carthage, Knightstown and Shirley Railroad

After departing from the old New York Central station, the CKS takes you on a 10-mile, 75-minute round trip from Knightstown to Carthage. When you pull back into the station, you can look over the railroad's assortment of antique railroad equipment. The CKS offers special events, including train robberies, during its season. It operates Friday to Sunday May through October.

ADDRESS: 112 W. Carey St., Knightstown, IN 46148
TELEPHONE: 765-345-5561
WEB SITE: www.cksrail.com

Linden   *Museum, Depot*
Linden Railroad Museum

The Linden Railroad Museum contains memorabilia from the two railroads it served, the Nickel Plate Road and the Monon Railroad. It displays a caboose from each railroad and several other pieces of equipment. Built in 1907, it is listed on the National Register of Historic Places. It is open May through September.

ADDRESS: 520 N. Main St., Linden, IN 47955
TELEPHONE: 765-339-7245
WEB SITE: www.crawfordsville.org/depot.htm

Connersville   *Train ride*

Whitewater Valley Railroad

ADDRESS: 455 Market St., Connersville, IN 47331
TELEPHONE: 765-825-2054
WEB SITE: www.whitewatervalleyrr.org

This surprising 19-mile line travels from Connersville to Metamora with much of the trip near the Whitewater Canal. The scenic route features good views of the forests and farms along the route.

CHOICES: The railroad offers standard, open-window coaches as well as caboose rides on its 32-mile, five-hour round trip. A two-hour layover gives you a chance to tour Metamora, a restored canal town.

WHEN TO GO: Regular excursion trains operate on Saturdays and Sundays from May to October. During the year, watch for special event trains, such as the one to Metamora Canal Days or the Civil War Train.

GOOD TO KNOW: The railroad is in the early stages of developing an interpretive museum site. The Metamora community is a popular getaway spot with plenty of art galleries, shops, and restaurants.

WORTH DOING: Inspect the operating diesel built by the Lima Locomotive Works of Lima, Ohio. Believed to be the last of its kind in operation today, locomotive no. 25 was one of only 174 diesels built by this company, one of the most famous steam locomotive manufacturers of all time. The museum also owns three others from this builder.

DON'T MISS: Take time to explore the historic buildings of Metamora, watch its water-powered grist mill in action, and take a boat ride along the canal.

GETTING THERE: Connersville is about 65 miles southeast of Indianapolis and accessible from all directions. If coming from the north, take Hwy. 1 off I-70 into Connersville. The depot is on your left between Fourth and Fifth Streets.

Indiana Railway Museum

ADDRESS: 1 Monon St., French Lick, IN 47432
TELEPHONE: 800-748-724 or 812-936-2405
E-MAIL: museumstore@indianarailwaymuseum.org
WEB SITE: www.indianarailwaymuseum.org

For many years, the Southern Railway and the Monon Railroad brought scores of vacationers to the mineral spring baths in the southern Indiana hill country. Today, the French Lick, West Baden & Southern Railway offers the chance to take a 20-mile round trip ride, leaving from the 1907 depot that served both railroads, through beautiful forested country and through the 2,200-foot Burton tunnel to Cuzco.

CHOICES: Located in a historic depot, the Indiana Railway Museum operates the French Lick, West Baden & Southern Railway. Two-hour excursions through the Hoosier National Forest travel along lakes and limestone cuts. Train robbery specials occur throughout the season, and Santa trains and haunted trains also run. The museum features exhibits housed in the depot as well as an impressive collection of equipment. The collection includes steam and diesel locomotives and more than 65 passenger and freight cars.

WHEN TO GO: The museum is open year-round Monday through Friday and on weekends April through November. Trains operate weekends April through November and on Tuesdays between June and October. Trips in October feature beautiful fall colors of the scenic Hoosier National Forest.

GOOD TO KNOW: Southern Indiana is home to a variety of caves ready to explore, including Squire Boone Caverns, Wyandotte Caves, and Marengo Cave.

WORTH DOING: Be sure to check out the former Louisville, New Albany & Corydon Railroad boxcar no. 14023 repainted as a Pluto water car that shipped Pluto mineral water that was bottled by the French Lick Springs Hotel.

DON'T MISS: Tour or stay at the newly restored historic French Lick Springs Resort, listed on the National Register of Historic Place, or the West Baden Springs Hotel that features a 200-foot domed atrium and is a National Historic Landmark.

GETTING THERE: French Lick is in southern Indiana, easily accessible from Bloomington (60 miles), Columbus (90 miles), and Indianapolis (110 miles). From Indianapolis or Bloomington, take Hwy. 37 to Hwy. 56. Take Hwy. 56 west to French Lick and the museum. From Columbus, take I-65 to Hwy. 56.

DISCOUNT: Receive $1 off a regular adult ticket for up to four adults.

La Porte   *Museum, Train ride*

Hesston Steam Museum

ADDRESS: 1201 E. 1000 N, La Porte, IN 46350
TELEPHONE: 219-872-5055
WEB SITE: www.hesston.org

This unique museum features steam trains of two narrow gauges – two-foot and three-foot – in a parklike setting that also offers miniature live steam operations and other steam-powered attractions such as a sawmill and a steam crane.

CHOICES: Ride a steam locomotive, in your choice of gauges, through the museum's 155-acre site. Each train travels over a different route. Wander through a unique collection of steam equipment. Be sure to look for an 1889 Scottish-built locomotive and a Czech 0-4-0 built in 1940.

WHEN TO GO: Trains run weekends and holidays, Memorial Day through Labor Day and Sundays-only from Labor Day through October. On Memorial Day weekend, additional steam equipment runs, and the sawmill operates over the July 4 weekend. In fall, you can enjoy apple cider made from an antique press.

GOOD TO KNOW: The railroad's geared Shay locomotive, New Mexico Lumber Company no. 7, was the last narrow gauge model built back in 1929. After years of restoration due to fire damage, the Shay recently returned to operation.

WORTH DOING: Watch the 92-ton, steam-powered log crane feed logs to the steam-powered lumber mill. Take a walk down by the pond near the depot for a scenic photo of a steam train.

DON'T MISS: The annual Hesston Steam & Power Show takes place over Labor Day weekend. Beside trains, the event features the operation of antique farm machinery, cars, and other machinery.

GETTING THERE: The museum is in northern Indiana near the Michigan border and is about a 90-minute drive from Chicago. It is easily accessible from either I-94 (Exit 1) or the Indiana toll road (Exit 49) on Hwy. 1000.

New Haven

TrainTown

ADDRESS: 15808 Edgerton Rd., New Haven, IN 46774
TELEPHONE: 260-493-0765
E-MAIL: contact@765.org
WEB SITE: www.765.org

TrainTown, operated by the Fort Wayne Railroad Historical Society, is home to one of the nation's largest operating steam locomotives, Nickel Plate Road 2-8-4 no. 765, which runs occasionally.

CHOICES: On weekends, you can tour TrainTown and check out the 400-ton no. 765 and other historic rail equipment. Make sure to visit the shops and talk with the volunteers who restore everything from baggage carts to locomotives. Several times a year, the society conducts operating days with rides aboard a vintage caboose.

WHEN TO GO: TrainTown is open on Saturdays and Sundays. Excursions on the 765 are scheduled as the opportunities to run the locomotive become available.

GOOD TO KNOW: The 765, a 1944 Berkshire type, is one of the most modern and powerful steam locomotives still capable of operation. It has pulled excursion trains in 16 states and was rebuilt at a cost of more than $800,000.

WORTH DOING: The group offers an engineer-for-an-hour program with its 44-ton diesel. For a fee, you can operate the engine under supervision.

DON'T MISS: Get a conductor's eye-view from the newly restored Nickel Plate caboose 141.

GETTING THERE: TrainTown is just east of Fort Wayne in the village of New Haven. From Fort Wayne, take I-469 to Exit 21. Turn right on Harper Road, then right on Ryan Road, and left on Edgerton Road.

Noblesville   *Museum, Train ride, Dinner train*

Indiana Transportation Museum

ADDRESS: 325 Cicero Rd., Noblesville, IN 46061
TELEPHONE: 317-773-6000
E-MAIL: nkp587@iquest.net
WEB SITE: www.itm.org

The Indiana Transportation Museum offers a wide variety of historic displays and educational programs along with several rail excursions over 30 miles of track. The museum offers passengers an array of riding options, from casual to formal.

CHOICES: The *Weekend Express*, which operates on Saturday and Sunday afternoons, takes passengers on a 22-mile round trip through the bucolic Indiana countryside. The Hamiltonian Dinner Train, operating on select Friday evenings, lets passengers disembark along the route to enjoy the wide range of cuisine offered at several outstanding area restaurants. On various Saturday evenings, the Pizza Train runs to Tipton, the end of the line, for a casual pizza dinner. The museum also offers Dinner in the Diner, where diners are served a four-course meal aboard the *Cross Keys Tavern*, the restored Louisville & Nashville dining car no. 2728.

WHEN TO GO: Indiana Transportation Museum's operating season begins in mid-April and continues through October with its pumpkin patch specials. Holiday charters and the *Polar Bear Express* take place in December.

GOOD TO KNOW: The museum grounds are open to the public Saturdays and Sundays during the operating season. Museum admission fees apply to visit the grounds and are included in train fares purchased at the museum.

WORTH DOING: Bring a picnic lunch and enjoy the beautiful setting of Forest Park. For the kids, there is a carousel, playground, and miniature golf. For the adults, walking trails cover the park, and two golf courses are nearby.

DON'T MISS: Indiana Transportation Museum is home to two stately business cars, the recently restored Nickel Plate Road 1 and Florida East Coast no. 90. Advance arrangements are suggested for touring these magnificent examples of executive travel.

GETTING THERE: The museum is located in Noblesville's Forest Park, which is just north of Hwy. 32 on Hwy. 19. Just 20 miles north of Indianapolis, the area is easily accessible from I-69 and Hwy. 31. Amtrak serves Indianapolis from both Chicago and Washington D.C. Air transportation is provided by several national carriers at the Indianapolis International Airport.

Madison   *Museum, Depot*
Madison Railroad Station

This restored 1895 Pennsylvania Railroad station is known for its unique octagon waiting room with stained glass windows. Exhibits describe the Madison Railroad Station and the Madison Railroad Incline. You can visit an agent's office, reconstructed to 1903, and try its functioning telegraph key and walk through a restored, wooden caboose.

ADDRESS: 615 W. First St., Madison, IN 47250
TELEPHONE: 812-265-2335
WEB SITE: www.jcohs.org

Monon   *Museum*
Monon Connection Museum

The museum features a completely furnished, full-size replica of an Illinois Central depot and outdoor displays. Exhibits include a large collection of dining car china, hundreds of hand-held lanterns, and restored brass steam locomotive bells and whistles. It is open Tuesday through Sunday.

ADDRESS: 10012 N. Hwy. 421, Monon, IN 47959
TELEPHONE: 219-253-4100
WEB SITE: www.mononconnection.com

North Judson   *Museum, Train ride*
Hoosier Valley Railroad Museum

The museum's collection consists of 30 pieces of rolling stock, former Chesapeake & Ohio 2-8-4 steam locomotive no. 2789, and various types of restored railroad signals. The museum is open Saturdays, and train rides featuring cabooses are available May through September.

ADDRESS: 507 Mulberry St., North Judson, IN 46366
TELEPHONE: 574-896-3950
E-MAIL: hvrm@yahoo.com
WEB SITE: hvrm.railfan.net

Terre Haute   *Museum*
Wabash Valley Railroaders Museum

The museum features two interlocking towers with operating machines, a depot, and a viewing platform adjacent to CSXT mainlines. Haley Tower was one of the last manned interlocking towers in the Midwest, and the 1910 Spring Hill Tower was the last lever interlocking machine on the CP. It is open weekends May through October.

ADDRESS: 1316 Plum St., Terre Haute, IN 47804
TELEPHONE: 812-238-9958
WEB SITE: www.haleytower.org

IOWA

Marquette   *Museum*
Marquette Depot Museum

Housed in a renovated Milwaukee Road depot, the museum contains Milwaukee Road exhibits and general railroad artifacts. A restored caboose is on display. The museum is open daily May through October, and the depot also contains a travel information center.

ADDRESS: 216 Edgar St., Marquette, IA 52158
TELEPHONE: 563-873-1200

Train ride, Dinner train, Museum

Boone & Scenic Valley Railroad

ADDRESS: 225 10th St., Boone, IA 50036
TELEPHONE: 800-626-0319 or 515-432-4249
E-MAIL: info@bsvrr.com
WEB SITE: www.scenic-valleyrr.com

Iowa isn't known for rolling terrain, but this fascinating railroad provides a scenic ride with interesting landscape through the Des Moines River Valley. The railroad runs across two impressive bridges, with the 156-foot-tall Bass Point Creek High Bridge being the highlight of a 15-mile round trip. The railroad's dinner and dessert trains run on a slightly longer route.

CHOICES: The railroad is among the few in the country that offer steam-, diesel-, and electric-powered trains. You can ride a standard excursion in coach class or opt for the *Valley View* car, which was formerly a C&NW transfer caboose. There is also limited seating in the train's caboose. Hop the restored 1915 Charles City & Western electric trolley for an interurban run through downtown Boone. And browse the railroad equipment displayed on the grounds or inside the depot's museum.

WHEN TO GO: Between Memorial Day through the end of October, excursion trains run daily, while trolleys operate on weekends. Dinner trains are scheduled on various Fridays and Saturdays. The museum grounds are open year-round. The indoor museum is open daily during the summer season and weekdays November through May.

GOOD TO KNOW: The railroad's Chinese steam engine, built in 1989, is one of two built at that time and imported to the United States for tour and excursion service.

WORTH DOING: Boone celebrates its railroad heritage during Pufferbilly Days, an annual event with train rides, a model train display, a parade, and a spike-driving contest.

DON'T MISS: On the dinner or dessert trains, step outside on the *City of San Francisco's* rear observation deck to experience the sights and smells.

GETTING THERE: The railroad is in central Iowa, an hour's drive northwest of Des Moines. Take I-35 to Ames and travel west on Hwy. 30 to Boone. Go north on Story Street through the business district to 10th Street and go west six blocks to the depot.

IOWA

Union Pacific Railroad Museum

ADDRESS: 200 Pearl St., Council Bluffs, IA 51503
TELEPHONE: 712-329-8307
E-MAIL: upmuseum@up.com
WEB SITE: www.uprr.com/aboutup/history/museum

Few railroads have gone to the great lengths of the Union Pacific to preserve and document their past. The Union Pacific Railroad Museum houses one of the oldest corporation collections of any kind in the country. Visitors will not find lines of steam locomotives, diesels, or rolling stock. Rather, they will be inundated with a tasteful display of artifacts, photographs and documents that trace the development of the UP and the role it played in the American West.

CHOICES: The museum can be taken in whole or digested by specific eras depending on your interests. The Union Pacific's history is a history of the American West. The collection dates from the mid-1800s and features original manuscripts such as reports from survey teams searching for the best land route to lay tracks. Surveying equipment, early rail equipment, and other artifacts fill the building. Docents are available to show and explain everything within the museum's walls.

WHEN TO GO: With the exception of a raging snowstorm, even winter is a good time to visit the museum. Events and special exhibits are changed periodically during the year.

GOOD TO KNOW: Council Bluffs is a quiet, modern city across the Missouri River from Omaha, Neb. There are numerous motels, hotels, restaurants, and parks in both cities.

WORTH DOING: The museum has a combination of static and interactive displays. The working locomotive simulator will fuel your thirst in thinking about a career in railroading. Plan to spend many hours here.

DON'T MISS: Take time to tour both Council Bluffs and Omaha. Both are culturally rich cities with much to offer visitors. Council Bluffs has several casinos and is Iowa's leading gaming spot. The Henry Doorly Zoo in Omaha is a world-class zoo that appeals to adults as well as children.

GETTING THERE: Omaha is an important regional airline hub with numerous flights from all directions daily. Amtrak also serves Omaha.

Midwest Central Railroad

ADDRESS: 405 E. Threshers Rd., Mount Pleasant, IA 50322
TELEPHONE: 319-385-2912
WEB SITE: www.mcrr.org

The Midwest Central Railroad was established when volunteers built a 1.25-mile of track around the Midwest Old Threshers Reunion site and acquired several steam locomotives and cars. Later, to bring visitors and exhibitors into the grounds, a counter-clockwise trolley loop line was built, dubbed the Midwest Electric Railway. On this loop line, streetcars from around the world operate frequently, often with standing room only.

CHOICES: Both the Midwest Central Railroad and the Midwest Electric Railway are in full operation during the Old Threshers Reunion, which takes place over the Labor Day weekend. The Museum and Education Center houses the railroad's antique equipment. Both the railroad and the electric line operate ghost rides each October, and the railroad also runs a *Polar Express*.

WHEN TO GO: The Midwest Old Threshers Reunion begins the Thursday before Labor Day and ends on Labor Day. The railroad begins operating on the Wednesday prior to the reunion, and the trolleys begin running on the Saturday before the reunion.

GOOD TO KNOW: The Midwest Old Threshers Reunion is the largest gathering of agricultural and tractor enthusiasts in the United States. It's like an old-fashioned state fair with tractor pulls, a steam-powered merry-go-round, and other fun activities. But its emphasis is on living agricultural history, and there are demonstrations of steam tractors, early gas tractors, and other period farm implements.

WORTH DOING: Take an international trolley ride. Midwest Electric Railway international streetcars include two open-air cars from Rio de Janeiro, Brazil, and car no. 1945 from Milan, Italy.

DON'T MISS: If you're a camper, stay at the Old Threshers campground and take the trolley into the grounds, then ride the train. You can take in the whole show without the hassle of parking and enjoy the sites and sounds of steam as you camp. Just be sure to make campground (or hotel) reservations early.

GETTING THERE: Probably the best way to visit Mount Pleasant is by driving. Located in southeastern Iowa, Mount Pleasant is south of Iowa City on Hwy. 218. The city is also served daily by Amtrak trains 5 and 6, the *Chicago-Emeryville (California) Zephyr*.

KANSAS

Abilene   *Train ride, Dinner train*
Abilene & Smoky Valley Railroad

A 90-minute, 10-mile round trip goes through the Smoky Hill River Valley from historic Abilene to Enterprise. The track crosses the river on a high-span steel bridge. The diesel-powered excursion train includes a restored 1902 wood Katy passenger car converted to a dining car, two open-air gondola cars with canopy tops, and a caboose.

ADDRESS: 200 S. Fifth St., Abilene, KS 67410
TELEPHONE: 888-426-6687 or 785-263-1077
E-MAIL: info@asvrr.org
WEB SITE: www.asvrr.org

Kingman   *Museum, Depot*
Santa Fe Depot

Dating to 1911, the former Santa Fe depot is on the National Register of Historic Places. It contains railroad memorabilia, some found within the depot itself, and a model train display. The stylish brick building also houses the Cannonball Welcome Center. It is open year-round, Monday through Friday.

ADDRESS: 201 E. Sherman Ave., Kingman, KS 67068
TELEPHONE: 620-532-2142
E-MAIL: thedepot@websurf.net
WEB SITE: skyways.lib.ks.us/towns/Kingman/depot

Wichita   *Museum*
Great Plains Transportation Museum

The museum features an outdoor display of locomotives, cabooses, and cars, including Santa Fe steam locomotive no. 3768 and Santa Fe FP45 diesel no. 93. Indoor exhibits feature railroad signs, lanterns, tools, and other artifacts. It is open year-round on Saturdays and also on Sundays from April to October.

ADDRESS: 700 E. Douglas Ave., Wichita, KS 67202
TELEPHONE: 316-263-0944
WEB SITE: www.gptm.us

Baldwin City　　　　　　　　　　　　　　　　　　　　*Train ride, Depot*

Midland Railway

ADDRESS: 1515 W. High St., Baldwin City, KS 66006
TELEPHONE: 800-651-0388 or 913-371-3410
WEB SITE: www.midland-ry.org

The Midland is a growing tourist line near Kansas City, offering 20-mile round trips in the pleasant Kansas countryside between Baldwin City and Ottawa. The Midland has an impressive roster of first-generation diesels for a line this size, including an Alco RS-3 in its original New York Central livery, an E-6 and an E-8 from the Rock Island, a Burlington NW-2, and a rare RS-3m from the Katy.

CHOICES: Regular service includes one-hour excursions from Baldwin City to Norwood that cross two 200-foot trestles and two-hour trips to the end of the line at Ottawa Junction, where the line meets BNSF's Transcon. Group charters and caboose charters are available. Midland also offers a mystery train, Thomas the Tank Engine, and other specials. The Midland has recently rehabilitated several miles of new trackage.

WHEN TO GO: The Midland operates primarily on weekends from June to October, with seasonal trains around Easter, Halloween, and Christmas. The annual Railfan Weekend is a big draw, with rides available in diesel cabs, on track speeders, or on a Railway Post Office car. The Midland also participates in a variety of community festivals, including the annual Planes, Trains, and Automobiles celebration on Father's Day weekend and the Maple Leaf Festival, the third weekend in October.

GOOD TO KNOW: Baldwin City has a pair of B&Bs, plus a host of independent and chain restaurants, all within two miles of the Midland station. More extensive offerings can be found within a 30-minute drive in Lawrence, Ottawa, or Olathe.

WORTH DOING: Look through the Midland's 1906 Baldwin City depot, which is on the National Register of Historic Places.

DON'T MISS: Visit the bridge near the Douglas-Franklin County line, which is a favorite photo location. Directions can be obtained at the Baldwin City station.

GETTING THERE: The closest Amtrak stops are Lawrence and Kansas City, Mo. The closest large airport is Kansas City. Baldwin City is 45 miles southwest of downtown Kansas City on Hwy. 56. The Midland depot is on High Street just west of the town square.

DISCOUNT: Take $1 off adult ticket (not good on specials).

KENTUCKY

Museum

Railway Museum of Greater Cincinnati

The museum collects, restores, and displays equipment that belonged to the seven railroads that served Cincinnati. The outdoor yard contains more than 70 cars and locomotives. It includes a large number of Pullman cars, several switchers, and a Pennsylvania Railroad E8A diesel locomotive. It is open Wednesdays and Saturdays year-round and on every fourth Sunday from May through October.

ADDRESS: 315 W. Southern Ave., Covington, KY 41015
TELEPHONE: 859-491-7245
E-MAIL: questions@cincirailmuseum.org
WEB SITE: www.cincirailmuseum.org

Paducah   Museum

Paducah Railroad Museum

Operated by the Paducah Chapter of National Railway Historical Society, the museum displays equipment and memorabilia from railroads including the three that served Paducah. It features replicas of a waiting room and freight office as well as section cars, tools, and an operating CTC system. A steam engine, a caboose, and a baggage combine are displayed a block away.

ADDRESS: 200 Washington St., Paducah, KY 42003
TELEPHONE: 270-519-7377
WEB SITE: www.paducahrr.org

Versailles   Train ride, Museum

Bluegrass Scenic Railroad

The railroad offers a six-mile round trip through the heart of Kentucky's Bluegrass region. The diesel-powered train is made up of vintage coaches from the 1920s and '30s and departs from Woodford County Park. Indoor and outdoor displays include a watchman's shanty, a working telegraph set, and Kentucky railroading artifacts.

ADDRESS: 175 Beasley Rd., Versailles, KY 40383
TELEPHONE: 800-755-2476 or 859-873-2476
WEB SITE: www.bgrm.org

Bardstown

My Old Kentucky Dinner Train

Dinner train

ADDRESS: 602 N. Third St., Bardstown, KY 40004
TELEPHONE: 866-801-3463 or 502-348-7500
E-MAIL: info@rjcorman.com
WEB SITE: www.kydinnertrain.com

My Old Kentucky Dinner Train operates in 1940s dining cars on 15 miles of former Louisville & Nashville track between Bardstown and Limestone Springs. The passenger waiting room is located in Bardstown's former limestone freight house, which dates from 1860 and is on the National Register of Historic Places.

CHOICES: The train operates year-round and offers both lunch and dinner trips, as well as occasional special events such as a mystery train. It offers two-hour lunch excursions on Saturdays. Other lunch and dinner excursions run Tuesday through Saturday on a varied schedule. Menu selections for the four-course meal include prime rib, seafood, and poultry. There are also vegetarian dishes and children's items. Trains are pulled by two ex-Southern FP-7a's. The Budd-built lightweight cars are of AT&SF, C&O, and PRR ancestry, including the former C&O 1921 that operated on President Dwight Eisenhower's funeral train. Two distilleries, several warehouses, and two restored depots, Deatsville and Limestone Springs, are on the line.

WHEN TO GO: The scenery is especially nice in spring and fall, and the temperatures are in the 70s and low 80s. Tobacco is grown from June through August and can be viewed along the route.

GOOD TO KNOW: Founded in 1780, Bardstown is Kentucky's second-oldest city and features a mix of old and new inns, restaurants, and shops. There are also accommodations in Elizabethtown, about 20 minutes away.

WORTH DOING: The area is rich in history and includes Civil War museums as well as Abraham Lincoln's birthplace and his boyhood home. Several local distilleries give tours, and the Kentucky Railway Museum is 15 minutes away.

DON'T MISS: The train passes through part of the Bernheim Forest, a private 14,000-acre nature preserve, a habitat for a variety of trees, vegetation, and wildlife. While in the forest, the train passes slowly over the 310-foot-long, 60-foot-high Jackson Hollow timber trestle built for predecessor Bardstown & Louisville Railroad in 1860.

GETTING THERE: Bardstown is about 40 miles south of Louisville and 55 miles southwest of Lexington. Air service is available to Louisville International Airport and Blue Grass Airport in Lexington. When driving from Louisville, take Hwy. 31E, and from Lexington, take Hwy. 60 west and then the Blue Grass Parkway.

KENTUCKY

KENTUCKY

New Haven　　　　　　　　　　　　　　　　*Museum, Train ride, Dinner train*

Kentucky Railway Museum

ADDRESS: 136 S. Main St., New Haven, KY 40051
TELEPHONE: 800-272-0152 or 502-549-5470
E-MAIL: info@kyrail.org
WEB SITE: www.kyrail.org

Housed in a replica of the original New Haven station, the Kentucky Railway Museum has more than 50,000 items in its collection and more than 120 pieces of rolling stock and engines. The museum also operates excursions on 17 miles of former Louisville & Nashville track.

CHOICES: The Kentucky Railway Museum's excursion trains take you on a 22-mile, 90-minute round trip through the scenic and historic Rolling Fork River Valley between New Haven and Boston. The museum's centerpiece is ex-L&N 4-6-2 no. 152, built in 1905 and listed on the National Register. The locomotive is currently under repair but is expected to be in operation by summer 2007. Other operating power includes ex-Monon BL-2 no. 32 and ex-AT&SF CF-7 2546. The museum also offers dinner trains, murder mystery trains, engine and caboose rides, train holdups, and Santa trains.

WHEN TO GO: The museum is open year-round, and excursions take place April through December. Trains run every day, except Monday, from the end of May through mid-August. The remainder of the schedule, April through May and August through December, excursions take place on weekends. Spring and fall scenery is nice, with temperatures in the 70s and low 80s. Open-air and air-conditioned coaches are available.

GOOD TO KNOW: Hotels and inns are available in Bardstown and Elizabethtown, both about 20 minutes away. The Sherwood Inn, a B&B, is adjacent to the museum.

WORTH DOING: Special events at the museum include days out with Thomas the Tank Engine, Kentucky Educational Television Day, and Iron Horse Festival Days.

DON'T MISS: Abraham Lincoln was born nearby, and historical sites to visit include his birthplace, boyhood home, and the Lincoln Museum. Mammoth Cave National Park, Fort Knox, the Patton Museum of Cavalry and Armor, and My Old Kentucky Home State Park are also close by. My Old Kentucky Dinner Train is 15 miles away.

GETTING THERE: The museum is located about 45 miles from Louisville and 65 miles from Lexington. If driving from Louisville, take I-65 south to Exit 105 and then take Hwys. 61, 62, 52, and 31E to New Haven. From Lexington, take Hwy. 60 west to the Blue Grass Parkway and then Hwy. 31E.

DISCOUNT: Receive 10 percent off train fares.

Stearns

Big South Fork Scenic Railway

ADDRESS: 100 Henderson St., Stearns, KY 42647
TELEPHONE: 800-462-5664 or 606-376-5330
E-MAIL: info@bsfsry.com
WEB SITE: www.bsfsry.com

In the 20th century, short lines and branches brought forth coal for use nationwide, and one of the primary locations was Stearns, home of the Kentucky & Tennessee short line. The coal is gone now, but the K&T has been reborn as a scenic railroad.

CHOICES: The railway offers three-hour trips through the Big South Fork National River and Recreation Area on the former Kentucky & Tennessee Railway. The train follows mountain streams, passes through a tunnel, and crosses a bridge as it descends 600 feet to the floor of the river valley. The ride includes a layover at the restored mining camp of Blue Heron.

WHEN TO GO: The railroad runs on a varied schedule from the end of March through December, but spring is especially beautiful in this part of the Appalachians because of all of the blooming plants that inhabit the mountains.

GOOD TO KNOW: The railroad is restoring a 1944 0-6-0 type steam locomotive for service on the line. Expansion of the line to the Worley mining camp is also underway.

WORTH DOING: Train fares include admission to the McCreary County Museum that is housed in the Stearns Coal and Lumber Company headquarters that was built in 1907.

DON'T MISS: Take the walking tour of the Blue Heron Mine at the end of the run. Built in 1937, this mine and coal tipple operated until it was abandoned in 1962 and restored with ghost structures and oral history exhibits in 1989 by the National Park Service as part of the Big South Fork River and Recreation Area. You can also camp, hike, fish, and raft the river.

GETTING THERE: Stearns is 70 miles from Knoxville, Tenn., and 120 miles from Lexington. From Knoxville, take I-75 north to Exit 141. Take Hwy. 63 west to the junction with Hwy. 27. Take Hwy. 27 north to Stearns. Turn left on Hwy. 92 and travel west one mile to the depot.

LOUISIANA

DeQuincy   *Museum, Depot*
DeQuincy Railroad Museum

Home to the DeQuincy Railroad Museum, the former Kansas City Southern depot is an outstanding example of Mission Revival architecture and is on National Register of Historic Places. It displays a 1913 Alco steam locomotive, a caboose, and a passenger coach as well as artifacts and memorabilia. The annual Louisiana Railroad Days Festival is held here in April.

ADDRESS: 400 Lake Charles Ave., DeQuincy, LA 70633
TELEPHONE: 337-786-2823

Jackson   *Train ride*
Old Hickory Railroad

The Old Hickory Railroad features a live steam locomotive pulling two open coaches on a six-mile trip through the town of Jackson, which has more than 100 historic buildings. It operates Saturdays and Sundays from March through November. The site also houses the G scale Little Hickory Railroad and the Republic of West Florida Museum.

ADDRESS: 3406 College St., Jackson, LA 70748
TELEPHONE: 225-634-7397
WEB SITE: www.louisianasteamtrain.com

Long Leaf   *Museum*
Southern Forest Heritage Museum

At this museum, a guided tour takes you around a 57-acre historic sawmill complex, where you'll see a roundhouse and other industrial structures, three early logging locomotives, two McGiffert loaders, a Clyde skidder, and other steam equipment. Motorcar rides on original Red River & Gulf railroad track are also available.

ADDRESS: Hwy. 497, Long Leaf, LA 71448
TELEPHONE: 318-748-8404
E-MAIL: longleaf@centurytel.net
WEB SITE: www.forestheritagemuseum.org

MAINE

Bangor   *Museum*

Cole Land Transportation Museum

The museum houses 200 antique land transportation vehicles and 2,000 photographs of life in early Maine. Its railroad collection includes one of the first Bangor and Aroostook diesels, a CP section shack, a Maine Central caboose, and a relocated station.

ADDRESS: 405 Perry Rd., Bangor, ME 04401
TELEPHONE: 207-990-3600
E-MAIL: mail@colemuseum.org
WEB SITE: www.colemuseum.org

Boothbay   *Museum, Train ride*

Boothbay Railway Village

A two-foot-gauge steam train ride takes you around a re-created historic village. Rail buildings include several stations, an engine house, a water tower, and a crossing tower. Exhibits include a history of Maine narrow gauge railroads, and various pieces of rolling stock and equipment are on display, as are more than 50 antique or classic automobiles and other vehicles.

ADDRESS: 586 Wiscasset Rd., Boothbay, ME 04537
TELEPHONE: 207-633-4727
E-MAIL: staff@railwayvillage.org
WEB SITE: www.railwayvillage.org

Kennebunkport   *Museum, Trolley ride*

Seashore Trolley Museum

The museum offers a 25-minute ride through the countryside aboard a restored early 1900s electric streetcar. There are more than 50 streetcars on display in three carbarns. Almost every state is represented as well as Canada, Japan, and several European countries. Special events, including a sunset ride with ice cream, are scheduled throughout the year.

ADDRESS: 195 Log Cabin Rd., Kennebunkport, ME 04046
TELEPHONE: 207-967-28712
E-MAIL: info@trolleymuseum.org
WEB SITE: www.trolleymuseum.org

Alna   *Museum, Train ride*

Wiscasset, Waterville & Farmington Railway

ADDRESS: 97 Cross Rd., Alna, ME 04535
TELEPHONE: 207-882-4193
E-MAIL: webmaster@wwfry.org
WEB SITE: www.wwfry.org

The railway is a faithful recreation of a portion of the original two-foot-gauge Wiscasset, Waterville & Farmington Railway, abandoned following a wreck in 1933. This line is being rebuilt by volunteers on the original right-of-way under the original charter, and the museum operates several pieces of preserved rolling stock from the original railway.

CHOICES: Trains operate between the Sheepscot station and Alna Center. Be sure to save some time to visit the railway's shop, where museum volunteers rebuild and maintain rolling stock using old-time skills and techniques, or take a walk beyond Alna Center to view the cleared grade where track will be constructed. Maine was famous for its two-foot gauge railways, a thrifty New England response to the expense of building and maintaining a railroad. Five two-foot-gauge railways once operated in Maine, but all were closed by 1941.

WHEN TO GO: The museum is open every Saturday year-round, as well as on Sundays beginning Memorial Day weekend through October. Trains operate when the museum is open. September and October are the best months to visit, after the summer crowds have diminished and the insects are dormant.

GOOD TO KNOW: The mid-coast region of Maine features plenty of motels and campgrounds, as well as numerous places to sample the bounty of the sea, especially lobsters, clams, and fish. Room rates are highest in July and August, and reservations are a must. Traffic on Hwy. 1, the main coastal artery, is very heavy and slow moving on summer weekends.

WORTH DOING: Visit the museum during the spring and fall "track meets," long weekends when volunteers from all over the country arrive to construct track, extending the railway a thousand feet or more during each session. You can even join in if you like.

DON'T MISS: Be sure to ride in Wiscasset & Quebec coach no. 3, a gem built by Jackson & Sharpe in 1894.

GETTING THERE: The closest airports are in Portland and Augusta. The museum itself is on

Train ride, Museum

MAINE

Maine Narrow Gauge Railroad & Museum

ADDRESS: 58 Fore St., Portland, ME 04101
TELEPHONE: 207-828-0814
E-MAIL: mngrr@maine.rr.com
WEB SITE: www.mngrr.org

The Maine Narrow Gauge Railroad & Museum operates along the Eastern Promenade fronting Casco Bay, offering spectacular views of ferries, sailboats, cruise ships, lobster boats, and freighters as well as the many islands dotting the bay.

CHOICES: The Maine Narrow Gauge Railroad operates with diesel and steam locomotives during most of the year. Both authentic open-window coaches and open-sided excursion cars are used. Tour the museum and see several beautifully restored passenger coaches, including *Rangeley*, the only two-foot-gauge private car ever built. Also on display is a railbus used on the Sandy River and Bridgton & Harrison.

WHEN TO GO: The Santa trains during the Christmas season are wonderful, operating into the evening hours. Steam locomotives are usually in service on weekends, especially in the summer and fall. Call ahead if steam is important.

GOOD TO KNOW: Most of the Maine Narrow Gauge equipment operated on either the Sandy River & Rangeley Lakes or the Bridgton & Harrison, two famed Maine two-footers. They were saved from the scrappers in the 1940s by industrialist Ellis D. Atwood and operated at the Edaville Railroad in Massachusetts until 1994, when it was returned to Maine.

WORTH DOING: Ride on the water side of the train for the best views. A walking and bike path follows the line for its entire length, making action photos easy.

DON'T MISS: The Portland waterfront is a busy area for tourists, and there are many other attractions in the area, including much of the original Federal-style architecture found in Maine's second largest city.

GETTING THERE: Portland International Airport is nearby, and Boston's Logan Airport is about two hours south. Amtrak's "Down Easter" trains run between Boston's North Station and Portland. I-95 passes just west of Portland.

MAINE

Oakfield   *Museum*
Oakfield Railroad Museum

Exhibits in the restored Oakfield station include hundreds of photographs dating to the beginning of the Bangor & Aroostook Railroad in 1891, vintage signs and advertising pieces, signal lanterns, original railroad maps, and telegraph equipment. A restored caboose and mail cars are also displayed. It is open Saturday and Sunday afternoons.

ADDRESS: Station St., Oakfield, ME 04763
TELEPHONE: 207-757-8575
E-MAIL: oakfieldmuseum@pwless.net
WEB SITE: www.oakfieldmuseum.org

Phillips   *Train ride, Museum*
Sandy River and Rangeley Lakes Railroad

You can ride along the original narrow gauge roadbed of the SR&RL Railroad in 1884 Laconia Coach no. 18, powered by a replica of SR&RL no. 4 or a Monson steam locomotive. You can also tour the eight-stall roundhouse to see ongoing restoration projects. Trains operate on select weekends June through October.

ADDRESS: 128 Bridge St., Phillips, ME 04966
TELEPHONE: 207-778-3621
WEB SITE: www.srrl-rr.org

Richmond   *Train ride*
New England Railroad

Take a relaxing New England vacation on a different type of train. A DMU self-propelled commuter rail car pulls glass-domed coaches and dining cars that offer panoramic views of the countryside. The railroad offers two levels of service. Service to Montreal is also available.

ADDRESS: 17 Church St., Richmond, ME 04357
TELEPHONE: 603-294-4367
E-MAIL: webmaser_newenglandrailroad@msn.com
WEB SITE: www.newenglandrailroad.com

MARYLAND

Baltimore Museum, Trolley ride
Baltimore Streetcar Museum

Relive Baltimore's history of rail transit from 1859 to 1963 by riding the museum's streetcars. Various cars are in service on the one-mile rides. In Trolley Theatre, you can view a short video about streetcars. Baltimore Transit Company's rare crane car 3715 is also available for touring. The museum is open Sundays year-round and Saturdays June through October.

ADDRESS: 1901 Falls Rd., Baltimore, MD 21211
TELEPHONE: 410-547-0264
WEB SITE: www.baltimorestreetcar.org

Chesapeake Beach Museum, Depot
Chesapeake Beach Railway Museum

From 1900 until 1935, the Chesapeake Beach Railway brought people to the resorts of Chesapeake Beach and North Beach. Housed in the railway's original station, the museum exhibits photographs, artifacts, and memorabilia from both railroad and the resort. A parlor car is also on display. It is open daily May through September and on weekends the rest of the year.

ADDRESS: 4155 Mears Ave., Chesapeake Beach, MD 20732
TELEPHONE: 410-257-3892
E-MAIL: cbrailway@co.cal.md.us
WEB SITE: www.cbrm.org

Colesville Museum, Trolley ride
National Capital Trolley Museum

Various cars from the museum's collection operate on a one-mile demonstration track. The 20-minute rides take you through Northwest Branch Park. The museum features exhibits of street railway artifacts and photographs, and it offers a video presentation and a full calendar of special events.

ADDRESS: 1313 Bonifant Rd., Colesville, MD 20905
TELEPHONE: 301-384-6088
WEB SITE: www.dctrolley.org

Baltimore

Museum, Train ride

Baltimore & Ohio Railroad Museum

ADDRESS: 901 W. Pratt St., Baltimore, MD 21223
TELEPHONE: 410-752-2490
E-MAIL: info@borail.org
WEB SITE: www.borail.org

Known as the birthplace of American railroading, the B&O Railroad Museum combines one of the most diverse and historic collections of railroad artifacts and rolling stock, one of the most historic settings for a railroad museum, and a unique focus upon a single railroad (the Baltimore & Ohio) and its subsidiaries and successors, all in an unusual urban setting.

CHOICES: The museum occupies several vintage buildings including a fully covered roundhouse and turntable built in 1884. The domed roundhouse is a distinctive feature of Baltimore's skyline. The museum houses the largest collection of 19th century locomotives in North America, including B&O locomotives dating back to 1836. Operable replicas of the 1831 *Tom Thumb* and the *Lafayette* are also on display. Later steamers and diesels are also well represented, and many passenger and freight cars round out the collection.

WHEN TO GO: The summer months are not only high tourist season in Baltimore but also months of typically muggy humidity. Late spring and fall are recommended, but the museum is open year-round, with special events spread throughout the year.

GOOD TO KNOW: The B&O museum is located in a residential neighborhood just west of downtown and the city's major stadiums. You can walk from downtown's Inner Harbor district, but a taxi or MTA transit bus is recommended.

WORTH DOING: Allow at least a half day for a full tour, including a train ride down the "first mile" of American intercity railroading (included with admission). Although the ride is through urban back lots and the now-empty sites of many B&O shops, if scheduling permits, stop at the museum's restoration facility and observe craftsmen restoring vintage rolling stock. Combined admission to the nearby Ellicott City Railroad Museum, the oldest railroad station in America, is also available.

DON'T MISS: Baltimore has a host of other attractions, including the Baltimore Streetcar Museum, a Civil War museum in the President Street Station, the National Aquarium, the Maryland Zoo, the Walters Art Gallery, and Fort McHenry.

GETTING THERE: Baltimore is served by many airlines, Amtrak, intercity bus, and mass transit, and the museum is only a few minutes off I-95.

DISCOUNT: Take $1 off the regular admission for each member of your party.

Western Maryland Scenic Railroad

ADDRESS: 13 Canal St., Cumberland, MD 21502
TELEPHONE: 800-872-4650 or 301-759-4400
E-MAIL: trainmaster@wmsr.com
WEB SITE: www.wmsr.com

Of all the Appalachian freight railroads, the Western Maryland was one of the most beloved because of its excellent steam power, which tackled difficult mountain grades. The trip out of Cumberland on the roadbed of the main line, with a short detour the last few miles onto a branch into Frostburg, is one of the best parts of the Western Maryland. The railroad also offers locomotive cab rides and caboose rides for an extra fee.

CHOICES: Ride in restored coaches pulled by a 1916 Baldwin steam locomotive or a vintage diesel through the mountains of western Maryland on a 32-mile round trip between Cumberland's restored Western Maryland Railway station and the 1891 Cumberland & Pennsylvania depot in Frostburg. First-class seating, which includes lunch, is available on some departures. The railroad also offers murder mystery and specialty trains.

WHEN TO GO: Trains run May through December. October, during the height of the fall color season, is especially beautiful, but make reservations in advance because the trains can fill up quickly.

GOOD TO KNOW: The Western Maryland station is home to the C&O Canal Museum. Both Cumberland and Frostburg have a variety of shops and restaurants.

WORTH DOING: When the train arrives in Frostburg, you have a 90-minute layover. Be sure to walk forward and find a spot to watch the locomotive change directions on the turntable.

DON'T MISS: Stick to the right side of the train. Leaving Cumberland, the train passes through the Narrows, a gap in the mountain that also allows the highway and paralleling CSX (the former B&O) an escape to the west. Just beyond is famous Helmstetter's Curve, a sharp turn in the railroad tracks to gain elevation. From here on, views remain mostly on the right side as the train makes its way higher into the mountains.

GETTING THERE: When driving, Cumberland is about two-and-a-half hours from Baltimore, Washington, or Pittsburgh. From either direction, the Western Maryland station is easily reached from Exit 43C off I-68 in downtown Cumberland.

Ellicott City   *Museum, Depot*
Ellicott City Station

Located on the B&O Railroad's historic Old Main Line, Ellicott City Station could be the oldest surviving railroad station in the country. The main depot building was completed in 1831, and the freight house was built in 1855. The museum displays a replica of the first horse-drawn passenger rail car, the *Pioneer*, and a 1927 caboose.

ADDRESS: 2711 Maryland Ave., Ellicott City, MD 21043
TELEPHONE: 410-461-1945
WEB SITE: www.ecbo.org

Gaithersburg   *Museum*
Gaithersburg Community Museum

Located in the restored 1884 B&O railroad station complex, the museum includes the historic freight house and an outdoor display of steam locomotives, rolling stock, and baggage wagons. The freight house contains permanent and rotating exhibits. Displayed are a 1918 Buffalo Creek and Gauley no. 14 steam locomotive, a B&O Wagontop, and a troop kitchen car.

ADDRESS: 9 S. Summit Ave., Gaithersburg, MD 20877
TELEPHONE: 301-258-6160
WEB SITE: www.gaithersburgmd.gov/museum

Hagerstown   *Museum*
Hagerstown Roundhouse Museum

The museum houses memories of the Western Maryland Railway with artifacts, photos, and model train layouts. A Baldwin diesel and Hagerstown & Frederick trolley are on display. It is open Friday through Sunday year-round.

ADDRESS: 300 S. Burhans Blvd., Hagerstown, MD 21741
TELEPHONE: 301-739-4665
WEB SITE: www.roundhouse.org

Walkersville   *Train ride, Museum*
Walkersville Southern Railroad

The Walkersville Southern Railroad takes you on a pleasant eight-mile, 70-minute round trip that travels through forests and farm country and crosses the Monocacy River. You can ride in an open-air excursion car, refurbished troop carrier, caboose, or passenger coach. It offers a murder mystery train and other special events. An 1880s station, freight house, and museum are also on the site.

ADDRESS: 34 W. Pennsylvania Ave., Walkersville, MD 21793
TELEPHONE: 877-363-9777 or 301-898-0899
E-MAIL: pres@wsrr.org
WEB SITE: www.wsrr.org

MASSACHUSETTS

Train ride
Edaville USA

This is a family fun park with a two-mile train ride through a 1,300-acre cranberry plantation. There are 11 amusement rides and an indoor play area. Special events include National Cranberry Festival, Holiday Festival of Lights, and many others.

ADDRESS: 7 Eda Ave., South Carver, MA 02336
TELEPHONE: 877-332-8455 or 508-866-8190
E-MAIL: info@edaville.com
WEB SITE: www.edaville.com

Chatham   *Museum*
Chatham Railroad Museum

This restored country depot is situated on its original site. Exhibits feature hundreds of railroad artifacts from the Chatham Railroad Company and other railroads, including a restored 1910 New York Central caboose and telegraph instruments.

ADDRESS: 153 Depot Rd., Chatham , MA 02633
TELEPHONE: 508-945-5199
WEB SITE: www.chathamrailroadmuseum.com

Hyannis   *Dinner train, Train ride*

Cape Cod Central Railroad

ADDRESS: 252 Main St., Hyannis, MA 02601
TELEPHONE: 888-797-7325 or 508-771-3800
E-MAIL: sales@capetrain.com
WEB SITE: www.capetrain.com

The Cape Cod Central Railroad operates diesel-powered scenic excursions and dinner trains, which also include luncheon and brunch outings. It runs from Hyannis over 23 miles of the former Old Colony Railroad that became part of the New York, New Haven & Hartford. Trains run from Memorial Day weekend through October in various combinations and with varying frequencies. Boarding is also possible at Sandwich.

CHOICES: For evening dining, passengers can select either the Elegant Dinner Train, involving multiple courses served with all the flourishes, or the Family Supper Train, which offers less formal service, a shorter ride, and special meals attractive to children.

WHEN TO GO: Sea breezes mean that Hyannis typically remains temperate throughout the railroad's operating season but visiting out of high summer may minimize crowds.

GOOD TO KNOW: Hyannis is quintessential Cape Cod, with all the sun, sand, salt – and tourists. Whale watching, beaching, fishing, golfing, and biking are among the available outdoor activities. The John F. Kennedy Hyannis Museum is located in town. There are many lodging choices and a wide variety of fine restaurants.

WORTH DOING: The Elegant Dinner Train offers one decided advantage – in addition to the cuisine – over the other meal trains (and scenic excursions as well). While the other trains are all two hours in length and run briefly along the Cape Cod Canal, only the three-hour Elegant Dinner Train crosses it on a lift bridge into Buzzards Bay. This bridge features outstanding aesthetics, with design touches supplied by the noted architectural firm of McKim, Meade, and White, and was the longest of its kind when completed in 1935.

DON'T MISS: The railroad offers a package fare with HyLine Cruises that includes a one-hour boat tour of Hyannis harbor and the Kennedy compound. The boats are little gems: Maine-style coastal steamers *Prudence* (the real McCoy, though now dieselized, built in 1911) and *Patience* (a convincing replica built in 1982).

GETTING THERE: Hyannis is located on the Atlantic Ocean at the elbow of Cape Cod. Barnstable Municipal Airport, right in town, hosts commercial flights from Boston and New York.

Lenox

Berkshire Scenic Railway

Museum, Train ride

MASSACHUSETTS

ADDRESS: 10 Willow Creek Rd., Lenox, MA 01240
TELEPHONE: 413-637-2210
E-MAIL: pieter.lips@berkshirescenicrailroad.org
WEB SITE: www.berkshirescenicrailroad.org

The Berkshire Scenic Railway Museum operates excursion trains that follow the scenic Housatonic River over part of the onetime New Haven Railroad's important passenger and freight route to Pittsfield. Operations are based out of the railway's beautifully restored New Haven station at Lenox, and trains run over 10 miles of freight-hauler Housatonic Railroad to Stockbridge. The adjacent museum includes many pieces of rolling stock.

CHOICES: Berkshire Scenic operates on Saturdays, Sundays, and major holidays from Memorial Day to late October. There are two departure times for a 90-minute, 20-mile round trip to Stockbridge. Well-suited for younger riders, there is also one 45-minute, narrated trip to Lee and back. Trains consist of former Delaware, Lackawanna & Western multiple-unit trailer coaches from the 1920s. Operating locomotives include former New York Central EMD SW8 8619, an ex-Maine Central Alco S1 now numbered 0954, former United Illuminating GE 50-ton no. 67, and borrowed Housatonic Alco/EMD RS3M 9935.

WHEN TO GO: New England's famed fall foliage peaks in this region in early October. Expect full trains, high lodging rates, and crowded roads during that time. Less congestion can be found at other times.

GOOD TO KNOW: There is abundant lodging in Lenox, Lee, and Pittsfield. The Berkshire Hills are ski country, but the area is a year-round tourist destination. Fine dining as well as fast-food chains can be found throughout the region.

WORTH DOING: The museum's Lenox station contains an impressive collection of local railroad historical artifacts. Also, the Gilded Age exhibit is housed in an old coach on the museum grounds and displays the history of Berkshire County.

DON'T MISS: Nearby attractions include weekend concerts at Tanglewood (the summer home of the Boston Symphony), the Hancock Shaker Village, and the Norman Rockwell Museum.

GETTING THERE: The Berkshire Scenic is located near Hwys. 7 and 20, five miles north of Massachusetts Turnpike (I-90) Exit 2. Amtrak's *Lake Shore Limited* stops daily at nearby Pittsfield. The nearest commercial air services are at Albany, N.Y., and Hartford, Conn.

DISCOUNT: Receive $1 off a regular adult ticket, good for up to four adults.

Fall River   *Museum*

Old Colony & Fall River Railroad Museum

The museum, located in railroad cars that include a renovated Pennsylvania Railroad coach, features artifacts of the New Haven, Penn Central, Conrail, Amtrak, and other New England railroads.

ADDRESS: 2 Water St., Fall River, MA 02721
TELEPHONE: 508-674-9340
E-MAIL: info@ocandfrrailroadmuseum.com
WEB SITE: www.ocandfrrailroadmuseum.com

Lowell   *Museum, Trolley ride*

Lowell National Historical Park

The park includes a variety of structures related to industry including 5.6 miles of canals and restored mill buildings. It displays a Boston & Maine 0-6-0 Manchester locomotive built in 1910, a combine/tool car, and two open-air trolleys. A trolley ride operates March through November.

ADDRESS: 67 Kirk St., Lowell, MA 01852
TELEPHONE: 978-970-5000
WEB SITE: www.nps.gov/lowe

Shelburne Falls   *Museum, Trolley ride*

Shelburne Falls Trolley Museum

The museum features a 15-minute trolley ride, complete with an interpretive talk by the motorman. Examine the excellent restoration work on car no. 10, which has been in the area since being built in 1896 (including 65 years as a chicken coop). The museum also displays railroad and trolley artifacts, a steam locomotive, a caboose, and other items.

ADDRESS: 14 Depot St., Shelburne Falls, MA 01370
TELEPHONE: 413-625-9443
E-MAIL: trolley@sftm.org
WEB SITE: www.sftm.org

MICHIGAN

Blissfield   *Dinner train, Train ride*
Adrian & Blissfield Rail Road

The railroad offers fine dining and fun entertainment from two locations, Blissfield and Charlotte. The murder mystery dinner trains provide a five-course dinner as you participate in a comical, interactive mystery show. The railroad also offers Saturday excursions out of Blissfield along a segment of the Erie & Kalamazoo Railroad.

ADDRESS: 301 E. Adrian St., Blissfield, MI 49228
TELEPHONE: 888-467-2451
WEB SITE: www.murdermysterytrain.com

Clinton   *Train ride, Museum*
Southern Michigan Railroad

The railroad offers nostalgic train tours over the remaining track of the early Palmyra and Jacksonburgh Railroad. Train tours are offered through the late spring and fall seasons with holiday trips available. The museum, which focuses on the Clinton Branch, is open Saturdays from mid-May through September.

ADDRESS: 320 S. Division St., Clinton, MI 49236
TELEPHONE: 517-456-7677
E-MAIL: trains@southernmichiganrailroad.org
WEB SITE: www.southernmichiganrailroad.org

Coopersville   *Train ride*
Coopersville & Marne Railway

Powered by a 1950s-era diesel locomotive, this railway's 14-mile, 75-minute excursion travels through farmland and crosses an open-deck girder bridge, four creeks, and a highway bridge. Before making the return trip, the engine is uncoupled, run along a passing siding, and coupled to the other end, which makes for fascinating watching.

ADDRESS: 311 Danforth St., Coopersville, MI 49404
TELEPHONE: 616-997-7000
WEB SITE: www.coopersvilleandmarne.org

Little River Railroad

ADDRESS: 29 W. Park Ave., Coldwater, MI 49036
TELEPHONE: 260-316-0529
E-MAIL: customerservice@littleriverrailroad.com
WEB SITE: www.littleriverrailroad.com

Whoever said bigger is better never visited the Little River Railroad. This railroad is home to one of the smallest standard gauge steam locomotives of its type ever built. No. 110 is a 57-ton Pacific that has all the charm of a ballerina. The railroad offers 90-minute trips behind it from Coldwater to nearby Quincy.

CHOICES: Ride in a coach or open-air car. During the 30-minute layover in Quincy, be sure to exit the train and watch as the locomotive is switched to the other end of the train. Also, look over the exhibits in the Coldwater depot.

WHEN TO GO: Trains run weekends Memorial Day through September. During Train Fest, on Labor Day weekend, Little River runs both of its engines as well as a motorcar. A second locomotive, 0-4-0T no. 1, is also in service. In October, the railroad offers a photo run as well as pumpkin and haunted trains. In December, the *Holiday Express* is in operation.

GOOD TO KNOW: Engine no. 110 started out on the Little River Railroad in east Tennessee. An Indiana family, the Blooms, rescued and rebuilt it for excursion work in the 1970s, and members of that same family continue this tradition of preservation.

WORTH DOING: The area features many antique shops and preserved buildings.

DON'T MISS: Take a locomotive cab tour, offered as conditions allow, during the layover between trips at Coldwater.

GETTING THERE: Coldwater is in south-central Michigan. Take I-69 to Exit 13 for Coldwater. Follow Hwy. 12 west and turn left onto Division Street and then turn right onto Park Avenue to the depot.

Greenfield Village at the Henry Ford

ADDRESS: 20900 Oakwood Blvd., Dearborn, MI 48124
TELEPHONE: 800-835-5237 or 313-982-6001
WEB SITE: www.thehenryford.org

The Henry Ford claims to be America's greatest history attraction, and even though it's in the capital of, and shrine to, the automobile, railroads are well represented here. The centerpiece for this is the Detroit, Toledo & Milwaukee Roundhouse, a reconstruction of the original in Marshall, Mich., believed to be one of only seven 19th century roundhouses left. A steam railroad encircles the historic 90-acre village.

CHOICES: You can ride the train around the village in open-air cars on a 30-minute narrated trip. Departing from the 1859 Smiths Creek depot, the train also makes stops at strategic locations throughout the village. The roundhouse includes hands-on railroading displays and a 1902 Atlantic engine. A mezzanine provides an excellent vantage point from which you can see work going on. Also, be sure to go inside the Henry Ford museum to view railroad cars and locomotives, including an Alleghany type, built for the Chesapeake & Ohio, one of the largest steam locomotives ever built.

WHEN TO GO: Greenfield Village is open daily mid-April through October. From November through December, it is open Friday through Sunday. It is closed the remainder of the year.

GOOD TO KNOW: Henry Ford had his own railroads: one to switch his car plant and another, the Detroit, Toledo & Ironton, to move parts as well as finished product.

WORTH DOING: Get to the roundhouse early in the day to help the crew turn the steam engine on the turntable. It's so well balanced that two people can do it, but it's more fun when you get to push a giant engine around.

DON'T MISS: Railroad Junction, where the roundhouse and depot are located, is one of seven different historic districts in Greenfield Village. In Henry Ford's Model T district, you can tour a replica of Ford's first factory and ride in a Model T.

GETTING THERE: Just west of Detroit, the Henry Ford is located in Dearborn on the corner of Village Road and Oakwood Boulevard, just west of the Southfield Freeway and south of Michigan Avenue (Hwy. 12). There is easy access from I-94 and I-75. You may also ride an Amtrak train that stops at the museum.

Flint   *Train ride*

Huckleberry Railroad

ADDRESS: 6140 Bray Rd., Flint, MI 48505
TELEPHONE: 800-648-7275 or 810-736-7100
E-MAIL: parkswebteam@gcparks.org
WEB SITE: www.geneseecountyparks.org

The Huckleberry Railroad is part of a historical village that is operated by Genesee County Parks in Flint. The narrow gauge railroad is built on an abandoned Pere Marquette Railway right-of-way. An eight-mile, 45-minute ride carries passengers through neighborhoods, by a lake, and into wooded areas.

CHOICES: Ride in one of the railroad's historic coaches or cabooses pulled by a Baldwin 4-6-0 or a Baldwin 2-8-2, two of the seven locomotives owned by the Huckleberry Railroad.

WHEN TO GO: Trains run Memorial Day weekend through Labor Day. In October, Halloween trains run, and in December, Christmas trains operate. During the railroad's rail-fan weekend, usually held in August, you can see all the trains, get great photos, and talk with the train crews.

GOOD TO KNOW: The Huckleberry Railroad was named because it ran so slow that a person could jump off the train, pick some huckleberries, and jump back on the train without breaking a sweat.

WORTH DOING: Look for Rio Grande 2-8-2 no. 464, one of a rare class of narrow gauge Mikado type steam locomotives on the Colorado railroad. Built in 1903 and restored in 2005, it was nicknamed *Mudhen* because it waddled like a chicken as it went down the tracks.

DON'T MISS: Take a stroll through Crossroads Village, which has 34 historic structures on 51 acres. Costumed interpreters will welcome you to the homes, mills, and shops that date back to the 1800s. Special events are scheduled throughout the summer, and you can take a ride on a paddle-wheel riverboat.

GETTING THERE: The railroad is located just north of Flint, about an hour from Detroit. From Detroit, take I-75 to I-475. Follow I-475 north to Saginaw Street (Exit 13). Take Saginaw Street north to Stanley Road, turn east on Stanley Road, and then turn south on Bray Road to the village and railroad.

Owosso   *Museum, Train ride*
Steam Railroading Institute

ADDRESS: 405 S. Washington St., Owosso, MI 48867
TELEPHONE: 989-725-9464
E-MAIL: mfolland@mstrp.com
WEB SITE: www.mstrp.com

The Steam Railroading Institute is all about preserving steam locomotives, and there is always restoration work going on. The institute displays equipment and offers some train rides.

CHOICES: The seven-acre site includes a roundhouse and turntable. Weekends during the summer, Flagg Coal Company 0-4-0T no. 75 operates short trips. Built in 1930, this small tank engine is typical of many industrial locomotives used across the land.

WHEN TO GO: In November and December, the *North Pole Express* is the big event, as the Pere Marquette Railway 1225 takes visitors on a 24-mile round trip to the North Pole and back.

GOOD TO KNOW: Pere Marquette 2-8-4 no. 1225 was the model and sound effects machine for the steam train in the movie *Polar Express*. It shows what a modern (1941) mainline steam locomotive is all about.

WORTH DOING: Don't miss work on a coming attraction. The institute is restoring a 2-8-0 steam locomotive, former Mississippian no. 76, which could be in operation during 2007. Built in 1920, it typifies a small shortline or branch-line locomotive.

DON'T MISS: The Michigan Railroad History Museum is housed in historic Durand Union Station, 20 minutes away.

GETTING THERE: Owosso is about 30 miles northeast of Lansing and 30 miles west of Flint. From Flint, take Hwy. 21 west to Owosso. From Lansing, take I-69 to Hwy. 52 north to Owosso. In Owosso, the Steam Railroading Institute is on south Washington Street.

Durand   *Museum, Depot*

Durand Union Station

This 100-year-old depot museum was the second busiest depot in Michigan, and its lower level has been restored to its former glory, with terrazzo floors and oak trim. Still functioning as a depot, the building also houses the Michigan Railroad History Museum. The museum contains exhibits showing railroading's role in lumber, mining, agriculture, and other industries.

ADDRESS: 200 Railroad St., Durand, MI 48429
TELEPHONE: 989-288-3561
E-MAIL: dusi@durandstation.org
WEB SITE: www.durandstation.org

Flushing   *Museum*

Flushing Area Museum

The museum's collection includes permanent displays of railroad artifacts as well as local historical exhibits. It is housed in the Flushing depot, which was built in 1888 and provided passenger service until 1971. The building was restored by the Flushing Area Historical Society to its former appearance.

ADDRESS: 431 W. Main St., Flushing, MI 48433
TELEPHONE: 810-487-0814
E-MAIL: fahs@att.net
WEB SITE: www.flushinghistorical.org

Grand Haven   *Museum, Depot*

Tri-Cities Historical Museum

The Tri-Cities Historical Museum operates out of two buildings including a former Grand Trunk Western depot. Located on the banks of the Grand River, the depot museum, built in 1871, contains two floors of railroad and other local historical artifacts. On display is a Pere Marquette Railway steam locomotive.

ADDRESS: 1 North Harbor Dr., Grand Haven, MI 49417
TELEPHONE: 616-842-0700
E-MAIL: tcmuseum@grandhaven.com
WEB SITE: www.tri-citiesmuseum.org

Howell *Train ride, Dinner train*

Lake Central Rail Tours

Lake Central Rail Tours operates a variety of passenger train excursions over the rails of the Tuscola & Saginaw Bay Railway. Excursions include dinner trains, fall color trips, and steam locomotive trips. Departure points include Howell, Owosso, Mount Pleasant, Cadillac, and Petoskey.

ADDRESS: 128 Wetmore St., Howell, MI 48843
TELEPHONE: 866-608-0746
E-MAIL: webmaster@lakecentralrailtours.com
WEB SITE: www.lcrt.homestead.com

Lake Linden *Museum, Train ride*

Houghton County Historical Museum

The museum includes the restored Mineral Range depot, which contains a collection of Copper County railroad artifacts. The museum operates the Lake Linden & Torch Lake Railroad. A narrow gauge, 0-4-0 Porter steam locomotive takes you to the end of a short section of track, which gets longer as work progresses. It is open June through September.

ADDRESS: 5500 Hwy. M-26, Lake Linden, MI 49945
TELEPHONE: 906-296-4121
E-MAIL: info@houghtonhistory.org
WEB SITE: www.houghtonhistory.org

Manistee *Museum*

SS City of Milwaukee

The SS *City of Milwaukee*, a national historic landmark, is the last surviving traditional Great Lakes railroad car ferry. Built in 1931, the *City of Milwaukee* served the Grand Trunk Western and Ann Arbor Railroads. The car deck houses five Ann Arbor boxcars that serve as exhibit spaces and a theater.

ADDRESS: 99 Arthur St., Manistee, MI 49660
TELEPHONE: 231-723-3587
WEB SITE: www.carferry.com

MICHIGAN

Mount Clemens   *Museum, Train ride*
Michigan Transit Museum

For a unique trolley ride, try one on at the Michigan Transit Museum. The 1920s interurban and rapid transit cars take you on a 45-minute round trip around the Selfridge Air National Guard Base, with an optional stop at the Selfridge Military Air Museum. The transit museum is open year-round, and train rides run June through September.

ADDRESS: 200 Grand Ave., Mount Clemens, MI 48043
TELEPHONE: 586-463-1863
WEB SITE: www.michigantransitmuseum.org

Royal Oak   *Train ride*
Bluewater Michigan Chapter, NRHS

This chapter of the National Railway Historical Society operates special events and excursions using its own equipment and fleet of historic passenger cars. It also offers rail-themed package tours.

ADDRESS: 300 E. Fourth St., Royal Oak, MI 48068
TELEPHONE: 800-594-5162 or 248-541-1000
E-MAIL: bluewaternrhs@bluewaternrhs.com
WEB SITE: www.bluewaternrhs.com

Saginaw   *Museum*
Saginaw Railway Museum

Located in a restored 1907 Pere Marquette Railway depot, this museum displays GP-9, RS1, and GE 25-ton locomotives, three cabooses, a combine coach, and various boxcars. It includes an 1898 Armstrong interlocking tower as well as a variety of smaller artifacts.

ADDRESS: 900 Maple St., Saginaw, MI 48602
TELEPHONE: 517-790-7994
WEB SITE: www.mercitrain.org/svrhs

Walled Lake   *Dinner train*
Train Travel

This group operates three different trains that provide a variety of rail experiences. The Michigan Star Clipper Dinner Train prepares five-course meals on-board. The Steel Wheels Entertainment Train provides a unique venue for comedy, music, and dancing. The Walled Lake Scenic Railway offers excursions aboard open-air coaches.

ADDRESS: 840 N. Pontiac Trail, Walled Lake, MI 48390
TELEPHONE: 248-960-9440
WEB SITE: www.rail-road.com
DISCOUNT: Take 10 percent off Michigan Star Clipper evening dinner excursions.

MINNESOTA

Chisholm   *Museum, Trolley ride*
Ironworld Discovery Center

The center offers a 2.4-mile trolley ride to a re-created mine location. The round trip, aboard a 1928 Melbourne trolley, offers fascinating views of the Pillsbury mine. The center, which preserves Iron Range mining history, includes a museum, outdoor exhibits, and preserved buildings. It is open Memorial Day weekend through Labor Day.

ADDRESS: 801 SW Hwy. 169, Chisholm, MN 55719
TELEPHONE: 800-372-6437 or 218-254-7959
E-MAIL: marketing@ironworld.com
WEB SITE: www.ironworld.com

Currie   *Museum*
End-O-Line Railroad Park & Museum

End-O-Line Railroad Park is a working railroad yard that includes a 1901 manually operated turntable, a rebuilt engine house on its original foundation, an original four-room depot, a water tower, an 1899 section foreman's house, a Grand Trunk Western caboose, and two steam locomotives. It is open Memorial Day to Labor Day.

ADDRESS: 440 N. Mill St., Currie, MN 56123
TELEPHONE: 507-763-3708
E-MAIL: info@endoline.com
WEB SITE: www.endoline.com

Dassel   *Museum*
Old Depot Railroad Museum

A former Great Northern depot, this museum contains two floors of artifacts and memorabilia. Displays include telegraph equipment, tools, signs, uniforms, and lanterns. Authentic railroad sounds add to your experience. You can also hop aboard a wooden caboose and sit in the brakeman's seat. The museum is open Memorial Day through September.

ADDRESS: 651 W. Hwy. 12, Dassel, MN 55325
TELEPHONE: 320-275-3876
WEB SITE: www.theolddepot.com

Minneapolis   Museum, Trolley ride
Minnesota Streetcar Museum

This museum operates two different streetcar lines from May through November.
Located southwest of downtown Minneapolis, the Como-Harriet line runs between
Lake Harriet and Lake Calhoun. The Excelsior line is about 15 miles west of downtown
Minneapolis. The museum exhibits electric streetcars that ran in the state.

ADDRESS: 2330 W. 42nd St., Minneapolis, MN
TELEPHONE: 952-922-1096
E-MAIL: info@msmuseum.org
WEB SITE: www.trolleyride.org

Minneapolis   Depot
Minnehaha Depot

The tiny Minnehaha depot's architecture features delicate gingerbread details. Built
in 1875, the building replaced an earlier Milwaukee Road depot on the first line into
the Twin Cities from Chicago. Managed by the Minnesota Transportation Museum, the
depot is open Memorial Day weekend through Labor Day.

ADDRESS: 4926 Minnehaha Ave., Minneapolis, MN
TELEPHONE: 651-228-0263
E-MAIL: minnehahadepot@mnhs.org
WEB SITE: www.mtmuseum.org

Stillwater   Dinner train
Minnesota Zephyr

As the Minnesota Zephyr winds along the river and wooded bluffs of the St. Croix River
Valley, you can enjoy the scenery and a five-course gourmet meal. This three-hour
journey takes you over a line that was first built more than 130 years ago. Each of
the train's five restored dining cars features a different design that harkens back to a
different era.

ADDRESS: 601 N. Main St., Stillwater, MN 55082
TELEPHONE: 800-992-6100 or 651-430-3000
E-MAIL: info@minnesotazephyr.com
WEB SITE: www.minnesotazephyr.com

Two Harbors   Museum
Depot Museum

Located in the 1907 headquarters of the Duluth & Iron Range Railroad, this museum
highlights the early history of Lake County. The Lake County Historical Society
operates the museum and displays a Mallet steam locomotive and a Baldwin 3-Spot.
The museum is open daily May through October.

ADDRESS: 520 South Ave., Two Harbors, MN 55616
TELEPHONE: 218-834-4898
E-MAIL: lakehist@lakenet.com
WEB SITE: www.northshorehistory.com/sites/depot

Lake Superior & Mississippi Railroad

ADDRESS: 6930 Fremont St., Duluth, MN 55816
TELEPHONE: 218-624-7549
E-MAIL: info@lsmrr.org
WEB SITE: www.lsmrr.org

Here's a laid-back operation that is a great complement to the marshlands near Duluth. A 90-minute ride on this railroad is a great way to relax and enjoy nature along the St. Louis River estuary, Spirit Lake, and Mud Lake.

CHOICES: While taking in the scenery and wildlife when riding in a restored, open-window coach, you can listen to narration of the area's rich history. For a truly outdoor experience, ride the Safari Car, a converted flat car. Power is provided by a General Electric industrial switcher built in 1946.

WHEN TO GO: Excursions operate on Saturdays and Sundays, beginning in June and running into October.

GOOD TO KNOW: The railroad takes its name from the first line built between the Twin Cities and Duluth and uses some of that line's original track.

WORTH DOING: Visit the nearby Lake Superior Railroad Museum or some of the many other museums in the area.

DON'T MISS: Keep your eyes on the marshes for egrets.

GETTING THERE: Duluth is on Lake Superior, about 150 miles from the Twin Cities. In Duluth, exit I-35 at Cody Street, turn right onto 63rd Avenue, and then turn right onto Grand Avenue to Fremont Street.

Duluth   *Museum, Train ride, Dinner train*

Lake Superior Railroad Museum

ADDRESS: 506 W. Michigan St., Duluth, MN 55816
TELEPHONE: 218-733-7519
E-MAIL: museum@lsrm.org
WEB SITE: www.lsrm.org

This is a combination of a great railroad museum and a great train ride. The Lake Superior Railroad Museum is located in the historic depot in downtown Duluth. Its extensive rolling stock collection rests in the train shed on the very tracks from which passenger trains once departed. Just outside, excursion trains ply the route to Two Harbors, with outstanding views along the way.

CHOICES: The Lake Superior Railroad Museum has a large collection of railroad equipment that changes annually. It includes steam, diesel, and electric locomotives as well as passenger coaches, freight cars, and cabooses. Much of the equipment was used on Minnesota railroads, including the first locomotive operated in the state. The museum also operates the North Shore Scenic Railroad, which conducts two excursions as well as several special trains. A 90-minute excursion runs along the shores of Lake Superior to Lester River. The six-hour round trip to Two Harbors takes you over seven bridges. Also operating are an elegant dinner train, a murder mystery train, a pizza train, and a Sunday afternoon tea train on which passengers often dress in period clothes.

WHEN TO GO: The museum is open year-round, with extended summer hours, and excursions are offered Memorial Day through October.

GOOD TO KNOW: You can buy a combined ticket for the museum and an excursion.

WORTH DOING: Take a close look at the *William Crooks*, the first locomotive operated in Minnesota. Built in 1861, it is one of a handful of engines remaining from before the Civil War. Sit in the diesel locomotive simulator and try your hand at running a big Wisconsin Central diesel. Climb into the cab of the Duluth, Missabe and Iron Range Railroad Yellowstone type locomotive. Pause a few moments because the clever museum folks have set up the engine so that its massive drivers and running gear rotate periodically.

DON'T MISS: Take time to tour historic Union Depot. Admission to the Lake Superior Railroad Museum also admits you to three other museums in the building: the Duluth Children's Museum, Duluth Art Institute, and St. Louis County Historical Society.

GETTING THERE: Situated on Lake Superior, Duluth is about 150 miles from the Twin Cities. To reach the museum, take Exit 256 off I-35 and follow Michigan Street to the depot.

Milwaukee Road 261

ADDRESS: 401 Harrison St., Minneapolis, MN
TELEPHONE: 651-765-9812
WEB SITE: www.261.com

The Friends of the 261 operate mainline excursion trips around the Midwest pulled by former Milwaukee Road steam locomotive no. 261, a 4-8-4 built by American Locomotive Company in 1944. The locomotive was donated to the National Railroad Museum in Green Bay, Wis., in 1956. Leased from the museum, the 261 was returned to active service in 1993 and has operated at least one excursion every year since restoration.

CHOICES: The Friends of the 261 offer several options for passengers. All trips include coach, first-class, and premium-class services. Premium class includes hors d'oeuvres and gourmet meals prepared on board and a ride in one of two former Milwaukee Road Hiawatha cars: Skytop lounge observation *Cedar Rapids* and full-length Super Dome no. 53. First-class includes an upscale meal plan with hors d'oeuvres and a ride in parlor or lounge cars. Both first- and premium-class include complimentary beverages.

WHEN TO GO: Generally 261 pulls trips as early as May and as late as October. One of the most popular and scenic routes is along the Mississippi River between Minneapolis and Winona operated in early autumn when the leaves are beginning to change.

GOOD TO KNOW: Downtown Minneapolis is near the 261 shop and has a variety of hotels and restaurants. For a complete Milwaukee Road experience, stay in one of the two hotels at the former Milwaukee Road Minneapolis passenger depot, built in 1898 and beautifully restored. Rail memorabilia and photographs can be found throughout the building.

WORTH DOING: Get a look at Skytop lounge observation car *Cedar Rapids*. Built by the Milwaukee Road in 1948, with their large glass area, the Skytops were unlike any other rail passenger car. The *Cedar Rapids* is the only Skytop still in operation.

DON'T MISS: Trains usually leave from the 261 shop facility in northeast Minneapolis. Head down to the shop the evening before a trip just to take in the sights and sounds of a large steam engine at night. Usually the crew has a donation box out, and for a small price, you can have a look in the cab.

GETTING THERE: Minneapolis/St. Paul has Amtrak, airline, and light rail and bus service. A short walk from the Metro Transit bus stop at Central Avenue and Broadway will get you to the shop, or you can take a taxi. Ample parking is available at the shop on excursion days.

St. Paul *Museum*

Jackson Street Roundhouse

ADDRESS: 193 E. Pennsylvania Ave., St. Paul, MN 55130
TELEPHONE: 651-228-0263
WEB SITE: www.mtmuseum.org

The former Great Northern Jackson Street Roundhouse was built in 1907 to service passenger locomotives. Closed in 1959, the roundhouse was converted to nonrailroad use and the tracks removed. In 1985, it was purchased by the Minnesota Transportation Museum and renovations began. One of the highlights was the reinstallation of the turntable and installation of new roundhouse doors built to the 1906 blueprint specs.

CHOICES: Visitors can roam the roundhouse and the outdoor grounds, take a short caboose ride pulled by a switch engine, and participate in interactive exhibits. Tours of the roundhouse, where equipment restoration takes place, are also available. Included in the collection are three Northern Pacific steam locomotives and Great Northern 400, the first production SD45 owned by the GN Historical Society. On Saturdays, take a ride on the miniature *Rock Island Rocket*, a perfect replica of the *Twin Star Rocket*. It was built in 1947 by Larry Sauter, a high school industrial arts teacher. The museum adds a few feet of special narrow gauge track for the train every year, and kids love its quick acceleration.

WHEN TO GO: The museum is open Wednesdays and Saturdays year-round, but it can be chilly inside the roundhouse in the winter – and downright cold outside. Summer or early fall are the best times to visit.

GOOD TO KNOW: St. Paul and Minneapolis have a wide diversity of restaurants and hotels for any taste and budget.

WORTH DOING: Walk inside the cab of Dan Patch Lines no. 100, built in 1913 by General Electric, and you've walked into history. It is one of the first locomotives that used an internal combustion engine and is the granddaddy of today's diesel locomotives.

DON'T MISS: After taking in the roundhouse, if you have a desire to learn more about the Great Northern Railway, visit the St. Paul home of James J. Hill, who founded the Great Northern. His mansion on Summit Avenue was completed in 1891 and was the largest and most expensive home in Minnesota at the time. The Minnesota Historical Society now owns it.

GETTING THERE: The Twin Cities have Amtrak, airline, and bus service. The roundhouse is located north of the Minnesota State Capitol. Take the Pennsylvania Avenue exit off I-35E and drive west two blocks to the roundhouse.

MISSISSIPPI

Water Valley Casey Jones Railroad Museum

The museum displays many of the artifacts from the defunct Casey Jones Railroad Museum State Park at Vaughan. The museum contains railroad memorabilia and photos and exhibits rolling stock. It is open Thursdays, Fridays, and Saturdays.

ADDRESS: 105 Railroad Ave., Water Valley, MS 38965
TELEPHONE: 662-473-1154
E-MAIL: jgurner@watervalley.net
WEB SITE: www.watervalley.net/users/caseyjones/home

MISSOURI

Belton   *Train ride*
Belton, Grandview & Kansas City Railroad

At this laid-back railroad, you can walk around the yard, look at displayed equipment, and talk to the crew before boarding a 5-mile excursion. The 45-minute round trip runs south from Belton. Rides in the caboose with the conductor and in the locomotive with the engineer are also available.

ADDRESS: 502 E. Walnut St., Belton, MO 64012
TELEPHONE: 816-331-0630
E-MAIL: info@beltonrailroad.org
WEB SITE: www.beltonrailroad.org

Branson   *Train ride, Dinner train*
Branson Scenic Railway

This railway operates a 40-mile round trip through the Ozark foothills and southwest Missouri wilderness. The train takes you over trestles and through tunnels into areas only accessible by rail, as narration describes landmarks, abandoned towns, and wildlife, before you return to the original 1905 Branson depot. The railway also operates dinner trains.

ADDRESS: 206 E. Main St., Branson, MO 65616
TELEPHONE: 800-287-2462 or 417-334-6110
WEB SITE: www.bransontrain.com

KC Rail Experience

ADDRESS: 30 W. Pershing Rd., Kansas City, MO 64108
TELEPHONE: 816-460-2000
E-MAIL: visitor@unionstation.org
WEB SITE: www.unionstation.org

Located in historic Union Station, the KC Rail Experience opened in 2005. This hands-on journey through railroading history is told through personal histories, vintage rail cars, and unique artifacts.

CHOICES: You enter the museum through one of the station's former train gates, duplicating the historic experience of descending the stairs and catching a train. After an award-winning orientation film by noted railfan filmmaker Rich Luckin, you immediately see a genuine SD40-2 simulator donated by BNSF. Three pieces of vintage rolling stock are located steps away, including the only cab-unit diesel in Kansas City Southern's historic *Southern Belle* livery, ex-Milwaukee Road dining car 170, and an observation car from the Great Northern's mid-century *Empire Builder*. Enhancing the experience are 20 ghostly figures from the station's past. These interactive "ghosts" come back to life to tell the story of the men and women of the railroads. They include architect Jarvis Hunt, a Harvey Girl, an engineer, a conductor, a gandy dancer, and a movie star boarding the *Super Chief*.

WHEN TO GO: The majority of the KC Rail Experience is indoors. Only the rolling stock is outside, and most of the cars are climate controlled.

GOOD TO KNOW: The Experience is still developing, and two streamlined cars, an Railway Post Office and a sleeper, will be placed on display as restoration funds allow. Union Station has three restaurants, ranging from fast food to elegant dining, including a Harvey House Diner.

WORTH DOING: More than 200 trains pass Union Station each day. A former Kansas City PCC streetcar is on display west of the station's Science City.

DON'T MISS: Union Station also contains a science museum and planetarium, an Extreme Screen theatre, a live theater, and traveling exhibits on loan from other museums.

GETTING THERE: Three Amtrak trains stop at Union Station including the *Southwest Chief* and *Missouri Mule*, which provides two daily round trips between St. Louis and Kansas City. Most major airlines serve Kansas City International Airport, 16 miles away. Interstates 29, 35, and 70 all intersect nearby in downtown Kansas City.

St Louis *Museum*

Museum of Transportation

ADDRESS: 3015 Barrett Station Rd., St. Louis, MO 63122
TELEPHONE: 314-965-7998
WEB SITE: www.museumoftransport.org

If you want to be surrounded by trains, this is the place. A visit here brings you in touch with more than 70 locomotives of steam, diesel, and electric power. You'll see scores of rail cars and even see one of the first railroad tunnels west of the Mississippi. The 150-acre site also houses airplanes, cars, and riverboats.

CHOICES: The museum features miles of switching and exhibition track and includes 10 buildings. Its collection of more than 30 steam locomotives is one of the largest around, and stairs let you climb into the cabs of many of them. Many rare and unusual items grace the site, including the world's largest tank car, an Aerotrain, and even a cast-iron turntable. A miniature train and a restored streetcar operate April to October.

WHEN TO GO: The museum is open year-round. It operates daily during its summer schedule, which begins in May and runs through Labor Day. During the rest of the year, the museum is open Tuesday through Sunday.

GOOD TO KNOW: Operated as a county park, the museum is located on the site of a man-made railroad tunnel that was used by the Missouri Pacific Railroad from 1853 until 1944 and is now listed on the National Register of Historic Places.

WORTH DOING: Climb into the cab of the Union Pacific Big Boy no. 4006 and see what it felt like to be the engineer on one of the world's largest steam locomotives. And climb aboard the Santa Fe 5011 and ring the engine's bell.

DON'T MISS: View the Union Pacific Centennial type diesel no. 6944. It's the modern equivalent of the Big Boy with two diesel engines, 6,600 horsepower, and a length of 98 feet. Also, be sure and check out the FT demonstrator, no. 103. It was the first mainline diesel locomotive built for freight service in North America back in 1939. A national tour it made proved the worth of diesel power and launched a full change of power from steam to diesel.

GETTING THERE: The museum is about 12 miles west of downtown St. Louis. When driving from I-270, either north or south, exit at Dougherty Ferry Road (Exit 8), go west about one mile to Barrett Station Road, and turn left. The museum is on the right.

Independence Museum, Depot
Chicago & Alton Railroad Depot

Built in 1879, the restored, two-story Chicago & Alton Railroad depot has two floors with seven rooms, including the stationmaster's residence. Each room is furnished in the period circa 1879. There are two original restored Railway Express baggage carts with camel-back top trunks, old railroad tools and equipment, and many other items.

ADDRESS: 318 W. Pacific Ave., Independence, MO 64050
TELEPHONE: 816-325-7955
WEB SITE: www.chicagoalton1879depot.com

Jackson Train ride, Dinner train
St. Louis Iron Mountain & Southern Railway

From April through December, this railway offers a variety of trips including sightseeing excursions, murder mysteries, train robberies, and holiday-themed rides.

ADDRESS: Hwy. 61 at Hwy. 25, Jackson, MO 63755
TELEPHONE: 800-455-7245 or 573-243-1688
WEB SITE: www.rosecity.net/trains/station

Springfield Museum
Railroad Historical Museum

Located in Grant Beach Park, this train museum is a train. It is housed in a locomotive, baggage car, commuter car, and caboose that contain artifacts from the St. Louis-San Francisco and other railroads. After touring the museum, you can enjoy the park's pool, playground, and picnic area. It is open Saturdays May through October.

ADDRESS: 1300 N. Grant St., Springfield, MO
TELEPHONE: 417-882-9106
E-MAIL: rrhistoricalmuseum@zoomshare.com
WEB SITE: www.rrhistoricalmuseum.zoomshare.com

MISSOURI

MONTANA

Anaconda   *Train ride, Museum*
Copper King Express

The *Copper King Express* is an excursion train that operates in the Butte-Anaconda area, where you'll see lost communities, abandoned homesteads, and pioneer cemeteries. The world's largest smokestack, on the Anaconda smelter, can be seen from 20 miles away. The story of the Butte, Anaconda & Pacific Railroad is shown on the train and in the railroad's museum.

ADDRESS: 300 W. Commercial Ave., Anaconda, MT 59711
TELEPHONE: 406-563-5458
E-MAIL: rarusrailway@yahoo.com
WEB SITE: www.copperkingexpress.com

Lewistown   *Dinner train*
Charlie Russell Chew-Choo Dinner Train

This dinner train takes you on a three-hour excursion over the old Milwaukee Railroad line from Kingston Junction to Denton. The ride crosses a 33-span bridge, passes through a 2,000-foot tunnel, and travels through the land that inspired artist Charlie Russell. Along the way, you'll enjoy a catered prime rib dinner.

ADDRESS: 211 E. Main St., Lewistown, MT 59457
TELEPHONE: 800-860-9646
WEB SITE: www.charlierussellchewchoo.com

Missoula   *Museum*
Historical Museum at Fort Missoula

Located in Fort Missoula, the Historical Museum includes 13 structures that depict the area's history. One is the Drummond depot, which was constructed by the Chicago, Milwaukee, St. Paul and Pacific Railroad in 1910. The museum also features a Rails through Missoula exhibit. Efforts are under way to house and restore Missoula's last streetcar.

ADDRESS: South Ave., Missoula, MT 59804
TELEPHONE: 406-728-3476
E-MAIL: ftmslamuseum@montana.com
WEB SITE: www.fortmissoulamuseum.org

Alder Gulch Short Line

ADDRESS: Wallace St., Virginia City, MT 59755
TELEPHONE: 406-843-5247
WEB SITE: www.virginiacitymt.com

The Alder Gulch Short Line is one of three operating 30-inch gauge tourist railroads in the United States. This narrow gauge railroad connects the former gold mining towns of Virginia City and Nevada City. The line winds along Alder Creek where you can view the remains of gold mining operations, dredge tailings, and wildlife. Grades approaching 4 percent challenge the little line.

CHOICES: Steam trains run weekends and holidays throughout the summer, while a gas-powered train operates on weekdays. Passengers may board the train at the depots in Virginia City or Nevada City for either a one-way or three-mile round trip. A round-trip ticket includes access to a walking tour of the historic collection of western buildings and displays in Nevada City. Also, round-trip passengers can lay over at either terminal, explore, and complete their trips later in the day.

WHEN TO GO: The operating season runs between Memorial Day and Labor Day weekends. Occasional moonlight rides are scheduled during the season.

GOOD TO KNOW: The line was completely rebuilt in the late 1990s when heavier motive power arrived. If you are interested in the Old West, mining, architecture, and history, plan on spending several hours exploring each town. With more than 100 historic buildings, Virginia City is one of best-preserved mining towns in the West.

WORTH DOING: Visit the historic Livingston depot, built in 1902, that provided access to Yellowstone National Park. The Italianate-style depot has been restored as a local museum. If interested in mining, the World Museum of Mining in Butte features more than 50 structures, including a re-created mining town.

DON'T MISS: The Alder Gulch Short Line is situated in scenic southwest Montana. Camping, fly-fishing, golf, day drives, hiking, biking, horse pack trips, nature watching, and gold-panning opportunities abound. The wonders of Yellowstone Park are also nearby.

GETTING THERE: Virginia City is located on Hwy. 287 approximately 80 miles south of Butte, and the Alder Gulch Short Line is located south of I-90 and east of I-15.

NEBRASKA

Fairbury   *Museum*
Rock Island Depot Railroad Museum

The museum is located in one of the state's only remaining Rock Island depots. Built in 1914, the building also housed the railroad's Western Division Headquarters. The collection features Rock Island artifacts and a restored baggage room. The site also includes the original freight house and gardens.

ADDRESS: 910 Bacon Rd., Fairbury, NE 68352
TELEPHONE: 402-729-5131
E-MAIL: fairburyridepot@alltel.net
WEB SITE: www.jeffersoncountyhistory.com

Fremont   *Train ride*
Fremont & Elkhorn Valley Railroad

This excursion train runs over a route laid out in 1869. The railroad offers a 16-mile round trip from Fremont to Nickerson. Diesel locomotives pull vintage railcars across historic paths. Excursions operate on weekends May through October. The Fremont Dinner Train also operates over the railroad's track.

ADDRESS: 1835 N. Somers Ave., Fremont, NE 68025
TELEPHONE: 402-727-0615
E-MAIL: fevr@fremontrailroad.com
WEB SITE: www.fremontrailroad.com

Grand Island   *Museum*
Stuhr Museum of the Prairie Pioneer

This interactive museum takes you back to an 1890s railroad town with more than
60 restored buildings. During the summer, townspeople dressed in period clothing
demonstrate daily life on the Plains. A 1901 steam locomotive, a 1912 caboose, an
1871 coach, and other railcars are on display.

ADDRESS: 3133 W. Hwy. 34, Grand Island, NE 68801
TELEPHONE: 308-385-5316
E-MAIL: info@sturhmuseum.org
WEB SITE: www.stuhrmuseum.org

Kearney   *Museum*
Trails & Rails Museum

The Rails portion of the museum includes an 1898 Union Pacific depot. The depot
houses transportation exhibits, and its waiting room and ticket office have been
restored. On display are a 2-8-0 Baldwin steam engine, a UP flatcar, a caboose, and
other equipment. Open year-round, the museum includes other historic buildings
including the distinctive Freighters Hotel.

ADDRESS: 710 W. 11th St., Kearney, NE 68845
TELEPHONE: 308-234-3041
E-MAIL: bchs@bchs.us
WEB SITE: www.bchs.us/museum.html

Omaha   *Museum*
Durham Western Heritage Museum

Built in 1931, Omaha's Union Station is a beautiful example of art deco style. This
historic railroad station now houses exhibits depicting the city's history. Rail displays
include an 1890 steam locomotive, a streetcar and a variety of railcars. Be sure to have
a malt, ice cream soda, or phosphate at the restored soda fountain as travelers did in
1931.

ADDRESS: 801 S. 10th St., Omaha, NE 68108
TELEPHONE: 402-444-5071
E-MAIL: info@dwhm.org
WEB SITE: www.dwhm.org

NEVADA

Boulder City   *Train ride*

Nevada Southern Railway

ADDRESS: 600 Yucca St., Boulder City, NV 89006
TELEPHONE: 702-486-5933
WEB SITE: dmla.clan.lib.nv.us/docs/museums/BoulderCity/rr.htm

The railway offers a train ride with a historical twist. This was part of the construction railroad from Las Vegas to Hoover Dam, with tracks having been laid in 1931. It's a nice ride in the desert and a break from the hustle of Las Vegas.

CHOICES: Located within former Union Pacific rail yards, the site includes a platform built to resemble a past structure. Along the 45-minute round trip, you get an up-close look at desert plant life, especially when riding in the train's open-air car. The other cars are air-conditioned, restored Pullman coaches dating back to 1911. A generator car behind the locomotive supplies power to the coaches. Operated by the Nevada State Railroad Museum, the railway's outdoor interpretative area displays a variety of equipment, including steam locomotive 264 with its unique Vanderbilt tender.

WHEN TO GO: The railway operates February through mid-December. Summer in Nevada can be hot, with temperatures hitting triple digits.

GOOD TO KNOW: You'll save money in Boulder City. It's the only community in Nevada where gambling is not legal.

WORTH DOING: Ride a train pulled by a historic diesel. One of the locomotives used, UP no. 844, is one of the last GP30 model diesel locomotives – the early 1960s type of diesel that replaced the first generation of diesel locomotives that had themselves replaced steam power.

DON'T MISS: Take a trip to nearby Boulder Dam and tour this technological wonder. Boating on Lake Mead is a popular activity any time of the year.

GETTING THERE: Boulder City is a 30-minute drive from Las Vegas and McCarran International Airport. It is an easy drive from Las Vegas along Hwy. 93 into Boulder City. Once there, turn left on Yucca Street to the museum.

Carson City   *Museum*

Nevada State Railroad Museum

NEVADA

ADDRESS: 2180 S. Carson St., Carson City, NV 89701
TELEPHONE: 702-486-5933
WEB SITE: dmla.clan.lib.nv.us/docs/museums/rr/ccrr.htm

Few states can claim as rich a railroading heritage as Nevada, and this museum does an admirable job interpreting it. The first transcontinental railroad, the state's many mining railroads, and the historic Virginia & Truckee – which ran right past the museum property – are all represented here. The museum boasts a particularly fine collection of 19th century rolling stock, much of which originally came from the V&T and was used in dozens of Hollywood films and television shows.

CHOICES: Star of the museum's collection is *Inyo*, a wood-burning 4-4-0 built for the V&T in 1875, and the museum still steams it up several times a year. When *Inyo* isn't operating, it's on display along with other beautifully restored pre-1915 freight and passenger equipment. Other rolling stock can often be seen in the restoration shop, including an ex-V&T McKeen motorcar and a car that was believed to have carried Central Pacific president Leland Stanford to the Golden Spike ceremony in 1869.

WHEN TO GO: Steam trains or a 1926 motorcar operate most weekends from May to October. Mid-summer highs are usually in the 80s, with little chance of precipitation.

GOOD TO KNOW: Carson City's downtown area is very walkable. The state capitol grounds and surrounding neighborhoods of historic homes are particularly pleasant. A wide variety of hotels, motels, and restaurants can be found nearby.

WORTH DOING: For those whose interests run toward scholarly pursuits, the museum has impressive static displays exploring such topics as Chinese workers in Nevada railroading and the evolution of V&T motive power. Lectures by leading rail historians are offered several times a year, and the museum also hosts an annual V&T symposium.

DON'T MISS: For more insight on Nevada history, the Nevada State Museum is located at 600 N. Carson St., about a mile from the railroad museum.

GETTING THERE: The museum is on Hwy. 395 (Carson Street) on the south side of Carson City. Carson City is within a day's drive of most major cities on the West Coast. Amtrak's *California Zephyr* stops at Reno, about 35 miles away.

135

East Ely

Train ride, Museum

Nevada Northern Railway

ADDRESS: 1100 Avenue A, East Ely, NV 89315
TELEPHONE: 866-407-8326 or 775-289-2085
E-MAIL: nnry@mwpower.net
WEB SITE: www.nevadanorthernrailway.net

The Nevada Northern is often hailed as the best-preserved standard gauge railroad in the country. The operating railway museum is headquartered on a 56-acre complex composed of 49 historic buildings, set amid the vastness of the Great Basin. Completed in 1906 to haul copper from area mines and smelters to the outside world, most cars and locomotives have been on the line since day one of their service lives, and they're maintained in the company's own shops.

CHOICES: The Nevada Northern offers something for everyone, railfan or not. Steam engines run every day between July 4 and Labor Day and frequently at other times of the year. The railroad operates a variety of special and seasonal trains, including haunted ghost trains that feature stories from the region's colorful past, barbecue trains, and wine trains. The railway's roster features three steam engines, nine first- and second-generation diesels, wooden passenger cars, a steam-powered rotary plow and a steam-powered wrecking crane. Structures include the original depot and office building, engine house, freight shed, coaling tower, and water tower. Diesels include everything from an SD9 to a Baldwin VO1000 to a trio of Alco RS-model road switchers.

WHEN TO GO: Summer is the busiest time, with three or four trains running most days. Temperatures are usually in the 80s. The railroad also operates on weekends through most of the winter, which has typically brisk but not frigid temperatures.

GOOD TO KNOW: The Hotel Nevada in downtown Ely dates from 1929 and was once a favorite of Hollywood stars. Ely also has a wide selection of motels.

WORTH DOING: The shop tour, which is included with every train ticket, features any historic equipment that's not on the road at the time of your visit.

DON'T MISS: An annual highlight for photographers is the Winter Steam Spectacular held in February. Dry desert air often makes for spectacular photos.

GETTING THERE: Ely is at the junction of Hwys. 6, 50, and 93 in east-central Nevada. Amtrak's *California Zephyr* stops at Elko, 188 miles away. The nearest air service is also at Elko, with Delta Air Lines offering commuter jets from Salt Lake City. The closest major airports are Salt Lake, Las Vegas, and Reno, in that order.

DISCOUNT: Buy one adult ticket and get one free.

Virginia & Truckee Railroad

ADDRESS: Washington and F Sts., Virginia City, NV 89440
TELEPHONE: 775-885-6833
E-MAIL: info@steamtrain.org
WEB SITE: www.steamtrain.org

The famous Comstock Lode yielded more than $400 million of silver and gold during a roughly 30-year period beginning in 1859 – and it led to the creation of both Virginia City and the Virginia & Truckee Railroad. Historically, the V&T ran from Reno south to Carson City, and soon the railroad may again make the spectacular descent to Carson City. Plans are underway to expand the line 17 miles to Carson City over much of the original, historic right-of-way and through the spectacular Carson River Canyon.

CHOICES: As the railroad expands, the train ride will be lengthened as new sections are rebuilt. The existing 2.5-mile segment makes an enjoyable 40-minute round trip between historic Virginia City and Gold Hill. Special trains include wine trains with vintners on board and Halloween trains. Try a special moonlight train, which is quite spectacular on V&T's mountain right-of-way, far removed from city lights. The railroad powers its trains with a 1916 Baldwin 2-8-0 from the Longview, Portland & Northern, a 1907 Baldwin 2-6-2 from the Hobart Southern, and an ex-Army, 80-ton diesel built in 1953.

WHEN TO GO: V&T operates on weekends during April and May and then daily from Memorial Day to the end of October. Temperatures are comfortable throughout the operating season, with average highs topping out in the low 80s during July and August.

GOOD TO KNOW: Virginia City boasts a variety of restaurants, hotels, and B&Bs that recall the town's frontier heritage. Many of them are within walking distance of the V&T station. A campground is also located in the historic area of Virginia City.

WORTH DOING: The Nevada State Railroad Museum in nearby Carson City displays more than 30 pieces of equipment that operated on the V&T.

DON'T MISS: The historic Virginia City walking tour provides a good sense of the Comstock mining boom. It includes historic mansions, churches, the Piper Opera House, and the *Territorial Enterprise* newspaper, where young Mark Twain worked as a reporter.

GETTING THERE: Virginia City is on Nevada Hwy. 341, 25 miles south of Reno and 15 miles north of Carson City. Amtrak's *California Zephyr* stops at Reno, 25 miles north. Several major airlines also serve Reno.

NEW HAMPSHIRE

Ashland   *Museum, Depot*
Ashland Railroad Station Museum

The museum was built by the Boston, Concord & Montreal Railroad as a station
around 1869. It is one of the state's best preserved examples of a 19th century
passenger station. The museum contains rail artifacts and photo displays.
Occasionally, an excursion train departs from the museum. It is open Saturdays during
July and August.

ADDRESS: 69 Depot St., Ashland, NH 03217
TELEPHONE: 603-968-3902
WEB SITE: www.ashlandnh.org/histsoc.html

Gorham   *Museum*
Gorham Rail Station Museum

This 1907 former Grand Trunk railroad station houses a museum that exhibits rail and
local historical items. It displays a 1911 Baldwin steam locomotive, a 1949 F-7 diesel
locomotive, and several boxcars. Operated by the Gorham Historical Society, the
museum is open Memorial Day weekend through mid-October.

ADDRESS: 25 Railroad St., Gorham, NH 03581
TELEPHONE: 603-466-5338
WEB SITE: www.aannh.org/heritage/coos/gorhamhist.php

Lincoln   *Train ride*
Hobo Railroad

Located in the White Mountains, the excursion train goes over the Pemigewasset
River, through the woods, and past Grandma's Crossing. For a unique meal on the
80-minute ride, grab a hobo lunch, complete with bindle stick. Near scenic Franconia
Notch, the railroad operates May through October and includes fall excursions.

ADDRESS: 64 Railroad St., Lincoln, NH 03251
TELEPHONE: 603-745-2135
WEB SITE: www.hoborr.com

Bretton Woods

Mount Washington Cog Railway

ADDRESS: Base Rd., Bretton Woods, NH 03589
TELEPHONE: 800-922-8825 or 603-278-5404
E-MAIL: info@thecog.com
WEB SITE: www.thecog.com

England may have invented the railroad, but the United States invented the cog railroad. The first such successful cog – a standard railroad with flanged wheels but with the addition of a gear engaging a cog down the center of the tracks – is credited to the Mount Washington Cog Railway in 1869, and it has been in operation since. The trip is to the top of 6,288-foot Mount Washington, infamous for its bad weather but famous for its great views.

CHOICES: Sit back and enjoy the views during the three-hour trip as a coal-fired steam engine takes you to the summit and back. On good days, you can see four states, Canada, and the Atlantic Ocean. You can view the railway's original cog engine, *Old Peppersass*, on display at the base.

WHEN TO GO: Excursion trains operate April through November, but fall in the White Mountains is always spectacular. During summer, trains run hourly. The ski train operates November through April.

GOOD TO KNOW: The trains operate on a track so steep that it resembles a ladder plunked down on the mountainside. Because of this, locomotive boilers are tilted as are the passenger cars so that passengers can ride upright.

WORTH DOING: The railway offers winter skiing and snowboarding. You can ride the train up and ski back down. There are trails for beginners and intermediate skiers. Catch a train ride on the Conway Scenic Railroad, which is 30 miles away.

DON'T MISS: Explore the mountains. Mount Washington State Park is at the summit and contains hiking trails, an observatory, and the stone Tip Top House. It is surrounded by the White Mountain National Forest, which is filled with a variety of recreational activities.

GETTING THERE: The Cog Railway is a pleasant drive from Boston, Hartford, New York, or Montreal. It is 90 miles from Portland off Hwy. 302. In Bretton Woods, follow Base Road for six miles to the railway.

Lincoln

Train ride

White Mountain Central Railroad

ADDRESS: Hwy. 3, Lincoln, NH 03251
TELEPHONE: 603-745-8913
E-MAIL: info@clarkstradingpost.com
WEB SITE: www.clarkstradingpost.com

The White Mountain Central Railroad is part of the popular family-owned Clark's Trading Post amusement park deep in New Hampshire's White Mountains. The railroad offers 30-minute excursions across the Pemigewasset River over a 1904 Howe-Truss covered bridge that was moved from the Barre & Chelsea Railroad in Vermont.

CHOICES: Once a center for the logging and paper industries, the region now caters to tourists. But four decades ago, the Clark family added a 1.25-mile railroad to its small amusement park and acquired an impressive collection of geared steam locomotives. A wood-burning International Shoe two-truck Heisler 4 and Beebe River Railroad two-truck Climax 6 are the star attractions, joined by East Branch & Lincoln Baldwin 2-4-2 no. 5, a Porter 0-4-0T, and a GE 65-ton diesel. Admission to Clark's Trading Post includes the train ride as well as other activities.

WHEN TO GO: Operations are daily through July and August and weekends in June and September through mid-October. The best New England fall foliage usually occurs in early October, which is also the peak tourist season. Special excursions and displays occur on Railroad Days, scheduled during a September weekend.

GOOD TO KNOW: Lodging, including motels and B&Bs, and restaurants can be found in Lincoln and surrounding communities. Rates will be the highest during fall, so reservations should be made far in advance for this season.

WORTH DOING: Nearby railroading attractions include Mount Washington Cog Railway, Hobo Railroad, and Conway Scenic Railroad.

DON'T MISS: The White Mountain National Forest is worth visiting any time of year for camping, hiking, history, and scenic drives.

GETTING THERE: There is limited commercial air service to Manchester, N.H. The Kangamangus Highway from Conway is a favorite drive for visitors during fall.

North Conway

Conway Scenic Railroad

Train ride, Dinner train

ADDRESS: 38 Norcross Circle, North Conway, NH 03860
TELEPHONE: 800-232-5251 or 603-356-5251
E-MAIL: info@conwayscenic.com
WEB SITE: www.conwayscenic.com

Here is a New England excursion train ride bursting with great scenery and Yankee character. The setting is in the Mount Washington Valley in the charming village of North Conway. With three different trips to choose from, this railroad offers a bounty of great journeys.

CHOICES: Two Valley Train excursions are offered: a 55-minute, 11-mile round trip to Conway and a longer 21-mile round trip to Bartlett. Passengers may choose from coach or lounge service. The Notch Train carries passengers from North Conway into the rugged Crawford Notch, as the first trains did more than 130 years ago. This train offers coach, first-class, and dome car seating. Some Valley Train departures include lunch or dinner options aboard *Chocorua*, the railroad's elegant dining car.

WHEN TO GO: Valley Trains operate excursions April through November, and the Notch Train runs June through October. What can be better than an autumn train ride in New England? Special trains operate throughout the year.

GOOD TO KNOW: Steam locomotive no. 7470 returned to service in 2006. Look for it on the Valley Trains.

WORTH DOING: Stick to the right side of the Notch Train as it ascends Crawford Notch and crosses the Frankenstein Trestle and Willey Brook Bridge for excellent views of bluffs, ravines, and streams. The later in the fall you travel, the fewer colors you'll see, but the better the vistas from the train.

DON'T MISS: Well, you can't miss the Victorian station in North Conway. Just take some time to appreciate this ornate structure that's been at work as a railroad depot since 1874.

GETTING THERE: The Conway Scenic Railroad is less than a three-hour drive from Boston. From Boston, take 1-95 to Hwy. 16, which runs to North Conway.

DISCOUNT: Take $1 off each regular adult ticket.

Meredith   *Train ride, Dinner train*
Winnipesaukee Scenic Railroad

Operated by the Hobo Railroad, this scenic railroad operates along the shores of Lake Winnipesaukee. It offers one- or two-hour train rides, lunch trips, and dinner trains. Special events include murder mysteries and fall foliage runs. The train features an ice cream parlor car and caboose rides.

ADDRESS: 154 Main St., Meredith, NH 03254
TELEPHONE: 603-279-5253
WEB SITE: www.hoborr.com

North Woodstock   *Dinner train*
Café Lafayette Dinner Train

Ride aboard a restaurant with a view of mountains and forests. This two-hour, 20-mile round trip follows the Pemigewasset River over a 100-year-old spur of the Boston and Maine Railroad. Enjoy a five-course dinner in several restored Pullman cars, including the *Granite Eagle*, a dome car that rode on the *City of New Orleans*.

ADDRESS: Hwy. 112, North Woodstock, NH 03262
TELEPHONE: 800-699-3501 or 603-745-3500
WEB SITE: www.cafelafayette.com

Sandown   *Museum*
Sandown Depot Museum

The museum is located in the restored Sandown railroad depot that was built in 1873. It contains a stationmaster's room with a working telegraph key and a waiting room with a pot-bellied stove. The museum also features two Flanger cars. It is open weekends May through October.

ADDRESS: 1 Depot Rd., Sandown, NH 03873
TELEPHONE: 603-887-6100
WEB SITE: www.sandown.us/historical%20society/museum_main.htm

NEW JERSEY

Cape May   *Train ride*

Cape May Seashore Lines

Take a ride on either of this railroad's two excursions, and you'll take a ride on the Reading, or over lines where the Reading used to operate, to the Jersey shore. There is a 30-mile round trip between Richland and Tuckahoe and a 22-mile round trip between Cape May Court House, Cold Spring Village, and Cape May City.

ADDRESS: 101 W. Pacific Ave., Cape May, NJ 08250
TELEPHONE: 609-884-2675
E-MAIL: info@capemayseashorelines.org
WEB SITE: www.capemayseashorelines.org

Maywood   *Museum, Depot*

Maywood Station Museum

The station has been restored, inside and out, to preserve its Victorian style, including its original colors. The station museum features local railroad artifacts and displays. Also on display is a restored caboose, which also contains exhibits.

ADDRESS: 269 Maywood Ave., Maywood, NJ 07607
E-MAIL: info@maywoodstation.com
WEB SITE: www.maywoodstation.com

Whippany   *Museum*

Whippany Railway Museum

A restored 1904 freight house contains railroad artifacts and memorabilia. Outdoor exhibits include rolling stock, a passenger depot, a wooden water tank, and a coal yard. During special events, a 10-mile, 45-minute excursion train operates.

ADDRESS: 1 Railroad Plaza, Whippany, NJ 07981
TELEPHONE: 973-887-8177
E-MAIL: wrym-web@comcast.net
WEB SITE: www.whippanyrailwaymuseum.org

Farmingdale   *Museum, Train ride*

New Jersey Museum of Transportation

ADDRESS: 4265 Route 524, Farmingdale, NJ 07727
TELEPHONE: 732-938-5524
WEB SITE: www.njmt.org

The museum is home to many rare pieces of equipment and offers a short ride on a narrow gauge train on the grounds of Allaire State Park.

CHOICES: Besides looking at the equipment on display, you have the opportunity to tour the museum's shops and see progress on the various restoration projects. The train travels through the scenic state park, which is home to the Manasquan River.

WHEN TO GO: The vintage locomotives run weekends, April through December. During the Railroader's Weekend Celebration in mid-September, all the equipment in running shape runs.

GOOD TO KNOW: One of the oldest all-volunteer railroad preservation groups, the museum began as the Pine Creek Railroad in 1952. The museum is the custodian of two 1850s steam locomotives submerged in 90 feet of water off the coast of New Jersey. How they got there is a mystery, but museum officials hope to raise them one day. The only other known engine of their kind is in the Smithsonian.

WORTH DOING: Look for the Ely-Thomas Lumber Company Shay locomotive. While not operable at present, it is one of the smallest Shays left in existence.

DON'T MISS: In the park, explore Allaire Village, a historic 19th century ironmaking town. The park also contains hiking and biking trails.

GETTING THERE: The museum is located in Allaire State Park not far from the ocean. It is easily accessible from the Garden State Parkway or I-195 off Exit 31B. Signs show the way to the park.

Flemington

Black River & Western Railroad

Train ride

ADDRESS: Stangle Rd., Flemington, NJ 08822
TELEPHONE: 908-782-9600
E-MAIL: psgrinfo@brwrr.com
WEB SITE: www.brwrr.com

The Black River & Western, which also hauls freight, operates hour-long passenger excursions over a short segment of the former Pennsylvania Railroad's Flemington Branch between Flemington and Ringoes.

CHOICES: Recent trains have been diesel-powered, but the railroad hopes for a return to service of American Locomotive 2-8-0 no. 60, which has done the honors for most years since 1963, when it arrived on the property. In addition to the standard excursions, there's a Great Train Robbery and special Octoberfest, Easter Bunny, and Halloween trains. The railroad also offers a *Santa Express* on two post-Thanksgiving weekends.

WHEN TO GO: The Black River & Western operates on weekends from May through October, and the fall foliage season is an ideal time to take this idyllic ride.

GOOD TO KNOW: Flemington is a mixture of quaint and commercial, with 60 percent of its buildings on the National Register of Historic Places. There are also plenty of shops and a handful of B&Bs.

WORTH DOING: Just 15 miles away, across the Delaware River into Pennsylvania, is the New Hope & Ivyland Railroad, which makes it easy to ride two excursion trains in the same day.

DON'T MISS: Nordlandz, an extraordinary model railroad rich in spectacle, is located in Flemington. Don't expect prototypical authenticity, but with eight miles of track, dozens of trains moving at once, and 35-foot-tall model mountains, it's acres of often whimsical fun.

GETTING THERE: Flemington is roughly 35 miles from Philadephia and 50 miles from New York City. Both Ringoes and Flemington are located just off Hwy. 202.

NEW MEXICO

Belen Harvey House Museum

Adjacent to the BNSF Division yard, the museum contains permanent exhibits
on Harvey Houses, Harvey Girls, and the Santa Fe Railroad. Exhibits change
monthly throughout the year. Listed on the National Register of Historic Places,
the Southwestern-style structure is one of state's few surviving Fred Harvey eating
establishments. The museum is open Tuesday through Saturday.

ADDRESS: 104 N. First St., Belen, NM 87002
TELEPHONE: 505-861-0581
E-MAIL: museum@belenharveyhouse.com
WEB SITE: www.belenharveyhouse.com

Cumbres & Toltec Scenic Railroad

ADDRESS: 500 Terrace Ave., Chama, NM 87520
TELEPHONE: 888-286-2737 or 505-756-2151
E-MAIL: info@cumbrestoltec.com
WEB SITE: www.cumbrestoltec.com

If you have ever craved going back in time to the 1920s to see what railroading was like, here's your chance. The Cumbres & Toltec operates 64 miles of track through the San Juan Mountains. Once part of the Denver & Rio Grande's vast narrow gauge railroad network, it has the feel of a working railroad from 80 years ago. Steam locomotives still labor up steep grades, cross 100-foot-tall trestles, and hug narrow shelves above yawning gorges.

CHOICES: The railroad offers a choice of excursions, and you can leave from either Chama or Antonito, Colo. From either station, there is a round trip to Osier, Colo., where a hot meal is provided. To see the scenic area in two different ways, you can ride the train one way and return by motor coach. The ride from Chama to Antonito offers a real show of the steam locomotives at work as the 2-8-2 Mikado type engines original to this line dig in and work as they go upgrade for several miles. Outbound trains occasionally require helpers.

WHEN TO GO: Excursion trains operate daily from the end of May until mid-October. During the summer, the *Cinder Express* runs weekly. The three-hour trip provides a fun and educational experience for children (and adults) that features Cinder Bear, surprises, and a picnic lunch.

GOOD TO KNOW: For more than 125 years, excursion passengers have ridden over Cumbres Pass, and the line crosses the border between Colorado and New Mexico 11 times.

WORTH DOING: Walk the Chama shop complex and yard and return to the 1920s. You'll see the coal tower, water tank, back shop and all sorts of clutter that is natural to a railroad yard.

DON'T MISS: Ride an open-window coach or a first-class car, and as your train moves along, be sure and walk back to the open gondola car. It's a great view and a lot of fun.

GETTING THERE: The railroad is located between Santa Fe and Colorado Springs. To reach Chama from Santa Fe, take Hwy. 285 to Hwy. 84. Hwy. 285 also takes you to Antonito.

Santa Fe

Train ride, Depot

Santa Fe Southern Railway

ADDRESS: 410 S. Guadalupe St., Santa Fe, NM 87501
TELEPHONE: 888-989-8600 or 505-989-8600
E-MAIL: depot@sfsr.com
WEB SITE: www.sfsr.com

One of the most famous railroad names of all is the Atchison, Topeka & Santa Fe Railway, usually known simply as the Santa Fe. This journey offers the chance to ride through the desert from Santa Fe along a historic spur to the junction city of Lamy.

CHOICES: Even if it wasn't a beautiful trip through the desert, the Santa Fe Southern offers something special: a chance to ride a working freight train. The railroad's scenic Day Train is a four-hour round trip aboard a real working mixed train. Along with vintage coaches, the train will most likely pull boxcars between Santa Fe and Lamy. You have the choice of riding in coach, silver, or dome class. Silver-class cars are vintage AT&SF *Super Chief* cars. The railroad also offers shorter excursions that travel to the Galisteo Basin overlook.

WHEN TO GO: The excursion trains operate year-round. There are numerous special events scheduled throughout the year, especially around holidays, as well as barbecue dinners and evening runs.

GOOD TO KNOW: If you would like to see one of the last surviving Harvey Houses, you can visit La Fonda Hotel located in Santa Fe's historic plaza.

WORTH DOING: The Lamy depot, built in 1880, has been renovated to match the style of the depot in Santa Fe.

DON'T MISS: Santa Fe is well known for its Southwest culture and art galleries, which number more than 200. Be sure and see the Georgia O'Keeffe Museum.

GETTING THERE: Santa Fe is 60 miles northeast of Albuquerque on I-25 and Hwy. 285. In Santa Fe, the station is on Guadalupe Street between Cerrillos Road and Agua Fria Street.

NEW YORK

Arcade   *Train ride*
Arcade & Attica Railroad

The Arcade & Attica Railroad offers a two-hour, 7.5-mile scenic excursion. Power is provided by a 1947 GE diesel. The railroad offers numerous special events throughout the year including fall foliage runs through western New York farmlands.

ADDRESS: 278 Main St., Arcade, NY 14009
TELEPHONE: 585-492-3100
WEB SITE: www.anarr.com

Arkville   *Train ride*
Delaware & Ulster Railroad

This 100-minute round trip from Arkville to Roxbury takes you along the Delaware River and through the scenic Catskill Mountains. The railroad also offers a dinner train and special events. The Arkville depot features an exhibit on the area's rail history. Excursions take place late May through October.

ADDRESS: 43510 Hwy. 28, Arkville, NY 12474
TELEPHONE: 800-225-4132 or 845-586-3877
WEB SITE: www.durr.org

Brooklyn   *Museum*
New York Transit Museum

Housed in a 1936 subway station, the New York Transit Museum features 19 restored subway cars and other exhibits related to urban transit. Exhibits highlight elevated rail lines and the construction of New York City's first subway line. The museum also offers special subway tours and events during the year.

ADDRESS: Boerum Pl. at Schermerhorn St., Brooklyn, NY 11201
TELEPHONE: 718-693-1600
WEB SITE: www.mta.info/mta/museum

NEW YORK

Central Square   *Depot*
Central Square Station Museum

The museum has various pieces of rail equipment on outdoor display including two 0-4-0 steam locomotives, a 1929 Brill car, a circus car, and a 25-ton diesel locomotive. Indoor exhibits are housed in an early 20th century depot. It is open Sundays May through October.

ADDRESS: 132 Railroad St., Central Square, NY 13036
TELEPHONE: 315-676-7582
E-MAIL: cnynrhs@aol.com
WEB SITE: www.cnynrhs.org/CentralSq.html

Dunkirk   *Museum*
Alco-Brooks Railroad Display

Located at the Chautauqua County Fairgrounds, this display features an Alco-Brooks 0-6-0 locomotive built in 1916, a Delaware & Hudson wood-sided boxcar, a wooden New York Central caboose, and other railroad artifacts.

ADDRESS: 1089 Central Ave., Dunkirk, NY 14048
TELEPHONE: 716-366-3797
E-MAIL: davrr@netsync.net
WEB SITE: www.wnyrails.org/cities/dunkirk/display.htm

Geneva   *Train ride*
Finger Lakes Scenic Railway

The railway offers a variety of scenic excursions in central New York. Also a freight hauler, the railway operates on 118 miles of track. Special themed excursions run all year from various locations in the Geneva-Syracuse area. Its popular Blues-n-Brew Train runs monthly.

ADDRESS: 68 Border City Rd., Geneva, NY 14456
TELEPHONE: 315-781-1234
E-MAIL: events@fingerlakesscenicrailway.com
WEB SITE: www.fingerlakesscenicrailway.com

Railroad Museum of Long Island, Greenport

Located in a Victorian-style LIRR freight station, the museum exhibits photos and artifacts of Long Island rail history. It displays an 1898 snowplow and a 1927 wooden caboose. An operating tower and turntable are also on site. The museum restores its rolling stock at its Riverhead location.

ADDRESS: 440 Fourth St., Greenport, NY 11944
TELEPHONE: 631-477-0439
E-MAIL: info@rmli.org
WEB SITE: www.rmli.org/Pages/Greenport_Site_main.htm

Hyde Park   *Depot*
Hyde Park Railroad Station

Built in 1914, the Hyde Park Railroad Station is listed on the National Register of Historic Places. You can tour the restored station, which was designed by the same architects who designed Grand Central Station, and view displays on the area's railroading history. It is open weekends during the summer and on holidays.

ADDRESS: 34 River Rd., Hyde Park, NY 12538
TELEPHONE: 845-229-2338
E-MAIL: webmaster@hydeparkstation.com
WEB SITE: www.hydeparkstation.com

Kingston   *Museum, Trolley ride*
Trolley Museum of New York

The museum operates a trolley ride from Kingston to the banks of the Hudson River, where you can enjoy a picnic lunch. With a stop at the museum, you can learn about trolleys and see them being restored. The museum's collection dates back to 1897 with its Oslo, Norway, car that was built in Germany.

ADDRESS: 89 E. Strand St., Kingston, NY 12402
TELEPHONE: 845-331-3399
E-MAIL: info@tmny.org
WEB SITE: www.tmny.org

Medina   *Train ride, Museum*

Medina Railroad Museum

ADDRESS: 530 West Ave., Medina, NY 14103
TELEPHONE: 585-798-6106
E-MAIL: office@railroadmuseum.net
WEB SITE: www.railroadmuseum.net

The area east of Buffalo provides a pleasant distraction with small towns, farms, and a relaxed existence. Here on a former New York Central main line is an opportunity to ride a streamlined passenger train behind a historic Alco Century diesel locomotive. The two-hour, 34-mile round trip parallels and then crosses the Erie Canal.

CHOICES: Housed in the old New York Central freight house, the museum exhibits a wide array of railroad displays. The freight house is huge – 301 feet long and 34 feet wide – and contains memorabilia, models, and artifacts. Enter the Union Station archway, and you'll see displays dedicated to the trains and railroads that helped develop the area including the *Empire State Express*, *20th Century Limited*, and Pennsylvania Railroad.

WHEN TO GO: The museum is open year-round Tuesday through Sunday. Fall foliage trips during October and Santa trains during December are the most popular train rides. Excursion trains run on other special events during the year.

GOOD TO KNOW: Ask about the bridge at Lockport, which according to legend was built upside down so as to limit the size of barge traffic on the competing Erie Canal

WORTH DOING: Watch a large HO scale model railroad in action. The prototypical railroad layout measures 14 feet by 204 feet. Also, take a close look at the lobby, which is refinished as the freight depot office.

DON'T MISS: Take a unique ride in a mule-drawn packet boat on the Erie Canal.

GETTING THERE: Medina is situated between Buffalo and Rochester, not far from Lake Ontario. From Buffalo, take I-90 east to Hwy. 77. Continue north on Hwy. 77/63 to downtown Medina. There, turn left onto at North Avenue and then right onto West Avenue.

DISCOUNT: Receive $1 off each adult admission.

Upper Hudson River Railroad

ADDRESS: 3 Railroad Place, North Creek, NY 12853
TELEPHONE: 518-251-5334
E-MAIL: info@uhrr.com
WEB SITE: www.uhrr.com

Since opening in 1999, the Upper Hudson River Railroad has operated over 8.5 miles of the former Delaware & Hudson Railway's Adirondack Branch from North Creek to Riverside station in Riparius. Round trips last more than two hours and include a layover at Riparius, where there are historical displays, a gift shop, refreshments, and a park with a bridge over the Hudson River. The tracks follow the river, here a scenic, rushing whitewater stream near its headwaters. Trains are pulled by a pair of Alco diesels – a road switcher built for the Delaware & Hudson and a yard switcher that Alco used at its own plant in Schenectady.

CHOICES: In 2006, a major new stretch of line was opened, 27 miles south from North Creek, past Thurman toward Hadley, allowing excursions from Riverside to 1000 Acres Ranch for luncheons, BBQs, rodeos, and other events. Soon there will be stations at Thurman and Hadley, 40 miles from North Creek. Eventually, an additional 15 miles of line, into Saratoga, will be rehabilitated as well.

WHEN TO GO: The Upper Hudson River Railroad operates in summer and fall, and the brilliant foliage makes autumn the season of choice for a visit.

GOOD TO KNOW: Nestled in the Adirondack Mountains, North Creek offers many opportunities for outdoor recreation, such as hiking, canoeing, or kayaking on the Hudson. Just a few miles away are the historic Barton Garnet Mines, where tours are offered, and the Gore Mountain Ski Center.

WORTH DOING: Leave time to visit the North Creek Depot Museum, which contains exhibits about ski trains and President Theodore Roosevelt's famous train ride from North Creek. The depot is on the National Register of Historic Places.

DON'T MISS: Sit on the left when departing, so you don't miss the views of the Hudson River.

GETTING THERE: North Creek is 18 miles from Exit 25 on the Adirondack Northway (I-87). Albany, the nearest city with a major airport, is 82 miles away.

Marcellus   *Museum, Depot*
Martisco Station Museum

This restored 1870 New York Central station contains two floors of local railroad artifacts. On the first floor of this Victorian-style brick structure, you'll enter a replica of a small-town railroad station. Items are displayed outside as well. It is open Sunday afternoons May through October.

ADDRESS: Martisco Rd., Marcellus, NY 13108
TELEPHONE: 315-673-1749
E-MAIL: cnynrhs@aol.com
WEB SITE: www.cnynrhs.org/Martisco.html

Milford   *Train ride, Depot*
Cooperstown & Charlotte Valley Railroad

On a 16-mile round trip between Milford and Cooperstown, the railroad takes you through a variety of landscapes found in the Upper Susquehanna River Valley. You cross the river twice over two steel-truss bridges. In the restored 1869 Milford depot, you can view an array of rail exhibits and displays.

ADDRESS: 136 E. Main St., Milford, NY 13807
TELEPHONE: 607-432-2429
E-MAIL: lrhs@lrhs.com
WEB SITE: www.lrhs.com
DISCOUNT: Take $1 off a regular adult ticket for up to four adults.

North Creek   *Museum, Depot*
North Creek Railway Depot Museum

Step into the North Creek Depot Museum and you'll relive a piece of presidential history. The depot was where Theodore Roosevelt learned he had become president at the death of President McKinley. The museum also tells the story of the Adirondack Railroad and the central Adirondack Mountains. The Upper Hudson River Railroad boards from the building's platform.

ADDRESS: 5 Railroad Pl., North Creek, NY 12853
TELEPHONE: 518-251-5842
E-MAIL: mail@northcreekdepotmuseum.com
WEB SITE: www.northcreekdepotmuseum.com

North Tonawanda   *Museum*
Railroad Museum of the Niagara Frontier

Housed in the restored Erie Railroad freight depot, which was built in 1922, the museum contains a collection of artifacts that recognize the region's railroading heritage. Also on display are several industrial locomotives, an Erie caboose, and a New York Central caboose.

ADDRESS: 111 Oliver St., North Tonawanda, NY 14120
TELEPHONE: 716-694-9588
E-MAIL: museum@nfcnrhs.com
WEB SITE: www.railroadniagara.com

Adirondack Scenic Railroad

ADDRESS: 321 Main St., Utica, NY 13501
TELEPHONE: 315-724-0700
E-MAIL: train@adirondackrr.com
WEB SITE: www.adirondackrr.com

The Adirondack Scenic Railroad currently operates excursions over two sections of line – 52 miles of the former New York Central's Adirondack Division from Utica to Thendara (plus an additional six miles on to Carter Station) and 10 miles between Lake Placid and Saranac Lake, built by the Delaware & Hudson and later acquired by the New York Central.

CHOICES: For serious riders, the railroad offers all-day excursions from Utica to Thendara on many summer and fall Thursdays, Saturdays, and Sundays. There is time for visiting the adjacent resort town of Old Forge and taking a two-hour cruise on the Fulton Chain of Lakes. Shorter round trips (of 20 miles, either south to Otter Lake or north to Carter Station) are offered from Thendara. Similar trips operate between Saranac Lake and Lake Placid at the other end of the railroad.

WHEN TO GO: In late November through mid-December, the railroad offers *Polar Bear Express* trains in emulation of the Chris Van Allsburg children's book. The brilliant foliage of fall makes that season perhaps the choicest time to ride.

GOOD TO KNOW: Thendara (adjacent to the resort community of Old Forge), Saranac Lake, and Lake Placid are all deep in the Adirondacks, replete with natural beauty. The region's history is interestingly presented at the Adirondack Museum in Blue Mountain Lake. The six-million-acre Adirondack Park offers 2,000 miles of hiking trails and hundreds of miles of canoe routes.

WORTH DOING: The Adirondack Scenic Railroad offers a whole smorgasbord of special trains and events throughout the year such as wine tastings and ghost trains.

DON'T MISS: The Adirondack Scenic Railroad shares Utica's grand 1914 Union Station with Amtrak, making it among the few excursion railroads with rail connections. Predating the station by two years and an easy walk away is the Hotel Utica, the city's grande dame hostelry, beautiful again after a recent refurbishing.

GETTING THERE: Served by multiple Amtrak trains each day, Utica also has excellent highway access, being located right on the New York State Thruway (I-90). The nearest major airport is in Syracuse, 56 miles away. Lake Placid is 30 miles from the Adirondack Northway (I-87). Adirondack Regional Airport is in Clear Lake, 15 miles away.

NEW YORK

Mount Pleasant Train ride

Catskill Mountain Railroad

The railroad offers a 90-minute excursion along Esopus Creek in the beautiful Catskills. Along the 12-mile round trip, you'll view peaks such as Mount Tremper, Mount Pleasant, and Romer Mountain. The trip also includes a stop at the Empire State Railway Museum in Phoenicia. Trains operate late May through October.

ADDRESS: Hwy. 28, Mount Pleasant, NY 10570
TELEPHONE: 845-688-7400
E-MAIL: cmrrinfo@hvc.com
WEB SITE: www.catskillmtrailroad.com

Phoenicia Museum, Depot

Empire State Railway Museum

Through photos, films, and artifacts, the museum highlights the history of railroads that served the Catskills. The museum, located in a restored 1899 Ulster & Delaware Railroad station, is also restoring several railway cars and a 1910 2-8-0 locomotive. It is open weekends and holidays Memorial Day through Columbus Day.

ADDRESS: 70 Lower High St., Phoenicia, NY 12464
TELEPHONE: 845-688-7501
WEB SITE: www.esrm.com

Riverhead Museum

Railroad Museum of Long Island, Riverhead

At its Riverhead location, where it restores rolling stock, the museum displays several steam locomotives and various rail cars. A miniature train ride also operates around the site. On weekends between May and October, you can take the LIRR and tour both Riverhead and the museum's Greenport facility.

ADDRESS: 416 Griffing Ave., Riverhead, NY 11944
TELEPHONE: 631-727-7920
E-MAIL: info@rmli.org
WEB SITE: www.rmli.org

Roscoe Museum

Roscoe O&W Railway Museum

This museum complex features a station building, a restored Ontario & Western caboose, a Beaverkill trout car, and watchman shanties. The museum specializes in O&W memorabilia and artifacts but also contains other railroad and local historical items.

ADDRESS: 7 Railroad Ave., Roscoe, NY 12776
TELEPHONE: 607-498-4346
E-MAIL: wilsip@frontiernet.net
WEB SITE: www.nyow.org/museum.html

Rush   *Museum*

Rochester & Genesee Valley Railroad Museum

The Rochester & Genesee Valley Railroad Museum is housed in a restored 1918 Erie Railroad train station. Inside, you'll see the original stationmaster's office and artifacts. You can also ride a track car to a second site, where you can inspect various early diesel and steam locomotives, freight cars, and passenger cars. It is open on Sundays from late May through October.

ADDRESS: 282 Rush-Scottsville Rd., Rush, NY 14626
TELEPHONE: 585-533-1431
E-MAIL: info@rgvrrm.org
WEB SITE: www.rgvrrm.org

Salamanca   *Museum*

Salamanca Rail Museum

This Buffalo, Rochester & Pittsburgh depot has been fully restored right down to the telegraph key in the ticket office, and it includes a ladies retiring room and a baggage room. Artifacts and photos show the history of railroads in western New York and Pennsylvania. A boxcar, a crew camp car, and two cabooses are on display.

ADDRESS: 170 Main St., Salamanca, NY 14779
TELEPHONE: 716-945-3133
E-MAIL: salarail@localnet.com
WEB SITE: www.wnyrails.org/cities/sal/sal_srm.htm

Utica   *Depot*

Utica Union Station

Built in 1914, the station serves the Adirondack Scenic Railroad and Amtrak. Restoration of the historic station is ongoing. On display is a rare New York Central steam locomotive, which is maintained by the Utica & Mohawk Valley Chapter of the National Railway Historical Society. That organization also maintains the railroad equipment displayed next door at the Children's Museum.

ADDRESS: 321 Main St., Utica, NY 13501
TELEPHONE: 315-787-8199
WEB SITE: www.uticarometrains.org

West Henrietta   *Museum, Trolley ride*

New York Museum of Transportation

The museum exhibits 11 trolley cars, a steam locomotive, a caboose, and rail artifacts as well as highway and horse-drawn vehicles. It features trolley rides and a short track-car ride that takes you to the nearby Rochester & Genesee Valley Railroad Museum. The New York Museum of Transportation is open year-round.

ADDRESS: 6393 E. River Rd., West Henrietta, NY 14586
TELEPHONE: 585-533-1113
E-MAIL: info@nymtmuseum.org
WEB SITE: www.nymtmuseum.org

NORTH CAROLINA

Bonsal   *Train ride, Museum*
New Hope Valley Railway

On this railway's train ride, you'll travel over a nine-mile stretch of historic railroad through the quiet woodlands of Chatham and Wake Counties. Each month at the North Carolina Railroad Museum, the railway operates ride days with activities and special events. The museum features artifacts and an impressive roster of locomotives.

ADDRESS: 5121 Daisey St., Bonsal, NC 27562
TELEPHONE: 919-362-5416
E-MAIL: info@nhvry.org
WEB SITE: www.nhvry.org

Charlotte   *Trolley ride, Museum*
Charlotte Trolley

Riding on Car 85 today is like going back to 1938. It is Charlotte's only original electric trolley car that remains in operation. Offering trolley service through the city's center, Charlotte Trolley also restores vintage electric streetcars and operates a museum highlighting the use of streetcars in the South.

ADDRESS: 2104 South Blvd., Charlotte, NC 28203
TELEPHONE: 704-375-0850
WEB SITE: www.charlottetrolley.org

Wilmington   *Museum*
Wilmington Railroad Museum

The museum is housed in a historic Atlantic Coast Line building, where you can view an extensive artifact collection. Outside, you can inspect a 1910 Baldwin steam locomotive, a hobo display in a boxcar, and a red caboose. Although it may be under renovation, the museum plans to remain open year-round.

ADDRESS: Nutt St., Wilmington, NC 28401
TELEPHONE: 910-763-2634
WEB SITE: www.wilmingtonrailroadmuseum.org

Tweetsie Railroad

ADDRESS: 300 Tweetsie Railroad La., Blowing Rock, NC 28605
TELEPHONE: 800-526-5740 or 828-264-9061
E-MAIL: info@tweetsie.com
WEB SITE: www.tweetsie.com

One of the original Wild West theme parks of the 1950s, when TV cowboys were popular, Tweetsie has roots in one of the most famous Southeastern narrow gauge railroads, the East Tennessee & Western North Carolina. The three-mile train ride gives the historic, coal-fired engines a chance to work and show that they are still the real thing.

CHOICES: The train is pulled by steam locomotive no. 12. The native engine worked for the East Tennessee & Western North Carolina and is listed on the National Register of Historic Places. Ride in a coach close to the engine, so you can hear it work up grade and listen to the whistle echo about the mountains.

WHEN TO GO: The park is open May through October. Memorial Day weekend through August, it is open daily. An annual railfan weekend is held in September, and a ghost train runs in October.

GOOD TO KNOW: The East Tennessee & Western North Carolina ran from Elizabeth City, Tenn., to Boone, N.C., for many years. Its whistle sounded a "tweet," and from that, locals nicknamed the railroad Tweetsie.

WORTH DOING: Bring the entire family along – there's lots to see and do for kids in the park. Admission to the railroad includes amusement rides, live shows, and other attractions.

DON'T MISS: Visit the actual Blowing Rock and learn its legend. Hike or drive through the scenic Blue Ridge Mountains. At Grandfather Mountain, you can cross the Mile High Swinging Bridge, a 228-foot long suspension bridge that spans an 80-foot chasm.

GETTING THERE: The railroad is west of Winston-Salem in the Blue Ridge Mountains near the Tennessee border. It is located off Hwy. 321 between Boone and Blowing Rock.

Bryson City   Train ride, Dinner train
Great Smoky Mountains Railroad

ADDRESS: 225 Everett St. Bryson City, NC 28713
TELEPHONE: 800-872-4681 or 828-586-8811
E-MAIL: info@gsmr.com
WEB SITE: www.gsmr.com

Few mountain railroads in the southeastern United States traverse such splendid scenery as this line does. Created from a portion of Southern Railway's Murphy Branch, the GSMR hugs the Tuckaseegee and Nantahala Rivers, climbs a mountain at Red Marble Gap, and rolls out over a 700-foot-long trestle at Fontana Lake.

CHOICES: GSMR offers a variety of accommodations, from cabooses and open-air cars to traditional coaches and air-conditioned lounge cars. Excursions range from three-hour jaunts to all-day adventures, dinner trains, and even a combination package in which you ride the train from Bryson City into the Nantahala Gorge and then raft part of the way back. The railroad has stations at both Bryson City, its headquarters, and Dillsboro.

WHEN TO GO: The railroad runs year-round. Spring and fall offer mild weather best suited to open cars and being able to see beyond the trees and into the forest; summer can be humid, and the tremendous foliage of the Southeast can make views more restricted.

GOOD TO KNOW: The railroad offers numerous special events, including some ideal for kids (Thomas the Tank Engine and the *Polar Express*) and others for the enthusiast, such as the Railfest weekend each September. It also operates Smoky Mountain Trains in Bryson City.

WORTH DOING: A trip along the Tuckaseegee River route (Dillsboro-Bryson City) offers the chance to see the train-wreck site from the 1993 movie, *The Fugitive*. It also provides a ride through curved Cowee Tunnel, scene of an infamous disaster in which convicts who dug the tunnel drowned when their boat sank in the river.

DON'T MISS: Watch whitewater rafters in the Nantahala River. They'll put on a good show, while you stay dry. Also, take in the bluegrass and gospel show at the Bryson City depot before the train leaves. Sit in church pews and sample some mountain culture.

GETTING THERE: The railroad is about three hours from Atlanta and one hour from Asheville. Major highways to the area include I-40, Hwy. 19/23 and Hwy. 441. Stations in both Bryson City and Dillsboro are in the downtown areas.

Museum, Train ride

North Carolina Transportation Museum

ADDRESS: 411 S. Salisbury Ave., Spencer, NC 28159
TELEPHONE: 877-628-6386 or 704-636-2889
E-MAIL: nctrans@nctrans.org
WEB SITE: www.nctrans.org

The state's transportation museum is housed in shop buildings from Southern Railway's largest steam locomotive repair shop that date from before 1900 to 1924. But this is no static museum. Trains run most of the year on 2.5 miles of track, giving visitors the chance to experience a 20-minute train ride that covers most of the 57-acre site.

CHOICES: Among the giant structures you'll see are the nation's largest preserved round-house, the 37-stall Bob Julian Roundhouse, which houses railroad displays, a restoration shop, and active locomotives and rolling stock. You will also see the Back Shop, a 600-foot-long, 80-foot-tall building once used to overhaul steam locomotives that is under restoration as an exhibit hall. The museum is free, and the train ride is only a few dollars. On some trains, you'll have the choice of riding in open-window or air-conditioned coaches or possibly a caboose.

WHEN TO GO: Any time of the year is enjoyable, but take plenty of water along if you go during the sweltering summer. Rail Days, the annual railroad festival when all the trains run, is usually held in spring, but it can be wet. Falls are long and mild. From November until April, winter hours are in effect.

GOOD TO KNOW: There are plenty of pork barbecue places in the region if you want to sample real Piedmont food.

WORTH DOING: Ride the engine cab for an extra fare. You'll get a unique view and a personalized tour. You might even get to blow the horn. A new program offers you the chance to become a student engineer; it is available by appointment only.

DON'T MISS: Ride the turntable. The 100-foot-long lazy Susan is used to turn locomotives at the roundhouse, and it helps define the term "in the round."

GETTING THERE: About an hour's drive from Charlotte or Winston-Salem, the museum is a few minutes off I-85. Take Exit 79 and then follow the brown signs to the museum in Spencer.

NORTH DAKOTA

Mandan   *Trolley ride*
Fort Lincoln Trolley

A restored trolley car takes you on a nine-mile excursion along the Heart River. The restored American Car streetcar, which was built in the 1890s, takes you from Mandan to Fort Abraham Lincoln State Park and back. The park features several reconstructed buildings that would have been found in the original fort.

ADDRESS: 2000 Third St. SE, Mandan, ND 58554
TELEPHONE: 701-663-9018

Minot   *Museum, Depot*
Old Soo Depot Transportation Museum

This museum focuses on the transportation history of the American West and includes materials on trains, planes, and automobiles. Located in a completely restored 1912 Soo Line depot, it also offers an excellent location for train-watching. The museum is open Monday through Friday.

ADDRESS: 15 N. Main St., Minot, ND 58703
TELEPHONE: 701-852-2234
E-MAIL: soodepot@srt.com

West Fargo   *Museum*
Bonanzaville USA

The museum features more than 40 historic buildings and 400,000 artifacts that depict life when bonanza homes dotted the Plains. Rail structures include a vintage Northern Pacific train depot, a water tower, and a train shed. The train shed displays an 1883 NP 4-4-0 steam locomotive, a caboose, and a 1930s Pullman car.

ADDRESS: 1351 Main Ave. W, West Fargo, ND 58078
TELEPHONE: 701-282-2822
E-MAIL: info@bonanzaville.com
WEB SITE: www.bonanzaville.com

OHIO

Conneaut   *Museum*
Conneaut Railroad Museum

Located in a former New York Central depot, which was built in 1900, this museum
displays railroad memorabilia, photos, and artifacts such as lanterns and timetables.
Be sure to climb aboard and inspect the cab of Nickel Plate Berkshire no. 755
displayed outside.

ADDRESS: 363 Depot St., Conneaut, OH 44030
TELEPHONE: 440-599-7878

Dennison   *Museum, Train ride*
Dennison Railroad Depot Museum

Built in 1873, the depot played a key role in troop disbursement in World War II and
now houses a museum. The museum schedules a variety of train rides during the
year including all-day excursions, murder mysteries, fall foliage trips, and holiday rides.
Open year-round, it displays locomotives, freight cars, and passenger cars.

ADDRESS: 400 Center St., Dennison, OH 44621
TELEPHONE: 877-278-8020
E-MAIL: depot@tusco.net
WEB SITE: www.dennisondepot.org

Jefferson   *Train ride*
AC&J Scenic Line

The railway offers a one-hour round trip that takes you over the last remaining
portion of the New York Central's Ashtabula-to-Pittsburgh passenger line. On the 12-
mile excursion, you'll travel on 1920s passenger cars pulled by a first-generation diesel
through scenic forests and farmland and cross two bridges. Various special events are
scheduled throughout the year.

ADDRESS: 122 E. Walnut St., Jefferson, OH 44047
TELEPHONE: 440-576-6346
E-MAIL: info@acjrscenic.net
WEB SITE: www.acjrscenic.net

Bellevue   *Museum*

Mad River & NKP Railroad Museum

ADDRESS: 253 Southwest St., Bellevue, OH 44811
TELEPHONE: 419-483-2222
E-MAIL: madriver@onebellevue.com
WEB SITE: www.madrivermuseum.org

The Mad River & NKP Railroad Museum opened on our nation's bicentennial in 1976 as a lasting tribute to the transportation industry. The museum has a widely varied collection of railroad locomotives, coaches, freight cars, equipment, and structures. While the museum focuses on the Nickel Plate Road and its successors, many other unique pieces of equipment, such as CB&Q Silver Dome no. 4714 (the first dome car built in the United States), are presented.

CHOICES: The museum is composed of static exhibits; however, many pieces, especially the passenger equipment, have interiors that are open for inspection. In addition, some equipment is outfitted with museum displays.

WHEN TO GO: Since the museum operates a seasonal schedule, summertime from Memorial Day to Labor Day is best. In addition, the museum is open on weekends in May, September, and October.

GOOD TO KNOW: Bellevue is a thriving, quaint rural Ohio town, with ample amenities for food and lodging and many other options for tourists such as antique shops and flea markets. Henry Flagler, who built the Florida East Coast Railroad, once lived on the property where the museum is now located.

WORTH DOING: Many opportunities exist for watching and photographing trains from public property around town. It is a major hub for the Norfolk Southern and home of one of the largest classification yards in the eastern United States. Mainline tracks bisect the museum and also host regional Wheeling & Lake Erie Railway trains.

DON'T MISS: Bellevue is a 30-minute drive from Sandusky and the Cedar Point amusement park, known for its roller coasters and its steam-powered, narrow gauge railroad.

GETTING THERE: The nearest major airports are Toledo, Cleveland, and Detroit. Amtrak's *Lakeshore Limited* and *Capitol Limited* stop in Toledo. For those driving, Bellevue is 20 minutes from the Ohio Turnpike off Exit 110.

Peninsula

Cuyahoga Valley Scenic Railroad

Train ride

ADDRESS: 1664 Main St., Peninsula, OH 44264
TELEPHONE: 800-468-4070 or 330-657-2000
E-MAIL: cvsr@cvsr.com
WEB SITE: www.cvsr.com

The Cuyahoga Valley Scenic Railroad operates on 47 miles of ex-B&O trackage through northeastern Ohio, from Independence (near Cleveland) through Peninsula and Akron to Canton. Much of the railroad is in the picturesque Cuyahoga Valley National Park, along the Cuyahoga River, and the route of the abandoned Ohio and Erie Canal.

CHOICES: The CVSR runs an extensive schedule of regular trains from various boarding stations. In addition, themed charters, such as a monthly wine train, run February through November. Also, many special events, including Thomas the Tank Engine and one of tourist railroading's premier *Polar Express* trains, are offered.

WHEN TO GO: The summer months offer the most extensive schedule of regular trains, with three separate trains running on the railroad during weekends in June, July, and August. Mid-October offers an extensive schedule to view the beautiful fall foliage. Trains are less crowded and still offer spectacular scenery in April and September. The railroad generally does not operate on Mondays and Tuesdays.

GOOD TO KNOW: The Cuyahoga Valley National Park features the Towpath Trail, which was built along much of the Ohio and Erie Canal Towpath. It is excellent for hiking and biking, and CVSR trains usually include a baggage car if you want to bike one way and ride the train one way.

WORTH DOING: The east side of the train generally includes the best views of the Cuyahoga River, which essentially parallels the railroad, especially on the north end from Peninsula up to Independence. In addition, many photo opportunities abound, and the park has re-created the feel of the early 1900s by building many of the railroad's depots and shelters in a style modeled after the railroad's original structures.

DON'T MISS: Explore many of the restored historical buildings in the national park, including the Canal Visitor Center (accessible by train) that details the canal's history and includes an operating canal lock.

GETTING THERE: By air, Cleveland is closest, but Akron-Canton is a convenient and often more economical option. Amtrak's *Lakeshore Limited* and *Capitol Limited* stop in Cleveland. If driving, the Ohio Turnpike crosses the CVSR near Peninsula, and I-77 generally parallels the railroad from Cleveland to Canton.

Jefferson   *Museum*

Jefferson Depot

The Jefferson Depot is more than a depot. It is a small village. In addition to the restored 1872 Lake Shore & Michigan Southern Railroad station, the site features a 1918 caboose and several 19th century buildings including a one-room schoolhouse, a post office, and a church. From June through September, guided tours are offered on Sundays. The AC&J Scenic Line is right next door.

ADDRESS: 147 E. Jefferson St., Jefferson, OH 44047
TELEPHONE: 440-576-0496
WEB SITE: www.members.tripod.com/jeffersonhome

Marion   *Museum*

Marion Union Station

The station contains a museum, and a fully restored Erie Railroad tower is also on site. Located between two diamond crossovers, the station is a great place to watch trains. More than 100 go by daily. The museum is open Monday through Friday.

ADDRESS: 532 W. Center St., Marion, OH 43302
TELEPHONE: 740-383-3768
WEB SITE: www.mariononline.com/agencies/MUSA.htm

Nelsonville   *Train ride*

Hocking Valley Scenic Railway

The railway offers diesel-powered excursions between Nelsonville and Logan. Once part of the original Hocking Valley Railway's Athens Branch, the route is listed on the National Register of Historic Places. Regular excursions run on weekends during summer and include a stop at Robbins Crossing, a re-created pioneer village. Special trains also run throughout the year.

ADDRESS: 33 Canal St., Nelsonville, OH 45764
TELEPHONE: 800-967-7834 or 740-753-9531
WEB SITE: www.hvsry.org

Orrville   *Train ride*

Orrville Railroad Heritage Society

The society offers excursions of various length, including trips to Pittsburgh, as well as fall foliage and holiday trains The trips are run in conjunction with the Wheeling & Lake Erie Railway or the Ohio Central Railroad. Special events also take place at the depot.

ADDRESS: 145 Depot St., Orrville, OH 44667
TELEPHONE: 330-683-2426
E-MAIL: questions@orrvillerailroad.com
WEB SITE: www.orrvillerailroad.com

Waterville   Train ride

Toledo, Lake Erie & Western Railway

Board the *Bluebird* at a historic depot and take a ride over the last remaining 10 miles of track of the Nickle Plate Railroad. Along the way, you'll see an 1817 log cabin and other structures amid scenic views. Trains run Wednesdays and Thursdays during summer, and special events are also scheduled during the year.

ADDRESS: 49 N. Sixth St., Waterville, OH 43566
TELEPHONE: 866-638-7246 or 419-878-2177
E-MAIL: info@tlew.org
WEB SITE: www.tlew.org
DISCOUNT: Receive $1 off each admission and 10 percent off all gift shop purchases.

Wellington   Train ride

Lorain & West Virginia Railway

Excursion rides take you on a 12-mile round trip over a restored portion of the L&WV. Trains run weekends late July through October, with special service during Lorain County Fair week. Cab rides are available in the railway's E-8 locomotive.

ADDRESS: Hwy. 18, Wellington, OH 44090
TELEPHONE: 440-647-6660
WEB SITE: www.lakeshorerailway.org

Worthington   Museum, Trolley ride

Ohio Railway Museum

The museum's collection features more than 30 pieces and includes streetcars dating from the 1890s, interurban cars, passenger cars, steam locomotives, and a post office car. It also offers a one-mile demonstration ride on one of the streetcars or interurbans. The museum may also offer train rides from time to time.

ADDRESS: 990 Proprietors Rd., Worthington, OH 43085
TELEPHONE: 614-885-7345
E-MAIL: askorm@insight.rr.com
WEB SITE: www.ohiorailwaymuseum.org

OKLAHOMA

El Reno   *Trolley ride*
Heritage Express Trolley

This 25-minute trolley ride is the only rail-based trolley in operation in Oklahoma. It runs from Heritage Park to downtown. Heritage Park is also home of the Canadian County Historical Museum, which is based in a historical Rock Island train depot.

ADDRESS: 300 S. Grand Ave., El Reno, OK 73036
TELEPHONE: 888-535-7366
E-MAIL: info@elreno.org
WEB SITE: www.elreno.org/tour/attractions.asp

Enid   *Museum*
Railroad Museum of Oklahoma

Located in a former Santa Fe freight house, this museum houses a large collection of railroad artifacts and memorabilia. In the yard, you can climb aboard a 1925 steam locomotive, wander through cabooses from nine different railroads, and view an assortment of freight cars. The museum also sponsors two all-caboose excursions.

ADDRESS: 702 N. Washington St., Enid, OK 73701
TELEPHONE: 580-233-3051
E-MAIL: information@railroadmuseumofoklahoma.org
WEB SITE: www.railroadmuseumofoklahoma.org

Hugo   *Museum, Depot*
Frisco Depot Museum

Once a main hub for the Frisco, the depot in Hugo is now a museum. Listed on the National Register of Historic Places, the 1917 building also contains a Harvey House restaurant, where you can grab a bite to eat. The museum includes railroad artifacts and displays on local history.

ADDRESS: 309 N. B St., Hugo, OK 74743
TELEPHONE: 580-326-6630

Clinton

Farmrail

Train ride

ADDRESS: 1601 West Gary Blvd., Clinton, OK 73601
TELEPHONE: 580-846-9078
E-MAIL: cityoflonewolf@swoi.net
WEB SITE: www.farmrail.com

Farmrail's *Quartz Mountain Flyer* takes passengers through the scenic Wichita Mountains of southwestern Oklahoma. The two-hour narrated round trip on refurbished, air-conditioned coaches gives you a glimpse of the area as it was 100 years ago.

CHOICES: Scheduled on select weekends from April through December, passenger excursions run from Quartz Mountain to Lone Wolf and back. A limited number of one-way locomotive cab rides are available for an additional fee.

WHEN TO GO: The scenery is in bloom during the spring, and the fall colors can be spectacular. If you like it hot, plan a visit during the summer months. The grain rush is in full swing in late May and early June, which means the railroad is running unit trains to keep up with demand.

GOOD TO KNOW: Make a vacation of your trip by staying at Quartz Mountain Resort. The resort, on Hwy. 44A east of Lone Wolf, offers numerous activities including golf, fishing, and hiking. A 50-acre ATV riding area is located on the north shore of nearby Lake Altus-Lugert. The Quartz Mountain Lodge features 118 rooms, nine cabins (pets welcome), and a 64-person bunkhouse, as well as RV hookups and primitive campsites.

WORTH DOING: Follow the railroad all the way down to the Red River into Texas, where it meets the BNSF Railway at Quanah.

DON'T MISS: For the transportation fan, head north to Elk City and see the National Route 66 Museum. The Oklahoma Route 66 Museum is located east of Elk City in Clinton.

GETTING THERE: Quartz Mountain is 101 miles southwest of Oklahoma City. Train departs from Quartz Mountain at the intersection of Hwys. 44 and 44A. Leaving Oklahoma City, travel west on I-40 to Clinton and then take Hwy. 9 south to Lone Wolf. Travel west on Hwy. 44, which parallels Farmrail's tracks, to the intersection with Hwy. 44A.

Pauls Valley   *Depot, Museum*

Santa Fe Depot Museum

This 1905 Santa Fe depot has been restored and now contains a collection of railroad photos and other local historical artifacts. On display are a 1907 Baldwin steam locomotive, Santa Fe no. 1951, a coal tender, and a caboose. The museum is open daily, and it features a convenient picnic area.

ADDRESS: 204 S. Santa Fe Pauls Valley, OK 73075
TELEPHONE: 405-238-2244
WEB SITE: www.paulsvalley.com/test/santa_fe.html

Oklahoma City   *Museum, Train ride*

Oklahoma Railway Museum

The Oklahoma Railway Museum possesses an interesting collection of equipment that includes a Santa Fe diner, a Porter 0-6-0, and a Santa Fe FP45 with a Warbonnet paint scheme. It also operates a variety of train rides and special events. It is open Saturdays.

ADDRESS: 3400 NE Grand Blvd., Oklahoma City, OK 73111
TELEPHONE: 405-424-8222
WEB SITE: www.oklahomarailwaymuseum.org

Waynoka   *Museum, Depot*

Waynoka History Museum

The museum is housed in a restored 1910 Santa Fe depot and Harvey House, and one room remains as a Harvey Girl's bedroom. The museum contains displays on Fred Harvey and the Santa Fe Railroad as well as other subjects. It includes a section foreman's house, other historic buildings, and a diesel locomotive.

ADDRESS: 202 S. Cleveland, Waynoka, OK 73860
TELEPHONE: 580-824-1886
E-MAIL: waynokahs@hotmail.com
WEB SITE: www.waynoka.org

Yukon   *Museum*

Yukon's Best Railroad Museum

Located in the hometown of Garth Brooks, the museum, made up of a Rock Island boxcar and a UP caboose, contains artifacts of the Rock Island and other railroads.

ADDRESS: Third and Main Sts., Yukon, OK 73099
TELEPHONE: 405-354-5079
E-MAIL: nanaust@cox.net

OREGON

Canby Depot Museum

The Canby Depot Museum is housed in what could be the oldest railroad station in Oregon, which has been around since at least 1873. The museum's displays provide a look at 19th century life of this historic community. It is open Thursday through Sunday March through December.

ADDRESS: 888 NE Fourth Ave., Canby, OR 97013
TELEPHONE: 503-266-6712
E-MAIL: depotmuseum@canby.com
WEB SITE: www.canby.com/community/depot/depot.htm

Lake Oswego   *Trolley Ride*
Willamette Shore Trolley

You can ride an antique trolley along a scenic six-mile rail line between Lake Oswego and Portland. Traveling along the Willamette River, you'll go through parks, past mansions, over bridges, and through a tunnel. It is open mid-May through October. The trolley is operated by the Oregon Electric Railway Historical Society. The society also operates the Oregon Electric Railway Museum located in Brooks, which is 30 miles south of Lake Oswego. The museum's collection includes streetcars, interurbans, and several double-deck trams.

ADDRESS: 311 N. State St., Lake Oswego, OR 97034
TELEPHONE: 503-697-7436
WEB SITE: www.oregonelectricrailway.org

Hood River   *Train ride, Dinner train*

Mount Hood Railroad

ADDRESS: 110 Railroad Ave., Hood River, OR 97031
TELEPHONE: 800-872-4661 or 541-386-3556
E-MAIL: mthoodrr@gorge.net
WEB SITE: www.mthoodrr.com

The Columbia River Gorge is filled with magnificent scenery, and the area around Mount Hood especially so because of its abundant orchards and vineyards. The Mount Hood Railroad offers a 44-mile round trip to Parkdale that features spectacular views of its namesake mountain. The train ends at a park, where passengers can relax and picnic before the return trip.

CHOICES: The four-hour excursion departs in the morning and follows the valley between the Columbia River and Mount Hood, providing views of Mount Adams as well. For half the journey, narration provides information about local history. Afternoon excursions also run on weekends. Brunch and dinner trains offer meals prepared on-board restored rail cars.

WHEN TO GO: Excursion and dinner trains run April through December, and there are numerous special events scheduled throughout the year. The railroad operates five or six days a week, depending on the time of year.

GOOD TO KNOW: The railroad still carries a limited amount of freight so don't be surprised if you see a boxcar somewhere along the line. Not far out of the Mount Hood depot, the train traverses a switchback, where it zig-zags up the side of the mountain to gain elevation quickly. The rear of the train becomes the front for the rest of the trip into Parkdale.

WORTH DOING: On the excursion train, be sure to take in the open-air car *Lookout Mountain*, which offers you the chance to soak in the atmosphere of the ride.

DON'T MISS: There is much to do in the area. Sample apples and pears from orchards, visit a local winery, or watch wind surfers try to master the gusts from the Columbia River Gorge. You can also take a drive on the Mount Hood Loop, which gives you a view of many scenic waterfalls.

GETTING THERE: The Mount Hood Railroad is located 60 miles east of Portland off I-84. In Hood River, take Exit 63 to reach the depot. If driving from the south, Hwy. 35 also goes to Hood River.

Sumpter Valley Railway

ADDRESS: Hwy. 7, Sumpter, OR 97814
TELEPHONE: 866-894-2268 or 541-894-2268
E-MAIL: svrydepotstaff@eoni.com
WEB SITE: www.svry.com

A five-mile portion of one of the most charming narrow gauge lines of the Pacific Northwest has been re-created amid forests and the spoils of a former gold-mining dredge operation. It is a good approximation of a remote steam line in eastern Oregon, where snowcaps rise in the distance even in June.

CHOICES: The railway runs between McEwen and Sumpter. Both round-trip and one-way excursions are available at either station. The railroad offers two historic locomotives. No. 19, an oil-burning 2-8-2, or Mikado type, is indigenous to the railroad. The two-truck, geared Heisler is one of a handful of wood-burners running today.

WHEN TO GO: The railway is open on weekends and holidays from Memorial Day through September. A special fall foliage photography train runs in October.

GOOD TO KNOW: The Sumpter depot is a replica of the original depot. Located on the Elkhorn Scenic Byway, Sumpter is surrounded by the Elkhorn Mountains. The area is filled with history, and Baker City boasts at least 60 restored buildings.

WORTH DOING: The railroad offers an engineer-for-a-day program. Take the throttle, under supervision, and you'll have a unique experience as a steam locomotive engineer.

DON'T MISS: Near the Sumpter station, in the Sumpter Valley Dredge State Heritage Area, see the historic gold dredge that churned up all the rocks the railroad runs through – it's as big as a house and a monster of a machine well worth touring.

GETTING THERE: The railway is about 330 miles from Portland in northeast Oregon. From Portland, take I-84 to Baker City and then take Hwy. 7 22 miles south to McEwen.

DISCOUNT: Receive $1 off a regular adult ticket for up to three adults.

Tillamook   *Train ride, Dinner train*

Port of Tillamook Bay Railroad

ADDRESS: 4000 Blimp Blvd., Tillamook, OR 97141
TELEPHONE: 800-685-1719 or 503-842-8206
E-MAIL: lhogsett@potb.org
WEB SITE: www.potb.org/oregoncoastexplorer

The Port of Tillamook Bay Railroad is really two excursion railroads in one. Packed into 95 miles of this railroad are a mountain railroad with long tunnels, steep grades, and magnificent trestles and a coastal railroad meandering along Oregon's magnificent Pacific Coast. Set in a part of the Pacific Northwest where grandeur describes the scenery, this railroad is among the best for viewing it.

CHOICES: The railroad offers a variety of excursions, as well as brunch and dinner trains. Rides provide views of scenery that cannot be seen from Hwy. 101. Steam-powered round trips travel along the Pacific shore. For a full day of mountain railroading, you can take a diesel-powered run from Banks, climb over the Coast Range into Salmonberry Canyon, turn at Enright, and return.

WHEN TO GO: Excursions usually begin Memorial Day weekend and run through mid-September. On the steam excursions, Friday runs are added to the schedule in July and August. Fall foliage and other special also take place during the year.

GOOD TO KNOW: The line is a former Southern Pacific Railroad branch that is now an out-growth of the port. It is a working freight line most of the week and sometimes passenger trains may be delayed.

WORTH DOING: For a unique railroading experience, try to reserve one of the two available seats in the 1910 Heisler steam locomotive.

DON'T MISS: Diesel locomotive no. 101 is painted like a Holstein cow to honor the region's dairying heritage. The Tillamook area produces some of the region's best ice cream and cheese.

GETTING THERE: Tillamook is 75 miles from either Portland or Salem. Highway 101 provides a scenic drive along the coast to Tillamook. Most excursions and dinner trains depart from Garibaldi and Banks.

Redmond   *Dinner train*
Crooked River Dinner Train

Riding this three-hour, 38-mile round trip is murder – or robbery. As you travel through the Crooked River Valley on a Wild West dinner train you can enjoy a murder mystery, train robbery, or other entertainment with your four-course meal. Themed rides are offered year-round along with holiday trains and special events.

ADDRESS: 495 NE O'Neil Way, Redmond, OR 97756
TELEPHONE: 541-548-8630
WEB SITE: www.crookedriverrailroad.com

Garibaldi   *Train ride*
Oregon Coast Scenic Railroad

Experience the Pacific Ocean on a 10-mile, 90-minute excursion along the shores of Tillamook Bay. The train is pulled by a Heisler locomotive and runs between Garibaldi and Rockaway Beach. It operates weekends from Memorial Day through mid-September. A special fireworks train operates in July.

ADDRESS: Hwy. 101, Garibaldi, OR 97141
TELEPHONE: 503-842-7972
E-MAIL: info@ocsr.net
WEB SITE: www.ocsr.net

Wallowa   *Train ride*
Eagle Cap Excursion Train

Explore the wilderness of northeast Oregon on the Eagle Cap Excursion Train. It operates over a 63-mile line that connects Wallowa, Elgin, Enterprise, and Joseph. Various trips are available, ranging from four-hour to seven-hour round trips that travel through canyons and along the Grande Ronde and Wallowa Rivers.

ADDRESS: 209 E. First St., Wallowa, OR 97885
TELEPHONE: 541-886-3200
WEB SITE: www.eaglecaptrain.com
DISCOUNT: Receive a $5 discount on adult tickets.

PENNSYLVANIA

Ashland   Train ride
Pioneer Tunnel Coal Mine and Steam Train

Take a scenic ride along Mahanoy Mountain as you hear stories about mining, bootlegging, and the Centralia Mine fire. A 1927 narrow gauge 0-4-0 steam locomotive takes you around the mountain. You can also tour a real anthracite coal mine in open mine cars. It is open April through November.

ADDRESS: 19th and Oak Sts., Ashland, PA 17921
TELEPHONE: 570-875-3850
WEB SITE: www.pioneertunnel.com

Bellefonte   Train ride
Bellefonte Historical Railroad

This railroad offers 60-mile trips over the Nittany & Bald Eagle Railroad to Lemont, Pleasant Gap, Tyrone, and Lock Haven. The Bellefonte Station, a restored former Pennsylvania Railroad structure built in 1888 houses historical photos and memorabilia of area railroading.

ADDRESS: 320 W. High St., Bellefonte, PA 16823
TELEPHONE: 814-355-2917
E-MAIL: query@bellefontetrain.com
WEB SITE: www.bellefontetrain.com

Erie   Museum
Museum of Erie GE History

The museum displays models, pictures, and memorabilia related to the production locomotives at the General Electric plant in Erie. The collection includes materials from 1906, when the plant was being planned, to the present. It is open most Saturdays during the year.

ADDRESS: 2901 E. Lake Rd., Erie, PA 16531
TELEPHONE: 814-875-2494
E-MAIL: bakerie@aol.com
WEB SITE: www.members.aol.com/museriege

Gallitzin   *Museum*
Allegheny Portage Railroad

This national historic site preserves the remains of the Allegeny Portage Railroad that operated from 1834 to 1854. You can explore the 900-foot Staple Bend Tunnel, the first railroad tunnel built in the United States, visit the engine house, or take a hike. For bikers, a 2.5-mile trail takes you to the Staple Bend Tunnel.

ADDRESS: 110 Federal Park Rd., Gallitzin, PA 16641
TELEPHONE: 814-886-6150
WEB SITE: www.nps.gov/alpo

Gallitzin   *Museum*
Tunnels Park & Museum

From the nearby Jackson Street Bridge, you get a great view of the twin tunnels, which are 3,605 feet long. The site also features a museum and a restored 1942 Pennsylvania Railroad caboose. The museum includes railroad artifacts and photos. It is open Tuesday through Sunday.

ADDRESS: 411 Convent St., Gallitzin, PA 16641
TELEPHONE: 814-886-8871
E-MAIL: info@gallitzin.info
WEB SITE: www.gallitzin.info

Greenville   *Museum*
Greenville Railroad Museum

This railroad museum displays historic engine no. 604. Built in 1936, it is the largest, and only surviving, steam switch engine built. Several other cars are on display along with no. 604. The museum also includes a reconstructed dispatcher's office and stationmaster's quarters. It is open June through October.

ADDRESS: 314 Main St., Greenville, PA 16125
TELEPHONE: 724-588-4009
WEB SITE: www.greenvilletrainmuseum.org

Altoona   *Museum*

Horseshoe Curve National Historic Landmark

ADDRESS: 1300 Ninth Ave., Altoona, PA 16602
TELEPHONE: 888-425-8666 or 814-946-0834
E-MAIL: info@railroadcity.com
WEB SITE: www.railroadcity.com

Horseshoe Curve is an engineering marvel completed in 1854 as part of the Pennsylvania Railroad's main line over the Allegheny Mountains. By curving the track across the face of a mountain, builders were able to gain elevation without making the grade too steep for trains to climb. Today, the curve is as vital as ever, serving as a key link in the Norfolk Southern system; more than 50 trains pass over its three tracks each day. A trackside park established in 1879 received major improvements in 1992, making it a premier train-watching spot.

CHOICES: Attractions at Horseshoe Curve consist of a visitors center/museum at ground level and the trackside park, which is accessible by a 194-step walkway or by a funicular railway. First-timers will want to tour the visitors center, ride the funicular up to track level, and then take the stairway back down. The best show at the curve is the passage of a heavy westbound train, laboring up the grade with helper engines on the front and/or rear. Try to stay long enough to catch this spectacle.

WHEN TO GO: The visitors center and funicular are open daily April through October. In October, the fall colors can be brilliant. Freight traffic tends to build toward the end of each week, so there may be more trains to see on Thursday, Friday, and Saturday.

GOOD TO KNOW: The site is managed by the superb Altoona Railroaders Memorial Museum in downtown Altoona; combined admission tickets are available.

WORTH DOING: Continue west on Kittanning Point Road to Gallitzin and visit the small park at the west portal of one of the tunnels the railroad uses to pierce the spine of the Alleghenies. Cresson, a little further west is also a good place to watch trains. Both towns have trackside, railfan-oriented lodging.

DON'T MISS: The longer you stay at Horseshoe Curve, the greater the chances of seeing two or even three trains rounding the curve, a thrilling occurrence.

GETTING THERE: Horseshoe Curve is located five miles west of Altoona. Altoona is on I-99, 33 miles north of I-70/76. Amtrak's New York-Philadelphia-Pittsburgh *Pennsylvanian* stops at Altoona daily.

Railroaders Memorial Museum

ADDRESS: 1300 Ninth Ave., Altoona, PA 16602
TELEPHONE: 888-425-8666 or 814-946-0834
E-MAIL: info@railroadcity.com
WEB SITE: www.railroadcity.com

Of all the places in the United States deserving a first-rate railroad museum, Altoona is certainly at the top of the list. The museum here is among the best when it comes to providing an interactive experience and telling the story of this shop town that in the 1920s employed more than 15,000 Pennsylvania Railroad workers. Today, Altoona is still a shop city for Norfolk Southern, and the museum tells the story of how it became so important and the people who made it so.

CHOICES: Be sure to step into the bar exhibit and hear all about the lives of railroaders as they sit and sip a cold one. Also look at the exhibit on the PPR's testing and research lab. Some of its efforts were astounding.

WHEN TO GO: The museum is open daily April through October and weekends in November and December.

GOOD TO KNOW: The museum is housed in the Pennsylvania Railroad's former master mechanic's building, which was built in 1882.

WORTH DOING: The Allegheny Portage Railroad National Historic Site and Staple Bend Tunnel are both within 25 miles of Altoona.

DON'T MISS: Take a day and spend half of it in the museum and the other half watching trains at Horseshoe Curve.

GETTING THERE: Altoona is about 95 miles east of Pittsburgh. From Pittsburgh, take Hwy. 22 to I-99 north. Take Exit 33, 17th Street, and a right turn on Ninth Avenue takes you to the museum.

Gettysburg   *Train ride, Dinner train*

Pioneer Lines Scenic Railway

ADDRESS: 106 N. Washington St., Gettysburg, PA 17325
TELEPHONE: 717-334-6932
E-MAIL: pioneerlines@innernet.net
WEB SITE: www.gettysburgrail.com

Abraham Lincoln rode a train to Gettysburg to deliver his famous Civil War address. Today, Gettysburg visitors can take a train ride into history, passing through a portion of the battlefield and within sight of monuments marking the first day of the battle. From there, depending on the length of the excursion, it's a delightful trip through the Pennsylvania countryside.

CHOICES: The railroad's scenic train offers a 75-minute tour, with the conductor providing historic narration on the 16-mile round trip. Dinner and murder mystery trains are three-hour, 36-mile trips. The railroad offers the option of riding the engine cab with the engineer for a fantastic view of the railroad.

WHEN TO GO: The railroad's excursions begin in April and run through November. Fall is among the most pleasant seasons to ride the train and visit Pennsylvania, and the railroad offers added runs in October. Special theme trains operate throughout the year.

GOOD TO KNOW: The railroad uses a pair of streamlined F-units from the 1950s that provide a striking silhouette for the train.

WORTH DOING: Abe Lincoln Trains run the beginning of July. History buffs can ride with costumed characters, including the 16th president, aboard these 1863 scenic excursions.

DON'T MISS: After riding the train, visit Gettysburg National Military Park. Besides a self-guided tour, you can tour the park by bus, listening to an audio tape, or with a licensed battlefield guide.

GETTING THERE: Gettysburg is in south-central Pennsylvania, just across the border with Maryland and about 60 miles from Baltimore. The railroad is a few blocks north of the downtown square in Gettysburg.

Jim Thorpe   *Train ride, Depot*

Lehigh Gorge Scenic Railway

ADDRESS: Susquehanna St., Jim Thorpe, PA 18229
TELEPHONE: 570-325-8485
WEB SITE: www.lgsry.com

This 16-mile round trip into the Lehigh Gorge is among the most beautiful in Pennsylvania, a state blessed with numerous great tourist railroads and museums because of its abundant railroad development. Trains run on the tracks of the Reading & Northern regional railroad, paralleling a state bike path into an isolated, narrow chasm.

CHOICES: The one-hour excursion follows the winding Lehigh River, curve after curve, and crosses it in several places, until it reaches Old Penn Haven. Leaving from the renovated, unique Central Railroad of New Jersey depot, the diesel-powered trains consist of vintage 1920s open-air coaches.

WHEN TO GO: The railway operates on Saturdays and Sundays mid-May through mid-December. The mountains present a new look for each season, but fall offers beautiful foliage and an extended schedule in October.

GOOD TO KNOW: In 1953, the towns of Mauch Chunk and East Mauch Chunk merged into one town with the name of Jim Thorpe when that famous athlete was buried there. Looking for a place that would help develop a memorial for her husband, who had no previous ties to the area, Thorpe's widow received assistance from the two towns.

WORTH DOING: Ride the train one day, then get an outfitter to set you up with a bicycle and a shuttle to White Haven and ride back down the gorge the next day for a different perspective.

DON'T MISS: Explore the town of Jim Thorpe, a charming village of shops, stores, and B&Bs, many featuring Victorian architecture. The town was once known as the Switzerland of America for its steep hillsides, narrow streets, and terraced gardens.

GETTING THERE: In the heart of the Poconos, Jim Thorpe is approximately 90 miles from Philadelphia. From there, take I-476 to Exit 74. Then take Hwy. 209 south into Jim Thorpe, where it becomes Susquehanna Street, and follow it to the railway.

Honesdale   *Train ride*

Stourbridge Line Rail Excursions

Offering views of the Lackawaxen River and the Pocono Mountains, this scenic round trip runs from Honesdale to Hawley, closely following the route of the Delaware & Hudson Canal. A restored BL2 diesel locomotive pulls vintage cars on a variety of differently themed excursions throughout the year.

ADDRESS: Torrey Lane, Honesdale, PA 18431
TELEPHONE: 800-433-9008 or 570-253-1960
WEB SITE: www.waynecountycc.com

North East   *Museum*

Lake Shore Railway Museum

A restored 1899 New York Central passenger station, built by the Lake Shore & Michigan Southern, houses extensive rail displays. Displayed on the grounds are 24 pieces of rolling stock and an 1869 station. There are demonstrations of Heisler fireless locomotive on select weekends.

ADDRESS: 31 Wall St., North East, PA 16428
TELEPHONE: 814-725-1911
E-MAIL: lsrhs@velocity.net
WEB SITE: www.lsrhs.railway.museum
DISCOUNT: Take $1 off regular adult admission for up to four adults.

Philadelphia   *Museum*

Franklin Institute Science Museum

The museum features the Train Factory, a permanent, interactive exhibit showcasing Baldwin locomotive no. 60,000. You'll explore past and present railroad technology as you journey through the exhibit and even take no. 60,000 for a test run. The museum is open year-round.

ADDRESS: 222 N. 20th St., Philadelphia, PA 19103
TELEPHONE: 215-448-1200
WEB SITE: www.fi.edu

Portage
Museum, Depot
Portage Station Museum

The museum is located in a restored Pennsylvania Railroad train station, originally built in 1926. The stationmaster's office contains artifacts from the Pennsylvania Railroad, and on the second floor, there is a display of Allegheny Portage Railroad items. The building is listed on the National Register of Historic Places.

ADDRESS: 400 Lee St., Portage, PA 15946
TELEPHONE: 814-736-9223
WEB SITE: www.portagestationmuseum.org

Robertsdale
Museum
Friends of the East Broad Top Museum

Located at the former southern operating terminus of the East Broad Top Railroad, the museum includes two historic buildings, an EBT station and a post office, both constructed around 1915. Exhibits illustrate the history of the railroad and the people who constructed, maintained, and operated it. The museum is open on weekends June through mid-October.

ADDRESS: Main St., Robertsdale, PA 16674
TELEPHONE: 814-635-2388
E-MAIL: febt@aol.com
WEB SITE: www.febt.org/museum.html

Rockhill Furnace
Museum, Trolley ride
Rockhill Trolley Museum

The museum offers a three-mile ride aboard a vintage electric trolley car along the former Shade Gap Branch of the East Broad Top Railroad past the site of the Rockhill Iron Furnace. You can tour the museum's collection, which includes an operating open trolley, high-speed interurban cars, and maintenance-of-way cars, and watch restoration projects in progress. It is open weekends Memorial Day through October.

ADDRESS: 430 Meadow St., Rockhill Furnace, PA 17249
TELEPHONE: 610-437-0448
E-MAIL: info@rockhilltrolley.org
WEB SITE: www.rockhilltrolley.org

Kempton   *Train ride*

Wanamaker, Kempton & Southern Railroad

ADDRESS: 42 Community Center Dr., Kempton, PA 19529
TELEPHONE: 610-756-6469
E-MAIL: info@kemptontrain.com
WEB SITE: www.kemptontrain.com

The Wanamaker Kempton & Southern, while short on mileage, is long on atmosphere. The WK&S has been successful for more than 40 years by striving to preserve the feeling of a Reading Railroad branch line, operating authentically painted and lettered equipment.

CHOICES: Both steam and diesel locomotives are used on the 40-minute trips, with several departures each day. There are Easter Bunny, Harvest Moon, Halloween, and Santa specials scheduled throughout the seasons. Once each year, the WK&S hosts a Kids Fun Weekend that includes train rides, extra activities, and free ice cream for all train riders.

WHEN TO GO: The WK&S operates weekends May through October. Passing prosperous farms and crossing Ontelaunee Creek, the excursion takes you through beautiful scenery at any time of the year. The fall colors in late September and early October on the surrounding mountains can be breathtaking.

GOOD TO KNOW: The WK&S is much less formal than some tourist railroads and museums, and it features a picnic grove that is accessible only by train.

WORTH DOING: Ride the left side of the train as you leave Kempton for the best views of Ontelaunee Creek and the surrounding mountains. Be sure to leave the train at Wanamaker while the engine runs around the train for the return trip to Kempton.

DON'T MISS: A visit to the WK&S can easily be combined with a trip to Steamtown, where the Railroad Museum of Pennsylvania is located, or Strasburg and the Strasburg Rail Road.

GETTING THERE: The WK&S is located in eastern Pennsylvania, five miles north of I-78 just off Hwy. 737 in Kempton. In Kempton, follow the signs to the station, which is located at the north end of town.

DISCOUNT: Receive $1 off a regular ticket for each member of your party.

Middletown & Hummelstown Railroad

ADDRESS: 136 Brown St., Middletown, PA 17057
TELEPHONE: 717-944-4435
E-MAIL: traingal@mhrailroad.com
WEB SITE: www.mhrailroad.com

If you're looking for that relaxed train ride in central Pennsylvania, here's your ride. The M&H provides a trip along the Swatara Creek, past the ruins of a canal, and ends with a dramatic bridge crossing over the creek and a stop at another tourist attraction, Indian Echo Caves. A nice package in an 11-mile round trip.

CHOICES: The M&H offers plenty of different trips, from scenic outings to murder mystery barbecues. You have a choice of departure locations, as trains operate from both the 1891 freight station in Middletown and the Indian Echo Caverns platform. However, the special event trains operate only out of Middletown. Aboard the train's Delaware, Lackawanna & Western coaches, you'll hear informative narration about the area; be prepared to sing some railroading songs. You can even reserve a hobo sack lunch, complete with bandana and pole.

WHEN TO GO: Excursions begin Memorial Day weekend and end the beginning of October. There are numerous special events during the year.

GOOD TO KNOW: Formerly part of the Reading Railroad, the M&H also provides freight service. At the Middletown yard, the railroad displays a collection of rolling stock.

WORTH DOING: The railroad offers a combination ticket with Indian Echo Caves for an interesting rail-cavern outing.

DON'T MISS: This close to Hershey, how could you go wrong with a Sunday Sundae trip that includes a stop at the Cone-A-Cabana. And in Hershey, you can hop on more than 60 rides, including roller coasters and water rides, at Hersheypark amusement park.

GETTING THERE: Middletown is situated between Harrisburg and Hershey, both 10 miles away, and 100 miles from Philadelphia. From Philadelphia, take I-76 to Hwy. 283. Exit at Middletown and from Main Street, turn left on Pine Street and then left on Brown Street to get to the station.

New Hope *Train ride, Dinner train*

New Hope & Ivyland Railroad

ADDRESS: 32 W. Bridge St., New Hope, PA 18938
TELEPHONE: 215-862-2332
E-MAIL: info@newhoperailroad.com
WEB SITE: www.newhoperailroad.com

The New Hope & Ivyland Railroad provides a scenic, 45-minute trip through the rolling hills and valleys of Bucks County, leaving from the quaint resort village of New Hope on the Delaware River.

CHOICES: There are lots of trains to ride, from scenic excursions to dinner trains, as well as story-time rides for children. You can board regular excursion trains at either New Hope or Lahaska. The 1920s vintage passenger coaches are pulled by a steam engine, including Old Number 40, a 1925 Baldwin 2-8-0, or a diesel locomotive.

WHEN TO GO: The New Hope & Ivyland operates year-round. From January through March, excursions run on Saturdays and Sundays. In April, May, and November, Friday runs are added to the weekend schedule. And beginning Memorial Day weekend, excursions operate daily through the end of October. Special trains operate throughout the year, and the annual railfan weekend in September, when all trains run, is a great time to visit.

GOOD TO KNOW: The line follows the ex-New Hope Branch of the Reading Railroad, and way back in 1914, the silent movie series *Perils of Pauline* was filmed along these same tracks. The restored Victorian station at New Hope has been in operation since 1891. An original "witch's hat" station, it once housed the railroad's telegraph operator.

WORTH DOING: You can get off at either station and take a later train back to the originating station. At Lahaska, you can enjoy a family picnic, and in New Hope, you can take a mule-drawn boat ride in the Delaware Division of the Pennsylvania Canal or stroll along the Delaware River.

DON'T MISS: History buffs can visit Valley Forge National Historical Park, which is about 40 miles from New Hope.

GETTING THERE: New Hope is 45 miles northeast of Philadelphia. From Philadelphia, take the Pennsylvania Turnpike east to the Willow Grove exit. Then take Hwy. 611 to Hwy. 202. Turn north on Hwy. 202 and go 10 miles to Hwy. 179, which leads you into New Hope. In town, take a left onto Bridge Street to the station. Lahaska is five miles southwest of New Hope, and the station is on Street Road, one mile east of Hwy. 202.

DISCOUNT: Take $1 off each regular adult ticket and 50 cents off each regular child ticket.

Rockhill Furnace   *Train ride*

East Broad Top Railroad

ADDRESS: Hwy. 994, Rockhill Furnace, PA 17249
TELEPHONE: 814-447-3011
E-MAIL: ebtrr@innernet.net
WEB SITE: www.ebtrr.com

PENNSYLVANIA

The East Broad Top was the last common carrier narrow gauge railroad east of the Mississippi River. A National Historic Landmark, The EBT's line runs through a beautiful valley little changed since the line closed in 1956. The 4.5-mile excursion has been operating since the 1960s.

CHOICES: The railroad still uses one of six Baldwin Mikado steam locomotives and wooden coaches purchased second-hand in the 1920s over a line laid out in 1874. In addition to the wooden coaches, the train includes open cars, a caboose, and a wonderful observation car *Orbisonia*, which requires an extra fare. The Fall Spectacular, held in early October, is the railroad's biggest event. More than 20 trains run, all operational equipment is used, and guided tours of the shops and roundhouse are conducted. Take time to wander around the nearby roundhouse, yard and the sprawling shops complex where the railroad once built its own freight cars and maintained its fleet of locomotives.

WHEN TO GO: The EBT is open Saturdays and Sundays from the first weekend in June through the end of October. Three trips are scheduled each day.

GOOD TO KNOW: Several times a year, the all-volunteer Friends of the East Broad Top lead tours of the interior of the shops and roundhouse. The group is also restoring rolling stock and buildings.

WORTH DOING: Be sure to visit the adjacent Rockhill Trolley Museum, whose trolley cars traverse the former Shade Gap Branch of the EBT. Other nearby attractions include Horseshoe Curve and the Railroaders Memorial Museum in Altoona, as well as Raystown Lake, a 29,000-acre recreational area.

DON'T MISS: Since the railroad parallels a highway, follow a train for photos across the fields or from an overhead bridge. Stick around after the day's runs are over on Saturday to watch the hostlers clean the fires and prepare the engine for its overnight rest.

GETTING THERE: The East Broad Top is off the beaten track in central Pennsylvania. The closest commercial airport is in Altoona, about 50 miles away. The drive from Harrisburg or Altoona on Hwy. 22 parallels the former Pennsylvania Railroad main line, now operated by Norfolk Southern, with its heavy freight traffic.

187

Scranton Museum, Trolley ride
Electric City Trolley Museum

Located on the grounds of the Steamtown National Historic Site, the museum is housed in a restored mill building. In addition to displaying vintage regional trolleys, the museum features a unique under-the-skin look at a restored trolley and other interactive exhibits. Trolley excursions travel through a 4,747-foot interurban tunnel.

ADDRESS: 300 Cliff St., Scranton, PA 18503
TELEPHONE: 570-963-6590
E-MAIL: trolley@lackawannacounty.org
WEB SITE: www.ectma.org
DISCOUNT: Buy one museum entrance or trolley excursion and get one free.

Titusville Train ride
Oil Creek & Titusville Railroad

Go with the flow on this railroad's two-hour train ride. As it rolls through Oil Creek State Park, you'll see where towns sprung up to follow the first oil boom and then disappeared when the oil did. The railroad operates the only working post office car in the country. Special excursions and biking and canoeing opportunities are offered.

ADDRESS: 409 S. Perry St., Titusville, PA 16354
TELEPHONE: 814-676-1733
E-MAIL: ocandt@usachoice.net
WEB SITE: www.octrr.org

Washington Museum, Trolley ride
Pennsylvania Trolley Museum

A visit to the museum includes a guided tour of the carbarn and unlimited four-mile trolley rides. In the carbarn, you can see some trolleys and restoration projects. For an added fee, you can tour the trolley display building that houses 30 additional trolleys.

ADDRESS: 1 Museum Rd., Washington, PA 15301
TELEPHONE: 724-228-9256
E-MAIL: ptm@pa-trolley.org
WEB SITE: www.pa-trolley.org

West Chester Train ride
West Chester Railroad

The railroad offers special-events excursions during the year. The 16-mile round trip runs from West Chester to Glen Mills, following scenic Chester Creek. Events are scheduled around holidays and excursions include train robberies, summer Sunday picnics, and fall foliage runs.

ADDRESS: Market St., West Chester, PA 19380
TELEPHONE: 610-430-2233
WEB SITE: www.westchesterrr.net

Museum, Train ride

Steamtown National Historic Site

ADDRESS: Cliff Ave. Scranton, PA 18503
TELEPHONE: 888-693-9391 or 570-340-5200
WEB SITE: www.nps.gov/stea

The former Delaware Lackawanna & Western railroad shop complex is home to one of the East's most complete railroad history exhibits. Housed in several buildings on the site of the Lackawanna's roundhouse, Steamtown provides a shrine to steam-era railroading in the northeastern United States. It also offers both short and long train rides. The real treat is a walk through the active portion of the roundhouse, where steam locomotives are still maintained.

CHOICES: The site includes both a steam history museum as well as a technology museum. The orientation movie, hands-on exhibits about workers as well as hardware, and equipment displays are excellent. Demonstrations of the turntable and shop tours are also conducted. You can make a brief visit by walking through the exhibits and taking the *Scranton Limited*, a half-hour ride on vintage commuter coaches. But if you have time, schedule your visit when you can spend a day with the exhibits, then ride an excursion train to Moscow, a two-hour trip that includes a climb up the Poconos or through the countryside to Tobyhanna. This is one of the few places where a large, mainline steam locomotive can operate at track speed on a mountain railroad.

WHEN TO GO: Steamtown is open year-round. Summer can be sultry, but spring and fall are pleasant. Winter sees less activity. Steamtown's trains run seasonally on select days. The *Scranton Limited* usually runs May through November, and the longer excursions from Memorial Day weekend through October.

GOOD TO KNOW: The Union Pacific Big Boy, one of 25 of its type built in the early 1940s, is one of the largest steam locomotives ever built at 1.1 million pounds. Operated in Wyoming and Utah, this is the only one of its type on exhibit in the eastern United States. It is so big, you could hold a dinner party in the firebox.

WORTH DOING: The 45-minute shop tour, offered regularly, provides a good behind-the-scenes look at heavy-duty restoration work underway on several locomotives.

DON'T MISS: Nearby, you can view the Scranton Iron Furnaces or tour a coal mine.

GETTING THERE: From I-81, take Exit 185. Stay in the left lanes to downtown Scranton and turn left at first traffic light. Follow Lackawanna Avenue to Cliff Avenue, where the park entrance is located.

Strasburg   *Museum*

Railroad Museum of Pennsylvania

ADDRESS: Hwy. 741 E, Strasburg, PA 17579
TELEPHONE: 717-687-8628
E-MAIL: info@rrmuseumpa.org
WEB SITE: www.rrmuseumpa.org

The Railroad Museum of Pennsylvania boasts one of the top rolling stock collections in the United States. The highlight is a dozen steam locomotives preserved by the Pennsylvania Railroad in the 1950s; very few PRR engines exist elsewhere. The collection also includes about 100 other locomotives and cars from the PRR and other railroads serving the state, many displayed in a 100,000-square-foot exhibition hall.

CHOICES: Go up, down, and out: an elevated walkway gives a fine view of the Rolling Stock Hall, a pit between the rails allows inspection of the underside of one of the locomotives, and tours of the rolling stock yard are sometimes available. Be sure to see PRR 4-4-2 no. 7002, a beautiful example of a high-wheeled passenger speedster from the early 20th century; PRR GG1 no. 4935, one of the best-preserved of the most famous class of electric locomotives; and PRR E7 no. 5901, the only surviving example of General Motors' top-selling passenger diesel.

WHEN TO GO: The museum is open every day except for certain major holidays and most Mondays November through March. A variety of special events are scheduled throughout the year.

GOOD TO KNOW: Lancaster County is in the heart of Pennsylvania Dutch country and home to Amish communities. Driving through the area, you can discover scenic farmlands with covered bridges and experience the Amish culture.

WORTH DOING: Spend part of the day at the museum and then take a ride on a steam train on the Strasburg Rail Road, located right across the road.

DON'T MISS: If you would like to see trains on a smaller scale, the National Toy Train Museum is also located in Strasburg.

GETTING THERE: The museum is on Hwy. 741 (Gap Road) one mile east of Strasburg, which is about 15 minutes by car from Lancaster, one hour from Harrisburg or Reading, and 90 minutes from Philadelphia. Most folks take Hwy. 30 to Hwy. 896 south to Hwy. 741.

DISCOUNT: Receive $1 off regular adult admission for up to four adults.

Strasburg Rail Road

ADDRESS: Hwy. 741 E, Strasburg, PA 17579
TELEPHONE: 717-687-7522
E-MAIL: srrtrain@strasburgrailroad.com
WEB SITE: www.strasburgrailroad.com

Founded in 1832, the Strasburg Rail Road is the oldest railroad company in the nation. It might have died if not for the efforts of local railfans who resurrected it as a tourist line in 1959. The nine-mile, 45-minute round trip from Strasburg to Paradise through Amish farmland aboard authentic 19th century wooden coaches recalls travel before automobiles. Trains are nearly always powered by one of the Strasburg's four operable steam locomotives.

CHOICES: Several different types of accommodations are available on most trains, including coach, open-air, deluxe lounge, and first-class parlor. Lunch, dinner, and wine-and-cheese trains are offered as well. Get off the train at Groffs Grove for a picnic or just to watch the action, which in the busy season includes a meet between two trains every half hour. Tours of the shop and engine house are available.

WHEN TO GO: Steam trains run every day nearly all year. In summer, two trains run simultaneously. A rare, wooden self-propelled doodlebug from a long-abandoned Lancaster County short line runs on several days in March and November. Thomas the Tank Engine events draw immense crowds.

GOOD TO KNOW: Strasburg is located in the heart of Pennsylvania Dutch country, and a drive through the area gives you an opportunity to explore scenic farmlands with covered bridges and experience the Amish culture.

WORTH DOING: There are no turning facilities on the Strasburg, so locomotives pull trains tender-first east out of the Strasburg station and pilot-first, west. Sit on the right-hand side of the train out of Strasburg for the best view of the engine changing ends at Paradise.

DON'T MISS: Drive out to a country grade crossing to watch trains. At Cherry Hill Road, westbound trains work hard up a 1.5 percent grade. At Black Horse Road, an 18th century cemetery beside the track provides a fine vantage point for westbounds. Also, visit the Railroad Museum of Pennsylvania's world-class collection right across the road.

GETTING THERE: For a scenic ride, approach Strasburg on Hwy. 741 from either the east or west – just watch out for Amish buggies! The railroad is on Hwy. 741 one mile east of Strasburg.

PENNSYLVANIA

Wellsboro *Train ride*

Tioga Central Railroad

ADDRESS: Hwy. 287, Wellsboro, PA 16901
TELEPHONE: 570-724-0990
WEB SITE: www.tiogacentral.com

Here's a short railroad that still carries freight on its 34-mile route but also knows how to have some fun. The ride takes you along Crooked Creek, through forests, and to Hammond Lake, a large reservoir. It's a good trip at a brisk pace behind rare Alco diesels.

CHOICES: The Tioga Central, in addition to operating its regular, 24-mile, 90-minute excursions, offers several special trains during summer, including a Friday night ice cream train and a 40-mile, Saturday sunset outing along Lake Hammond to the New York state line. Ride the train's open-air car and keep a lookout for wildlife such as osprey, blue herons, deer, and even bald eagles.

WHEN TO GO: The railroad offers regular excursions on Saturdays and Sundays from Memorial Day weekend through October. In fall, there are special weekday excursions to take advantage of the spectacular foliage.

GOOD TO KNOW: The railroad owes its good views of Lake Hammond, which it parallels for much of its journey, to a dam project that almost resulted in the railroad's abandonment. Fortunately, the railroad was relocated to the side of the reservoir.

WORTH DOING: At the station, take a look at the railroad's oldest piece of rolling stock. Now an office, Car 54 was originally a double-ended, open-platform paymaster car built in 1894 for the Grand Trunk Western.

DON'T MISS: Explore the nearby Pine Creek Gorge however you like. You can take a hike, ride a bike, or raft a river. Called the Grand Canyon of Pennsylvania, the 1,000-foot-deep gorge winds its way through acres of scenic landscape. Various parks provide breathtaking views of the canyon from hiking trails. You can also bike the Pine Creek Trail, a former rail line, through the canyon. Rafting is best in spring.

GETTING THERE: Wellsboro is in north central Pennsylvania, 50 miles north of Williamsport. Trains leave from Wellsboro Junction, which is about three miles north of Wellsboro on Hwy. 287.

RHODE ISLAND

Newport Dinner Train

Aboard the Newport Dinner Train, you can enjoy a four-course dinner in elegantly restored 1940s Budd dining cars. The 22-mile round trip takes you along scenic Narragansett Bay. Lunch trains, murder mysteries, and entertainment specials are also available. One lunch package features a boat cruise of Newport harbor. The menu offers several entree choices including the train's specialty, baby back ribs.

ADDRESS: 19 America's Cup Ave., Newport, RI 02840
TELEPHONE: 800-398-7427 or 401-841-8700
E-MAIL: info@newportdinnertrain.com
WEB SITE: www.newportdinnertrain.com

SOUTH CAROLINA

Greenwood   *Museum*
Railroad Historical Center

A walk-through display of rolling stock includes a Mikado type steam engine, a dining car, a sleeper car, a caboose, and other cars. It is operated in partnership with the Museum, located four blocks north, which features a wide range of exhibits and programs. The Railroad Historical Center is open Saturdays April through October.

ADDRESS: 908 S. Main St., Greenwood, SC 29646
TELEPHONE: 864-229-7093
E-MAIL: themuseum@greenwood.net
WEB SITE: www.themuseum-greenwood.org/train.shtml

Museum, Train ride

South Carolina Railroad Museum

ADDRESS: 110 Industrial Park Rd., Winnsboro, SC 29180
TELEPHONE: 803-635-4242
E-MAIL: info@scrm.org
WEB SITE: www.scrm.org

A slice of Southeastern shortline history awaits visitors to the South Carolina Railroad Museum. Located on the former Rockton & Rion Railway, a granite quarry short line, this railroad brings the experience of a casual Southeastern short line to life through a 10-mile, one-hour ride, interesting exhibits, and rolling stock displays.

CHOICES: The museum operates the Rockton, Rion & Western Railroad on five miles of the former Rockton & Rion Railway line. The line runs west past antebellum plantation remains and through pine forests to Rion. Its collection showcases South Carolina's railroad heritage and includes exhibits of track tools, artifacts, and photographs. Rolling stock includes passenger cars, freight cars, cabooses, and other equipment from CSX, Norfolk Southern, the Lancaster and Chester, and other railroads.

WHEN TO GO: The museum is open the first and third Saturdays June through October, with regular train rides scheduled on those days. It is also open on several special days during the year. On Caboose Days in October, all trains run with a caboose, which is available for rides.

GOOD TO KNOW: The railroad's 100-ton General Motors diesel saw action in the Korean War. Late in the year, children can mail letters to Santa from a 1927 Railway Post Office car.

WORTH DOING: Check out the two steam locomotives in the collection, 4-6-0 no. 44 from the Hampton & Branchville, and no. 712, one of only five existing Atlantic Coast Line steam locomotives, and a veteran of the Rockton & Rion.

DON'T MISS: Wet a line in one of the state's top fishing lakes. Lake Wateree has more than 13,700 acres and contains bream, catfish, crappie, and bass. Dammed in 1919, it is also one of the oldest manmade lakes in the state.

GETTING THERE: About 30 miles from Columbia, Winnsboro is between Columbia and Rock Hill, just off I-77. Take Exit 34 and follow Hwy. 34 about five miles and turn left at the steam locomotive that marks the museum's entrance.

SOUTH DAKOTA

Prairie Village

Prairie Village is a collection of restored buildings, rail equipment, and farm machinery that preserves the past. Rail structures include several historical depots, a roundhouse, and a turntable. On Sundays, you can take a two-mile train ride around the village. Several steam and diesel locomotives, various cabooses, and a unique chapel car are featured. Railroad Days takes place in June.

ADDRESS: Hwy. 34, Madison, SD 57042
TELEPHONE: 800-693-3644 or 605-256-3644
E-MAIL: Info@prairievillage.org
WEB SITE: www.prairievillage.org

Hill City

Black Hills Central Railroad

Train ride

SOUTH DAKOTA

ADDRESS: 222 Railroad Ave., Hill City, SD 57745
TELEPHONE: 605-574-2222
E-MAIL: office@1880train.com
WEB SITE: www.1880train.com

This railroad gives you a chance to ride on a real mountain railroad with steep grades, mines, and scenic hills. Situated close to Mount Rushmore, the Black Hills Central, also known as the 1880s Train for the year of its inception, carries riders between stations in Keystone and Hill City.

CHOICES: The two-hour, 20-mile round trip is a beautiful journey through the historic, rugged landscape of the Black Hills. Ride a coach or pile into the drover's caboose, believed to be one of only two left from the Chicago & North Western Railroad and the only one in use. Cattlemen lived in these cabooses while following their herds, loaded onto stock cars, to market.

WHEN TO GO: With a few exceptions, trains operate several times daily between May and October, departing from both Keystone and Hill City. Some last-train departures from Keystone are one-way trips only.

GOOD TO KNOW: Keystone is rich in tourist offerings including restaurants, shows, and shops. Hill City has amenities but without the tourist hubbub. Engine no. 7, its tender, and the drover's car were used in TNT's 2005 miniseries *Into the West*.

WORTH DOING: Ride on steam locomotive no. 110, the nation's only operating Mallet locomotive. What makes this engine special is that it has two sets of cylinders and drivers, and the exhaust steam from the back set of cylinders moves the front set of drivers. The engine is like having two smaller engines (which Black Hills Central has, by the way) under one boiler. It's impressive as it tackles grades as steep as 5 percent for almost a mile but never breaks a sweat.

DON'T MISS: The Black Hills area is filled with must-see activities, including a trip to Mount Rushmore. You can experience the rugged beauty of the Badlands, see bison in Custer State Park, and visit the Wild West town of Deadwood.

GETTING THERE: Whether traveling east or west, I-90 gets you to the train. To reach Keystone from Rapid City, take Hwy. 16 to Hwy. 244. To reach Hill City from Deadwood, take Hwy. 385.

TENNESSEE

Cookeville   *Museum, Depot*
Cookeville Depot Museum

This railroad museum is housed in a Tennessee Central Railway depot. Built in 1909, the building is listed on the National Register of Historic Places. Inside, there are changing displays of railway artifacts and photos highlighting local railroad history. A renovated caboose contains additional exhibits. It is open year-round Tuesday through Saturday.

ADDRESS: 116 W. Broad St., Cookeville, TN 38501
TELEPHONE: 931-528-8570
E-MAIL: depot@cookeville-tn.com
WEB SITE: ls.cookeville-tn.org/depotmuseum.html

Cowan   *Museum*
Cowan Railroad Museum

Photos, relics, and memorabilia from the age of steam are located in a restored, century-old depot. Outdoor displays include a 1920 Porter-type locomotive, a flatcar and a caboose. Nearby is the Franklin-Pearson House, which was built in 1850 as a boarding house for workers constructing the Cumberland Mountain Tunnel.

ADDRESS: 108 S. Front St. Cowan, TN 37318
TELEPHONE: 931-967-3078
WEB SITE: www.visitcowan.com

Jackson *Museum*
Casey Jones Railroad Museum

Although Casey Jones has been dead for more than 100 years, his legend lives on. His former home has been turned into a railroad museum. The museum includes artifacts related to Casey Jones as well as Jackson's railroad history. A replica of no. 382, Casey's engine, is also on display.

ADDRESS: 30 Casey Jones La., Jackson, TN 38305
TELEPHONE: 731-668-1222
E-MAIL: cjtrainstore@iwon.com
WEB SITE: www.caseyjones.com

Jackson *Museum*
Nashville, Chattanooga & St. Louis Depot and Railroad Museum

The museum houses a collection of artifacts, photographs, and memorabilia associated with local as well as railroad history. The grounds feature a dining car and two cabooses. Built in 1907, the depot is listed on the National Register of Historic Places. It is open year-round Monday through Saturday.

ADDRESS: 582 S. Royal St., Jackson, TN 38301
TELEPHONE: 731-425-8223
E-MAIL: thedepot@cityofjackson.net
WEB SITE: www.cityofjackson.net/departments/recpark/facilities/special/depot.html

Townsend *Museum*
Little River Railroad

The museum holds a number of tools, artifacts, and photographs dedicated to the Little River Railroad and the lumber company it served. It displays a restored 1909 Shay locomotive, several pieces of rolling stock, logging equipment, and a water tower. It is open April through October.

ADDRESS: 7747 E. Lamar Alexander Pkwy., Townsend, TN 37882
TELEPHONE: 865-428-0099
WEB SITE: www.littleriverrailroad.org

TENNESSEE

Chattanooga

Tennessee Valley Railroad

ADDRESS: 4119 Cromwell Rd., Chattanooga, TN 37421
TELEPHONE: 423-894-8028
E-MAIL: info@tvrail.com
WEB SITE: www.tvrail.com

If you were to take a major steam railroad from the 1920s, shrink it and preserve it, you'd have the Tennessee Valley Railroad. It offers a steam-powered train ride that leaves from a magnificent station, crosses trestles over streams and another active railroad line, and passes through a tunnel before it reaches the terminal at the opposite end of the run.

CHOICES: The railroad offers a variety of excursions. You can take the *Missionary Ridge Local* on a six-mile round trip between Grand Junction and East Chattanooga, traveling through a unique horseshoe tunnel as you do. On the *Chickamauga Turn*, a six-hour ride takes you to Chickamauga and back. Departing out of Etowah, the railroad, with the Tennessee Overhill Association, also offers a trip through the Hiwassee River Gorge that rides to the top of the Great Hiwassee Loop.

WHEN TO GO: Excursions run March through December, with specials scheduled throughout the year. Anytime the steam train is running is a good time to go. Take a day to explore the railroad's equipment and then take a day-long ride on the same weekend.

GOOD TO KNOW: If you want an all-railroad experience, stay at the Chattanooga Choo Choo, a Holiday Inn in the former terminal station; there, you can eat at the station complex in one of several venues, including a real railroad dining car, and sleep on a train car.

WORTH DOING: Be sure to walk into the shop at East Chattanooga, where volunteers and professionals restore railroad equipment dating back to 1903. East Chattanooga features one of the few complete wheel shops in the country, and on any given visit, there's no telling what set of wheels from what engine is there for repairs.

DON'T MISS: In Chattanooga, activities include visiting the Tennessee Aquarium and taking a riverboat cruise on the Tennessee River. History buffs should explore both the Lookout Mountain and Chickamauga battlefields.

GETTING THERE: The railroad is in northeast Chattanooga. Take Hwy. 153 to Exit 3. At the end of the exit ramp, turn left over Hwy. 153 and turn right onto Cromwell Road.

DISCOUNT: Take $1 off each adult and 50 cents each child (Missionary Ridge trains only).

Knoxville   *Train ride*

Three Rivers Rambler

ADDRESS: Volunteer Landing on Neyland Dr., Knoxville, TN 37902
TELEPHONE: 865-524-9411
E-MAIL: info@threeriversrambler.com
WEB SITE: www.threeriversrambler.com

TENNESSEE

There are few perfect chances to ride a steam train in a beautiful part of the Appalachians, leaving from one of the more pleasant areas of a small city like Knoxville. But the *Three Rivers Rambler* offers just such an outing. From its departure point on the Tennessee River, it makes its way into the country to its namesake point: the confluence of the Holston and French Broad Rivers to create the mighty Tennessee. The train bridges this point on a magnificent trestle that puts an exclamation point on the trip.

CHOICES: On the 90-minute round trip, you'll have the choice of riding in an air-conditioned coach, an open-air car, or a caboose. The vintage cars are pulled by a restored 1925 Baldwin steam engine. No. 203 is decked out in historical attire as Washington & Lincolnton for the Georgia short line it first worked. Along the way, feel free to ask the conductor or volunteer staff questions about the train or local history.

WHEN TO GO: Excursions operate on weekends during summer and fall. You can't beat autumn, especially for the colors, but on Saturdays featuring University of Tennessee home football games, you may be swamped with orange-clad fans and find the train being used for railgate parties.

GOOD TO KNOW: The departure point on the Tennessee River is adjacent to the university in an area with several good restaurants (try Calhoun's cheesy spinach dip – it's delicious!).

WORTH DOING: The railroad offers the chance to ride in the locomotive's cab and help the crew with the engine as part of its Engineer-for-a-Day package.

DON'T MISS: Sports fans could try to catch a University of Tennessee football or basketball game or visit the Women's Basketball Hall of Fame.

GETTING THERE: From I-40, take Exit 386B to Neyland Drive and turn left. Drive two miles to the parking lot on your left and look for signs. After parking, cross under Neyland Drive and proceed left down the riverwalk to the train at Volunteer Landing.

DISCOUNT: Take $2 off regular ticket price.

Nashville

Museum, Train ride

Tennessee Central Railway Museum

ADDRESS: 220 Willow St., Nashville, TN 37210
TELEPHONE: 615-244-9001
WEB SITE: www.tcry.org

The museum offers day trips on a streamlined passenger train through scenic middle Tennessee over the tracks of the Nashville & Eastern Railroad to a variety of destinations.

CHOICES: The museum offers a variety of excursions throughout the year. Most depart from Nashville and travel to Watertown or Cookeville, but some also depart from the Cookeville depot. A typical excursion will carry about 400 passengers. You can ride coach, first-class, or dome seating. First-class offers reclining seats and large windows. With dome seating, you get a spacious ride with a panoramic view. The museum displays a representative selection of cars.

WHEN TO GO: The museum is open on Tuesdays, Thursdays, and Saturdays year-round. Excursions run at various times during the year. The majority of the longer, 180-mile round-trip excursions to Cookeville take place in the fall when the foliage is most brilliant.

GOOD TO KNOW: The museum is housed in the former Tennessee Central Railway's master mechanic's office, and it includes a large collection of Tennessee Central Railway artifacts.

WORTH DOING: If available, try riding on the Seaboard Air Line Railway sun-lounge car. With its curved oversize windows, the *Hollywood Beach* is a unique car that occasionally is seen in an excursion train consist. Be sure and photograph the museum's E and F units, which are 1950s streamliners.

DON'T MISS: There is much to see and do in Nashville. You can tour numerous mansions and historic buildings including the Hermitage, the home of Andrew Jackson, and Ryman Auditorium, the former home of the Grand Ole Opry. Make sure to sample some of the city's famous music and barbecue.

GETTING THERE: The museum is located near downtown Nashville on Willow Street one block north of Hermitage Avenue.

Train ride

Southern Appalachia Railway Museum

ADDRESS: Hwy. 58, Oak Ridge, TN 37831
TELEPHONE: 865-241-2140
WEB SITE: www.techscribes.com/sarm

For many years during World War II, the government did not acknowledge the existence of the huge nuclear research lab at Oak Ridge or the railroad that served it. Now that the lab is closed, the railroad to "Secret City" is now a tourist attraction, giving visitors some insight into this unusual bit of railroading as well as a nice ride through the east Tennessee hills.

CHOICES: Pulled by 1950s Alco diesels, the 14-mile, 60-minute round trip takes you through the former secret atomic facility. Once outside the Secret City, the train enters the countryside, where it crosses Poplar Creek and passes Watts Bar Lake before returning. Several two-hour dinner trains, as well as intrigue-filled mystery trains, are scheduled during the year.

WHEN TO GO: Excursions run several Saturdays a month from April to September. Special runs occur in February, November, and December, and fall foliage runs happen in October.

GOOD TO KNOW: Non-U.S. citizens must show a passport and visa before riding the train. When the train leaves, it passes through an enclosure used to check rail cars for hobos, and still provides a way to screen the train from unwanted spies.

WORTH DOING: Arrive 30 minutes early and you may be able to get a caboose seat of a coach seat.

DON'T MISS: To learn more about the secrets of atomic power, you can visit the American Museum of Science & Energy in Oak Ridge and take a self-guided auto tour of some Manhattan Project sites in the area.

GETTING THERE: Oak Ridge is about 30 miles west of Knoxville, and the Heritage Center is situated between Oak Ridge and I-40 on Hwy. 58. To get there from Knoxville, take I-40 west to Exit 356. Turn right and travel north on Hwy. 58 approximately five miles to the Heritage Center. Turn left into the main entrance and take the first left inside the plant.

TEXAS

Trolley ride

Dallas
McKinney Avenue Trolley

McKinney Avenue Trolley operates a fleet of vintage streetcars, built between 1909 and 1945. You can hop on and off a trolley and explore the city's Uptown area. Trolley rides are free, so you can hop all you want. They run daily, every 25 minutes on weekends and every 15 minutes on weekdays.

ADDRESS: 3153 Oak Grove Ave., Dallas, TX 75204
TELEPHONE: 214-855-0006
WEB SITE: www.mata.org

Museum

Diboll
History Center

The History Center features indoor and outdoor interpretive exhibits. Permanent displays include a 1920 Baldwin 4-6-0 from Texas Southeastern Railroad, a log car, a caboose, and two motorcars. Its research center is open to the public.

ADDRESS: 102 N. Temple Dr., Diboll, TX 75941
TELEPHONE: 936-829-3543
E-MAIL: info@thehistorycenteronline.com
WEB SITE: www.thehistorycenteronline.com

Museum

El Paso
Railroad and Transportation Museum of El Paso

A restored 4-4-0 1857 locomotive and other railroad exhibits are on display in the Transit Terminal of Union Plaza. A featured exhibit covers urban transit from the mule car through streamlined art deco streetcars. It is open daily.

ADDRESS: 400 W. San Antonio Ave., El Paso, TX 79901
TELEPHONE: 915-422-3420
WEB SITE: www.elpasorails.org

Galveston *Museum*
Galveston Railroad Museum

This impressive collection features three steam locomotives, including a Houston and Texas Central 4-6-0, and three operational diesel engines. There are more than 30 pieces of rolling stock including freight cars, passenger cars, and cabooses. It is open daily March through December.

ADDRESS: 25th St. at the Strand, Galveston, TX 77550
TELEPHONE: 409-765-5700
E-MAIL: galvrrmuseum@sbcglobal.net
WEB SITE: www.galvestonrrmuseum.com

Houston *Museum*
Houston Railroad Museum

The museum features a unique collection of locomotives, freight cars, and passenger cars with a Texas flavor. At the museum, you can tour a *Texas Special* coach and *Texas Eagle* sleeping car, view artifacts, and even blow a diesel's whistle. It is open on Saturdays April to November.

ADDRESS: 7390 Mesa Rd., Houston, TX 77028
TELEPHONE: 713-631-6612
E-MAIL: info@houstonrrmuseum.org
WEB SITE: www.houstonrrmuseum.org

Marshall *Museum*
Texas & Pacific Railway Museum

The museum is housed in a restored Texas & Pacific depot that was built in 1912. It contains artifacts and photos dating from the 1870s and a replica of an agent's office. For a panoramic view of the area, go to the depot's upper level and look out from the balcony. The Texas & Pacific Railway Museum is open Tuesdays through Saturdays. A UP caboose is also on the grounds.

ADDRESS: 800 N. Washington Ave., Marshall, TX 75670
TELEPHONE: 800-513-9495 or 903-938-9495
E-MAIL: tandprymuseum@marshalldepot.org
WEB SITE: www.marshalldepot.org

Cedar Park   *Train ride*

Austin Steam Train

ADDRESS: Discovery Blvd., Cedar Park, TX 78613
TELEPHONE: 512-477-8468
E-MAIL: info@austinsteamtrain.org
WEB SITE: www.austinsteamtrain.org

This tourist line was formed in 1989 to provide weekend service over a portion of a 167-mile route purchased from Southern Pacific. The train operates out of Cedar Park or Austin and rolls through the Texas hills and history.

CHOICES: The railroad's operating hub is in Cedar Park, 19 miles from downtown Austin. Austin passengers can board at either Brush Square or Plaza Saltillo. Currently there are four types of rides. From September to May, the *Hill Country Flyer* makes a 70-mile round trip between Cedar Park and Burnet, while summer visitors enjoy a 46-mile round trip on the *Bertram Flyer*. In August 2006, the *River City Flyer* was inaugurated to provide a round trip from Austin to the farming village of Littig, 18 miles east of the city. Rolling stock consists of six vintage Pennsy P-70 coaches plus an AT&SF high-cupola caboose, along with three first-class parlor cars of AT&SF, NKP, and MP heritage.

WHEN TO GO: Many visitors choose to ride during the spring and fall or enjoy special runs such as the *Polar Express*. The annual visit of Thomas the Tank Engine is held each fall in downtown Austin.

GOOD TO KNOW: Both Cedar Park and Burnet have numerous lodging and dining facilities for visitors, while Austin is famous for its museums, entertainment, and scenic drives. Initial power was provided by SP Mikado no. 786 (Brooks 1916), which operated regularly until cracks developed in its cylinder saddle. This required a complete overhaul that should be completed in 2008. To replace the steamer, The Austin Steam Train Association rebuilt an ex-Santa Fe Alco RSD-15 now adorned in a modern version of SP's famous Black Widow paint scheme.

WORTH DOING: *Twilight Flyers,* featuring nighttime entertainment, run periodically. Some incorporate storytellers for children while others feature adult-oriented murder mysteries.

DON'T MISS: Each June, the railroad hosts a day-long railfair at its Burnet terminal. This event, featuring 24-mile round trips to Bertram, also incorporates large numbers of hobby and book vendors, plus numerous outdoor activities for families.

GETTING THERE: Cedar Park can be reached from the north by leaving I-35 at Round Rock and using Hwy. 45 westward, while visitors arriving from the south will travel northward though Austin on I-35 and connect directly with Hwy. 183.

Dallas   *Museum*

Age of Steam Railroad Museum

ADDRESS: 1105 Washington St., Dallas, TX 75315
TELEPHONE: 214-428-0101
E-MAIL: info@dallasrailwaymuseum.com
WEB SITE: www.dallasrailwaymuseum.com

TEXAS

Founded in 1963, the museum's collection features 33 pieces of vintage equipment. It is located in downtown Dallas at Fair Park, home of the annual Texas State Fair. Despite its name, the museum contains an eclectic mixture of all types of locomotives from both the United States and Canada. Age of Steam also features one of the nation's largest collections of pre-World War II heavyweight passenger equipment (11 cars) plus six lightweight passenger cars, two freight cars, and three cabooses.

CHOICES: At few other locations can you find two of UP's largest locomotives, a Big Boy and a Centennial DD40AX, along with a Pennsy GG-1. Other engines range in size from a Frisco 4-8-4 down to a diminutive 0-6-0 from the Dallas Union Terminal, the museum's initial acquisition in 1962. The display also includes two historic structures from Dallas' rail history, the city's first depot (Houston & Texas Central, 1903) and a Santa Fe interlocker (Tower 19), along with a 1941 Ford truck used by the Railway Express Agency.

WHEN TO GO: The museum is open Wednesday through Sunday throughout the year and closed on all national holidays. A special August event is a Whistle Fair using the Museum's steam calliope and its many steam engine whistles. During the two-week State Fair, held in mid-October, the museum is open daily, but with the event's vast crowds, access to the rail site is more difficult.

GOOD TO KNOW: The Age of Steam collection rests on a half-dozen parallel tracks that, while offering close inspection (inside and outside), nevertheless may preclude a three-quarters or side perspective of certain pieces of equipment.

WORTH DOING: Rail enthusiasts may also wish to visit nearby Dallas Union Terminal, which is served by Amtrak, Dallas Area Rapid Transit, and Trinity River Express (commuter rail to Fort Worth). Vintage streetcars also ply the nearby McKinney Avenue Trolley lines.

DON'T MISS: Dallas' Fair Park is home to other museums and performance venues including the African American Museum, Museum of Nature and Science, Dallas Aquarium, Cotton Bowl, and Music Hall. Its 225-acre site is a registered National Historic Landmark and includes a large collection of Art Deco buildings.

GETTING THERE: Downtown Dallas is easily accessible by 10 major highways (including I-30, I-35, and I-45) plus two airports.

New Braunfels   *Museum*

New Braunfels Railroad Museum

Housed in the restored 1907 International & Great Northern depot, the museum displays a 0-6-0 Porter oil-fired steam locomotive, a Missouri Pacific caboose, and numerous railroad artifacts. It is open Thursday through Monday.

ADDRESS: 302 W. San Antonio St., New Braunfels, TX 78131
TELEPHONE: 830-627-2447
E-MAIL: info@nbhrmsmuseum.org
WEB SITE: www.nbhrmsmuseum.org

Rosenberg   *Museum*

Rosenberg Railroad Museum

The museum features Tower 17, the last manned interlocking tower in Texas, which was moved to the site. When it is fully restored, you will be able to work the interlocking machine. Other exhibits include signaling, station agent, and telegraph artifacts. Tours are also available of an 1879 business car that is being restored.

ADDRESS: 1921 Avenue F, Rosenberg, TX 77471
TELEPHONE: 281-633-2846
E-MAIL: rrm@texas.net
WEB SITE: www.rosenbergrrmuseum.org

San Angelo   *Museum, Depot*

Railway Museum of San Angelo

Located in the historic Kansas City, Mexico and Orient depot, which was completed in 1910, the museum highlights local railroad history. Static displays include two diesel locomotives, a boxcar, and a caboose. It is open on Saturdays.

ADDRESS: 703 S. Chadbourne, San Angelo, TX 76903
TELEPHONE: 325-486-2140
WEB SITE: www.railwaymuseumsanangelo.homestead.com

San Antonio   *Museum*
Texas Transportation Museum

The museum displays a variety of railroad structures and equipment. It features an SP depot built in 1913 that was moved from Converse. The two-room building contains memorabilia from the SP and two other railroads that served San Antonio. The museum also operates a short train ride. On display are two steam locomotives, two diesel engines, and a variety of rolling stock.

ADDRESS: 11731 Wetmore Rd., San Antonio, TX 78247
TELEPHONE: 210-490-3554
WEB SITE: www.txtransportationmuseum.org

Temple   *Museum, Depot*
Railroad & Heritage Museum

Housed in a 1910 Gulf, Colorado & Santa Fe depot, the museum features early Santa Fe and Missouri-Kansas-Texas station equipment, including a working telegraph. Outdoor exhibits feature a variety of cars, a steam locomotive, and a diesel engine. The museum is open Tuesday though Sunday.

ADDRESS: 315 W. Avenue B, Temple, TX 76501
TELEPHONE: 254-298-5172
E-MAIL: museum@rrhm.org
WEB SITE: www.rrhm.org
DISCOUNT: Take $1 off each admission for up to four admissions.

Wichita Falls   *Museum*
Wichita Falls Railroad Museum

The museum's collection includes a Fort Worth & Denver steam locomotive, a Missouri-Kansas-Texas switch engine, a 1913 Pullman all-steel sleeper, troop sleepers, cabooses, and other cars. Artifacts center on the railroads that served Wichita Falls, especially the Missouri-Kansas-Texas Railway. The museum is open year-round Tuesday though Sunday.

ADDRESS: 500 Ninth St., Wichita Falls, TX 76308
TELEPHONE: 940-723-2661
E-MAIL: wfrrm@hotmail.com
WEB SITE: www.wfrrm.com

Grapevine Vintage Railroad

ADDRESS: 709 S. Main St., Grapevine, TX 76051
TELEPHONE: 817-410-3123
E-MAIL: twayne@ci.grapevine.tx.us
WEB SITE: www.gvrr.com

With its home base at the restored 1888 Cotton Belt depot in downtown Grapevine, the GV Railroad operates over 21 miles of ex-Cotton Belt trackage into the famous Fort Worth Stockyards Mall. It also includes a six-mile branch line (ex-Frisco) running southward from the mall across the Trinity River into the western part of the city. Grapevine operates the only 19th century steam locomotive in Texas, an 1896 Cooke 4-6-0 used for decades by Southern Pacific in fire service on Donner Pass.

CHOICES: For maximum mileage, passengers can board at Grapevine, travel to the stockyards, and then ride the Trinity River turn that passes through Trinity Park and the Fort Worth Zoo. It connects with the return train to Grapevine. The two-hour layover allows ample time to explore the mall's many offerings. Trains carry four 1925-era day coaches (19th century décor) plus a pair of open-air excursion coaches.

WHEN TO GO: Four-day operation (Thursday through Sunday) is offered between April and Labor Day. Frequency is reduced to three days (Friday to Sunday) during February and March and September through December, while no service is offered during January. Steam power is generally used only for weekend operations.

GOOD TO KNOW: Grapevine features numerous lodging and dining opportunities as well as proximity to the Ballpark at Arlington (Texas Rangers) and Six Flags Over Texas. The stockyards complex includes the Texas Cowboy Hall of Fame and weekend rodeo shows. Just north of the city is Grapevine Lake, a mecca for water sports.

WORTH DOING: The line offers numerous trips that feature entertainment, including mock gunfights and train robberies, visits to historical frontier forts, and children's activities such as Easter Bunny runs, Thomas the Tank Engine, and North Pole trains with a storytelling Santa.

DON'T MISS: True to its name, Grapevine is home to numerous wineries with regular tours and a special Grapefest celebration in September.

GETTING THERE: The city of Grapevine is adjacent to the northwest corner of the DFW Airport, midway between the two hubs of the Metroplex. Three major highways (114, 121, and 360) intersect at Grapevine, with I-30 being only a few miles south of the airport.

Train ride

Texas State Railroad

ADDRESS: Park Rd. 76, Rusk, TX 75785
TELEPHONE: 800-442-8951 or 903-683-2561
WEB SITE: www.texasstaterailroad.com

Built in 1896 and operating as a state park since 1976, the Texas Sate Railroad offers a relaxing enjoyable ride through the piney woods region of east Texas between the small towns of Rusk and Palestine. Various steam and diesel locomotives with local history pull the trains through tall stands of timber in the I. D. Fairchild State Forest, giving riders a glimpse into the railroad's origin of hauling agricultural and timber products in the early 20th century.

CHOICES: The Texas State Railroad offers visitors several options for trips on the 25-mile ride. Riders can purchase tickets to ride in either open-air cars or in air-conditioned coaches (recommended during the summer months). Round trips and one-way jaunts are available from Rusk or Palestine, and kids ride free between June and September. Murder mystery dinner trains are also scheduled, and occasional photo freights are run. Each of the Victorian-styled stations have historical exhibits.

WHEN TO GO: Trains currently operate Thursday through Sunday during June and July and on weekends between August and December. Autumn and winter are generally mild and open-air seating is very enjoyable; however, east Texas weather changes rapidly, so have a jacket or coat handy.

GOOD TO KNOW: Of the two towns, Palestine is larger and offers more accommodations and services. Rusk is headquarters for the railroad and offers several small hotels and B&Bs. Additional lodging and amenities are located in nearby Jacksonville. Camping and picnic sites are available adjacent to each depot. Food service is offered in both depots on the days of operation.

WORTH DOING: Before the day's excursion, take a cab tour and meet the engineer and fireman. On selected weekends of each month, steam engine shop tours are available in Rusk as well as tours of Texas & Pacific 2-10-4 no. 610 housed in the shop at Palestine.

DON'T MISS: Several times a year, various historical western and military reenactments are presented by the railroad.

GETTING THERE: Major airlines to Dallas or Houston provide the closest air transportation. From there, a leisurely three-and-a-half hour drive is required to reach the east Texas towns.

UTAH

Helper   *Museum*

Western Mining and Railroad Museum

Museum exhibits feature the Denver & Rio Grand Western and Utah railways. Located in the old Helper Hotel, which was completed in 1914, the museum contains four floors of artifacts. The third floor contains a railroad office and two rooms of railroading artifacts. A 100-year-old caboose is also on display. Other exhibits focus on mining and workers and include a simulated coal mine. It is open year-round.

ADDRESS: 296 S. Main St., Helper, UT 84526
TELEPHONE: (435) 472-3009
E-MAIL: helpermuseum@helpercity.net
WEB SITE: www.wmrrm.org

Ogden   *Museum, Depot*

Ogden Union Station

Built in 1924, Ogden Union Station now houses a variety of museums and galleries, including the Utah State Railroad Museum and Eccles Rail Center. The museum contains artifacts of Utah railroading and the rail center displays a UP Northern 4-8-4 locomotive and other historic pieces of equipment. Other museums in the station focus on history, firearms, gems, classic cars and the arts.

ADDRESS: 2501 Wall Ave., Ogden, UT 84401
TELEPHONE: 801-393-9886
WEB SITE: www.theunionstation.org

Heber Valley Historic Railroad

ADDRESS: 450 S. 600 W, Heber , UT 84032
TELEPHONE: 435-654-5601
WEB SITE: www.hebervalleyrr.org

This railroad offers a scenic ride beside Deer Creek Reservoir and then down Provo Canyon in unspoiled country with the Wasatch Mountains as a backdrop over a line that began operating in 1899.

CHOICES: Heber Valley offers two regular excursions in the shadow of 12,000-foot Mount Timpanogos. The vintage-coach trains are pulled by a 1907 Baldwin steam locomotive or a diesel locomotive. The *Provo Canyon Limited* is a three-hour round trip that runs to Vivian Park and back. Along the way, you'll hear about the history of train and the area. The 90-minute *Soldier Hollow Express* goes to Deer Creek Reservoir and returns. Summer excursion packages combine river rafting or bike riding with a train ride. In winter, you can train to a 1,000-foot hill and tube down. Numerous special events take place throughout the year including comedic murder mysteries, moonlight runs, and western-themed rides.

WHEN TO GO: The railroad operates year-round. Each of the seasons has something special to offer, but summer is especially beautiful in Utah. And winter steam excursions provide excellent opportunities for exceptional steam photography.

GOOD TO KNOW: The railroad helped to move passengers and athletes to and from venues during the 2002 Olympics. For film fans, locomotive no. 75 and various cars have appeared in more than 30 movies including *A River Runs Through It*.

WORTH DOING: If you can, ride the caboose. It's the first steel caboose that belonged to the Union Pacific. The railroad also offers cab rides for a fee.

DON'T MISS: Take a scenic drive along the Provo Canyon Scenic Byway (Hwy. 189) that runs between Heber Valley and Provo. A short side trip on the Alpine Scenic Loop (Hwy. 92) takes you past Robert Redford's Sundance Resort.

GETTING THERE: The railroad is located between Salt Lake City and Provo. From Salt Lake City, take I-80 east to Exit 148 and then follow Hwy. 40 into Heber. Turn right on W. 300 S and then left on S. 600 W to the station.

DISCOUNT: Take $5 off an adult ticket, up to four adults, for the *Provo Canyon Limited*.

Promontory   *Museum*

Golden Spike National Historic Site

ADDRESS: Golden Spike Dr., Promontory, UT
TELEPHONE: 435-471-2209
WEB SITE: www.nps.gov/gosp

The construction of the transcontinental railroad is one of the pivotal events in the nation's history. Completed May 10, 1869, at this remote spot northwest of Ogden, the National Park Service does justice to the event by running replica locomotives and conducting reenactments.

CHOICES: Reenactments of the Last Spike Ceremony, complete with dignitaries in period dress, take place on Saturdays and holidays during the summer season. The two steam locomotive replicas, the coal-burning Union Pacific 119 and the wood-burning Central Pacific *Jupiter*, are accurate reproductions and fully functional. The visitor center offers informative films and exhibits.

WHEN TO GO: Except for Thanksgiving, Christmas, and New Year's Day, the visitor center is open daily. Between May and Labor Day, the steam locomotives are on display and operate demonstrations daily. During winter, when the locomotives are being maintained, rangers conduct engine house tours on Saturdays and Sundays.

GOOD TO KNOW: The correct name for the location of Golden Spike National Historic Site is Promontory Summit, not Promontory Point, which is 35 miles to the south. The summit is the highest point of Promontory Pass. For some reason, the wrong location was reported in some records in 1869 and perpetuated throughout history.

WORTH DOING: To the west, a dirt road leads to one of the original grades. Take your vehicle and put it on the grade pointed east. It's a one-lane, one-way road that goes back to the visitor center. Driving at 20 mph, you'll get a good sense of what it was like to ride an early 4-4-0 steam engine down these very tracks. At one point, you'll pass a spot where 14 miles of track were laid in one day during 1869, a record that has never been broken.

DON'T MISS: Drive through Brigham City and view the interesting Box Elder Tabernacle and stop at the restored early 20th century train depot.

GETTING THERE: Golden Spike National Historic Site is in northern Utah, 32 miles west of Brigham City. From Brigham City, take Hwy. 83 to the entrance, which is Golden Spike Drive. The area is still very rugged and sparsely populated. Food and fuel are available in Brigham City.

VERMONT

Bellows Falls
Green Mountain Railroad
Train ride

The railroad offers three distinct scenic excursions. Leaving Bellows Falls, the *Green Mountain Flyer* crosses two covered bridges on its way to Chester Depot. The *White River Valley Flyer* travels from White River Junction along the Connecticut River to Norwich and the Montshire Museum of Science. On the *Champlain Valley Flyer*, you'll see the state's two highest mountains and Lake Champlain.

ADDRESS: 54 Depot St., Bellows Falls, VT 05101
TELEPHONE: 800-707-3530 or 802-463-3069
E-MAIL: railtour@vermontrailway.com
WEB SITE: www.rails-vt.com
DISCOUNT: Receive 10 percent off any gift shop purchase.

Shelburne
Shelburne Museum
Museum

Outside the museum, you'll see the 1890 Shelburne passenger station, locomotive no. 220, which pulled the trains of four presidents, and an 1890 private luxury car. Other historic buildings, a steamship, and fine and folk art are also on display.

ADDRESS: Hwy. 7, Shelburne, VT 05482
TELEPHONE: 802-985-3346
E-MAIL: info@shelburnemuseum.org
WEB SITE: www.shelburnemuseum.org

White River Junction
New England Institute and Transportation Museum
Museum

The centerpiece of the museum's railroad exhibit is the renovated Boston & Maine no. 494. The museum also celebrates the railroad with annual Glory Days of the Railroad festival. Other exhibits are dedicated to aviation and river commerce.

ADDRESS: 100 Railroad Row, White River Junction, VT 05001
TELEPHONE: 802-291-9838
E-MAIL: info@newenglandtransportationmuseum.org
WEB SITE: www.newenglandtransportationmuseum.org

VIRGINIA

Eastern Shore Railway Museum

The museum is housed in a restored 1906 Pennsylvania Railroad passenger station. On the siding are two cabooses, a baggage car, a Pullman sleeper, a Budd dining car, and a touring car. The museum also includes an 1890s maintenance-of-way tool shed, a crossing guard shanty, and various railroad artifacts. It is open year-round.

ADDRESS: 18468 Dunne Ave., Parksley, VA 23421
TELEPHONE: 757-665-7245
WEB SITE: www.chincoteaguechamber.com/i-rail.html

Old Dominion Railway Museum

The Old Dominion Railway Museum tells the story of Virginia's railroading heritage through artifacts, videos, displays, and an HO layout. Located near the birthplace of Virginia railroad operations, it is open Saturdays and Sundays year-round.

ADDRESS: 102 Hull St., Richmond, VA 23224
TELEPHONE: 804-233-6237
WEB SITE: www.odcnrhs.org/docs/museum.asp

Suffolk Seaboard Station Railroad Museum

The restored 1885 Seaboard Airline passenger station features permanent and seasonal displays of railroad memorabilia and a caboose built for the Nickel Plate Line. It is open Wednesday through Sunday.

ADDRESS: 326 N. Main St., Suffolk, VA 23434
TELEPHONE: 757-923-4750
E-MAIL: info@suffolktrainstation.org
WEB SITE: www.suffolktrainstation.org

O. Winston Link Museum

ADDRESS: 101 Shenandoah Ave. NE, Roanoke, VA 24016
TELEPHONE: 540-982-5465
E-MAIL: programs@linkmuseum.org
WEB SITE: www.linkmuseum.org

Only two photographers in the United States have their own museums. One belongs to noted landscape photographer Ansel Adams. The other is O. Winston Link. A commercial photographer, Link was fascinated with steam locomotives and made a pilgrimage to record the last of these on the Norfolk & Western in the late 1950s.

CHOICES: The museum is housed in the former Norfolk & Western passenger station in downtown Roanoke. The station was the departure point for many of the trains Link photographed, making it an excellent departure point for a world of Link's photography. More than 300 of Link's photographs are on display. The museum includes interactive exhibits, Link's photography equipment, and his railroad sound recordings. Be sure to watch the documentary film on Link's life. It's an excellent look at the man and his work through his voice and those of many others.

WHEN TO GO: The museum is open daily except for Easter, Thanksgiving, Christmas, and New Years Day. Fall and spring in the Blue Ridge Mountains are magnificent.

GOOD TO KNOW: Famous for his nighttime scenes that record the passing railroad as well as slices of rural life, Link made many photos of the region in the late '50s and early '60s. For years, Link's work languished, but in the 1980s, his career rebounded as the art world discovered his genius of recording steam at night in (mostly) black and white.

WORTH DOING: The former station is a Virginia Historic Landmark and is listed on the National Register of Historic Places. It is one of several renovated railroad buildings in the area including the Virginia Museum of Transportation, which is a short walk away. The two museums offer a combined admission.

DON'T MISS: The Hotel Roanoke, directly behind the museum, is a former railroad hotel and a great place to spend the night. It offers packages that include the Link museum. Spend some time on the front lawn and watch the coal trains lumber by as they have for more than 120 years.

GETTING THERE: Roanoke is about 190 miles west of Richmond and near West Virginia and North Carolina. To reach the museum from I-81, take I-581 south and exit at Williamson Road and turn right on Shenandoah Avenue.

Virginia Museum of Transportation

ADDRESS: 303 Norfolk Ave. SW, Roanoke, VA 24016
TELEPHONE: 540-342-5670
E-MAIL: info@vmt.org
WEB SITE: www.vmt.org

Roanoke was once synonymous with the best steam locomotives in the land. The Norfolk & Western built many of them right here, just a few blocks away. While the museum's scope covers the broad subject of transportation, its heart is in railroading.

CHOICES: The museum is housed in a historic rail setting, the city's old N&W freight station. Through exhibits and rolling stock displays, you'll learn a lot about how people got around in the Old Dominion State. It displays steam and diesel locomotives, antique automobiles, trucks, and even a post office bus. The museum also includes several ongoing exhibits dedicated to railroading and a model railroad.

WHEN TO GO: The museum is open daily, except for various holidays, throughout the year.

GOOD TO KNOW: The museum also contains a research library that includes books, photographs, periodicals, blueprints, maps, and timetables.

WORTH DOING: Climb into the crew cab of the streamlined Norfolk & Western 4-8-4 Class J. Built in 1950, no. 611 is the last of its kind, one of 13 that pulled the railroad's named trains. Capable of sprinting faster than 100 mph, or climbing the mountains of West Virginia, these locomotives were considered to be among the best in the nation. You can stand in the cab and see the gauges, handles, and levers that made it all happen. Next door to no. 611 is no. 1218, a Class A. Built in 1943, this articulated locomotive features two sets of drivers and cylinders.

DON'T MISS: Stroll along the rail walk that connects the museum with the O. Winston Link Museum and Hotel Roanoke. The walk parallels the Norfolk Southern's mainline track.

GETTING THERE: Situated in the Blue Ridge Mountains, Roanoke is served by a regional airport and several major highways. The museum is located downtown on Norfolk Avenue between Second and Fifth Streets.

WASHINGTON

Museum

Pioneer Village and Museum

The village features 20 historical structures dating back to the late 1800s. Railroad displays include a caboose, a dining car, and a section house containing artifacts. The museum is open March through December.

ADDRESS: 600 Cotlets Way, Cashmere, WA 98815
TELEPHONE: 509-782-3230
WEB SITE: www.visitcashmere.com/pionvilandmu.html

Dayton *Museum, Depot*

Dayton Historical Depot

Built in 1881, this is the oldest surviving railroad station in Washington. The stylish Stick/Eastlake building is now a museum of local history. It includes artifacts from the Union Pacific and the Oregon Railroad and Navigation Company, and a UP caboose is also on display. It is open year-round.

ADDRESS: 222 E. Commercial St., Dayton, WA 99328
TELEPHONE: 509-382-2026
WEB SITE: dayton.bmi.net

Pasco *Museum*

Washington State Railroads Historical Society Museum

The museum features artifacts and photos of the railroads involved in the state. Outdoors, it displays a variety of locomotives, passenger cars, freight cars, and cabooses. It is open on Saturdays.

ADDRESS: 122 N. Tacoma Ave., Pasco, WA 99301
TELEPHONE: 800-465-5430 or 509-543-4159
E-MAIL: email@wsrhs.org
WEB SITE: www.wsrhs.org

Chehalis   *Train ride, Dinner train*
Chehalis-Centralia Railroad

ADDRESS: 1101 Sylvenus St., Chehalis, WA 98532
TELEPHONE: 360-748-9593
E-MAIL: info@steamtrainride.com
WEB SITE: www.steamtrainride.com

In the shadow of Mount Saint Helens, this relaxing train ride takes you into the forests of western Washington. You'll ride behind a steam locomotive that saw many years of service logging these very forests.

CHOICES: The railroad offers two different excursions. The 12-mile Milburn run takes you through forests and countryside. A longer 18-mile round trip to Ruth extends the ride by following the Chehalis River. The railroad's dinner train follows the Ruth route and serves a four-course meal in a refurbished 1920s dining car.

WHEN TO GO: Summer steam train rides begin Memorial Day weekend and operate Saturdays and Sundays through September. Dinner trains, murder mystery trains, and special events are scheduled throughout the year.

GOOD TO KNOW: Trains travel over trackage that was once part of the Milwaukee Road, and a restored Milwaukee Road depot serves as the boarding point.

WORTH DOING: On summer Saturdays, the railroad usually makes a 12-mile run to Milburn in the afternoon and then follows up with an 18-mile run to Ruth late in the afternoon. Here's a great opportunity to take pictures with Mount Saint Helens in the background of the early run and then ride the later trip.

DON'T MISS: Take time to visit Mount Saint Helens National Volcanic Monument and view the dramatic changes the area has undergone since the 1980 eruption. The 110,000-acre site contains hiking trails, several visitor centers, and an observatory.

GETTING THERE: The railroad is about a 90-minute drive from either Portland or Seattle. From I-5, take Exit 77 (Main Street) into Chehalis. Turn left on Riverside and then left again on Sylvenus. Nearby Centralia is also served by Amtrak.

Elbe   *Train ride*

Mount Rainier Scenic Railroad

ADDRESS: 54124 Mountain Highway E, Elbe, WA 98330
TELEPHONE: 888-783-2611 or 360-569-2351
WEB SITE: www.mrsr.com

Here's a chance to experience a real Pacific Northwest logging railroad at work. The locomotives, the setting, and the route all have the feel of a working railroad. You'll ride out over tall bridges on a 14-mile round trip to Mineral Lake.

CHOICES: A pure steam experience, a 2-8-2T logging engine usually pulls the passenger coaches through the foothills of Mount Rainier. For a longer day, you can ride an early train, have a picnic lunch in Mineral Lake, and take a later train back.

WHEN TO GO: The railroad operates weekends during June and September. In July and August, trains operate daily. October is filled with special events including autumn foliage trains, pumpkin runs, and ghost trains. The *Snowball Express* runs in November and December. The railroad has also begun to offer a winter photo outing with multiple locomotives, perfect for anyone who really likes trains.

GOOD TO KNOW: The railroad offers all three major types of geared logging locomotives as possible power: a Shay, a Climax, and a Heisler.

WORTH DOING: Ride one trip and photograph another one, especially if you can get Mount Rainier to peek out from behind the clouds.

DON'T MISS: Mount Rainier National Park provides scenic drives and hikes around the 14,410-foot active volcano. Most roads in the park are open from late May to early October.

GETTING THERE: Elbe is located in western Washington near Mount Rainier National Park, approximately 75 miles south of Seattle and 125 miles north of Portland. Elbe is on Hwy. 7, which is also known as the Mountain Highway. The train station is off the highway in Elbe.

Renton   *Dinner train*

Spirit of Washington Dinner Train

ADDRESS: 625 S. Fourth St., Renton, WA 98055
TELEPHONE: 800-876-7245 or 425-227-7245
E-MAIL: customerservice@swdtrain.com
WEB SITE: www.spiritofwashingtondinnertrain.com

Located in the Seattle metro area, this train combines magnificent scenery, excellent equipment, delicious food, and an unbeatable destination in one package. The *Spirit of Washington*, using streamlined locomotives from the 1950s and dome cars, rolls along the shores of Lake Washington and across the historic Wilburton Trestle.

CHOICES: The three-hour, 44-mile trip takes you along the eastern shore of Lake Washington, a 27-mile long freshwater lake, to Columbia Winery in Woodinville. Before returning, you have a 45-minute pause to sample the winery's offerings. For brunch, lunch, and dinner, you have a choice of parlor or dome seating in a variety of cars, including the one-of-a-kind *Columbia Winery*. Murder mystery and special events are also scheduled during the year.

WHEN TO GO: The *Spirit of Washington* operates year-round. In summer, June through September, there is daily service. During the rest of the year, the train runs Tuesday through Sunday. Weekends offer lunch as well as dinner departures.

GOOD TO KNOW: Built in 1891, the Wilburton Trestle in Bellevue is the longest wooden trestle in the Northwest. It is 975 feet long and 102 feet high.

WORTH DOING: If you reserve seats on the left side of a car, you get a sunset view of Lake Washington as you leave Renton.

DON'T MISS: Seattle has much to offer visitors. You can view Puget Sound by ferry, tour the underground below Pioneer Square, and of course, see the city from the top of the Space Needle.

GETTING THERE: The station is about 12 miles from Seattle and easily accessible from either I-5 or I-405. Take Exit 2 off I-405 and travel north on Rainier Avenue. Then turn right on Third Street and right again onto Burnett Avenue to the station.

Snoqualmie   *Museum, Train ride*

Northwest Railway Museum

ADDRESS: 38625 SE King St., Snoqualmie, WA 98065
TELEPHONE: 425-888-3030
E-MAIL: info@trainumseum.org
WEB SITE: www.trainmuseum.org

The museum is home to more than 70 pieces of rolling stock, the bulk of it from the Pacific Northwest. The museum also includes a collection of dining car china, tools, signs, and lanterns. It offers a short train ride from Snoqualmie or from North Bend.

CHOICES: The museum is headquartered at Snoqualmie depot, a restored 1890 Queen Anne-style building that is on the National Register of Historic Places. It features exhibits inside the depot and outdoor displays of restored equipment, including steam locomotives, passenger cars, freight cars, and maintenance equipment. It offers 10-mile round trips to Snoqualmie Falls in restored heavyweight coaches pulled by first-generation diesel locomotives.

WHEN TO GO: The museum is open daily year-round except for Thanksgiving, Christmas, and New Year's Day. It offers train rides on weekends April through October, with special events scheduled during the year. Railroad Days takes place the beginning of August.

GOOD TO KNOW: The museum has completed an 8,200-square-foot restoration and conservation center, the first step in the construction of an effort to put a cover over its rolling stock collection and to house its extensive library and archives.

WORTH DOING: Check out the nine steam locomotives in the collection, including the unusual Mallet engines used for logging – they're basically two locomotives under one boiler.

DON'T MISS: View Snoqualmie Falls, one of the state's most popular attractions. The waterfall cascades down 270 feet, which is 100 feet more than Niagara Falls. You can see the falls from a park with an observation platform.

GETTING THERE: The museum is 30 miles east of Seattle off I-90. From I-90 east, take Exit 27. Take North Bend Way to Meadowbrook Way. Turn left on Meadowbrook Way and then left again onto Railroad Avenue to King Street and the depot. To get to the North Bend depot, take Exit 31 off I-90. Follow Bendigo Street into North Bend and turn right on North Bend Way.

Toppenish *Museum*

Northern Pacific Railway Museum

The 1911 Northern Pacific railroad depot in Toppenish now serves as a museum to that railroad. The site's freight house has been converted to an engine house, where a 1902 locomotive is being restored. The museum offers several special events during the year. It is open Wednesday through Saturday May through October.

ADDRESS: 10 S. Asotin Ave., Toppenish, WA 98948
TELEPHONE: 509-865-1911
WEB SITE: www.nprymuseum.org

Wickersham *Train ride*

Lake Whatcom Railway

This 90-minute train ride takes you from the shores of Lake Whatcom into the wooded countryside and back. The vintage coaches and diesel were all used on the Northern Pacific. A 100-year-old steam engine and wooden Great Northern freight cars are also on site. For a good workout, you can try your hand at riding a hand car. Excursions run during summer and for special events.

ADDRESS: NP Rd., Wickersham, WA 98220
TELEPHONE: 360-595-2218
WEB SITE: www.lakewhatcomrailway.com

Yacolt *Train ride*

Chelatchie Prairie Railroad

Leaving from Yacolt, in rugged logging territory, round-trip excursions travel through a 330-foot tunnel, cross over a trestle bridging the Lewis River, and stop at Moulton Falls, where you can take in two waterfalls and a tall arched bridge. The railroad operates on weekends in summer as well as during special events.

ADDRESS: NE Railroad Ave., Yacolt, WA 98604
TELEPHONE: 360-686-3559
E-MAIL: admin@bycx.com
WEB SITE: www.bycx.com

WEST VIRGINIA

Museum, Train ride

Huntington Railroad Museum

This outdoor museum, located in Ritter Park, displays a Chesapeake & Ohio Mallet locomotive, a Porter 0-4-0, a C&O caboose made in Huntington, and other pieces of equipment. The museum is open Sundays during summer. Run by the Collis P. Huntington Railroad Historical Society, the group also operates *New River Train* excursions during October to view autumn foliage. The train travels over the former C&O main line from Huntington to Hinton through the New River Gorge for a scenic all-day trip.

ADDRESS: Memorial Blvd. and 14th St. W, Huntington, WV
TELEPHONE: 304-523-0364
E-MAIL: newrivertrain@aol.com
WEB SITE: www.newrivertrain.com

Cass   *Train ride*

Cass Scenic Railroad State Park

ADDRESS: Hwy. 66, Cass, WV 24927
TELEPHONE: 800-225-5982 or 304-456-4300
E-MAIL: cassrailroad@wvdnr.gov
WEB SITE: www.cassrailroad.com

The Cass Scenic Railroad is as close as you'll ever come to experiencing a mountain logging railroad – because it once was one. Leaving from the mill town of Cass along the beautiful Greenbriar River, trains climb steep grades out of the Leatherbark Creek area, negotiate two switchbacks, and hug hillsides to gain elevation. It was all about getting to the timber 100 years ago. Today, it's all about getting above it all. And Cass does that.

CHOICES: Got only a little time? Ride a 90-minute trip to Whitaker station and back for a taste. Got plenty of time? Sink your teeth into a half-day trip to Bald Knob and back. At an intermediate point, trains pause for servicing, and you can inspect a re-created railroad logging camp, complete with the big rigs that picked up tree trunks. Going further, trains powered by unusual geared steam locomotives work their way to Bald Knob, which, at 4,880 feet, is the second highest point in West Virginia. The view there is spectacular, and the trains climb an 11 percent grade. The railroad schedules special events during the season and runs a "fiddles and vittles" train with dinner and bluegrass music.

WHEN TO GO: The railroad runs Memorial Day through October, with heavy passenger counts during the colorful autumn.

GOOD TO KNOW: In spring, the railroad's support organization, the Mountain State Railroad and Logging Historical Association, holds a railfan weekend when all the Shay geared locomotives run; this and other association events cover tracks not normally used by Cass trains.

WORTH DOING: Stay in one of the restored mill workers' cabins. Most of the two-story cabins sleep eight, are fully furnished, and come with a fully equipped kitchen. Several motels are nearby, but the cabins add to the mill atmosphere.

DON'T MISS: Walk up to the shop where the unusual Shay and Heisler locomotives are maintained. It's a great opportunity to see the engines and meet the crews. Be sure to check out Western Maryland no. 6, the last Shay built, and at 162 tons, the largest one left.

GETTING THERE: Cass Scenic Railroad is located in eastern West Virginia, and I-64 is the closest major road. From there, narrow, winding two-lane roads are the rule, so take plenty of time and watch for deer. Hwy. 66 connects to Hwy. 219 at Slatyfork.

DISCOUNT: Take $1 off regular adult admission, good for up to four adults.

Durbin
Train ride

Durbin & Greenbrier Valley Railroad

ADDRESS: Main St., Durbin, WV 26264
TELEPHONE: 877-686-7245
E-MAIL: ticketinfo@mountainrail.com
WEB SITE: www.mountainrail.com

The Durbin & Greenbrier Valley Railroad operates three separate and distinct railways over 135 miles of scenic railroad through the Mountain State. The *Cheat Mountain Salamander* offers a ride on a replica Edwards rail car, the *Durbin Rocket* operates a 1910 Climax locomotive, and the *New Tygart Flyer* runs a diesel-powered train pulling coaches and first-class cars through the wilderness.

CHOICES: This railroad is all about choices. The *Salamander* provides two self-propelled rail car trips through the wilderness. The northern trip takes you down the Shavers Fork River Valley, through the Monongahela National Forest, and around two sharp curves. The other trip goes upriver and into a mountain forest. The *Rocket* is a peaceful ride behind a Climax geared steam locomotive, believed to be one of only three in operation in the United States, along the unspoiled Greenbriar River. The *Flyer* provides a dramatic trip across a mountain pass to the High Falls of the Cheat, an impressive waterfall that puts an exclamation point on the journey. It offers 46-, 78-, and 102-mile round trips.

WHEN TO GO: All three trains operate May through October.

GOOD TO KNOW: The *Flyer* has departures in both Belington and Elkins. The *Rocket* departs from the restored C&O Railway depot in Durbin, and the *Salamander* is located at Cheat Bridge.

WORTH DOING: You can spend the night at a remote spot aboard the *Durbin Rocket*'s Castaway Caboose, a restored Wabash caboose. The railroad's location is close to the Cass Scenic Railroad, so you can visit four great railroads in one impressive mountain setting.

DON'T MISS: The *Flyer*'s all-day, 102-mile tour of the line, offered select Saturdays out of Belington, shows you all of this wilderness railroad.

GETTING THERE: Hwy. 250 connects the railroad's locations. Durbin is 35 miles south of Elkins at the base of Cheat Mountain, and the *Rocket* leaves from the station on Main Street. Cheat Bridge is seven miles north of Durbin and 30 miles south of Elkins. The *Salamander*'s station is on Red Run Road. The *Flyer*'s station in Elkins is located at 12th Street and Davis Avenue. The Belington station is a half block west of Hwy. 250 in town.

DISCOUNT: Take $1 off each adult ticket.

Parkersburg *Train ride*

Potomac Eagle Scenic Railroad

ADDRESS: Hwy. 28 N, Parkersburg, WV 26104
TELEPHONE: 304-424-0736
WEB SITE: www.potomaceagle.info

Here's a three-hour train ride for the birdwatchers among us. After all, who doesn't enjoy the sight of a bald eagle floating on the currents. The Potomac Eagle goes in search of bald eagles down the remote South Branch of the Potomac just inside West Virginia.

CHOICES: All trains depart from the Wappocomo station, just north of Romney. The 40-mile excursion travels along the South Branch of the Potomac River and through the six-mile Trough, a narrow mountain valley, where eagles are often seen. You can ride coach, or better yet, ride in three first-class cars, where you get lunch as part of the package. Historic narration adds extra insight into the journey. Also, the railroad offers occasional 70-mile, all-day trips down the length of the railroad.

WHEN TO GO: Trains run mid-May through the beginning of November. Departures are on Saturdays with a few Sundays sprinkled in. Autumn makes an especially great time to visit this railroad and it offers trips almost daily during October. A special photo weekend in late October is perfect for train lovers.

GOOD TO KNOW: The railroad says eagles are spotted on 90 percent of its trains. General Motors locomotives provide power for the trains.

WORTH DOING: As it enters the most remote and steepest portion of the South Branch valley, the train pauses so you can find a seat in the open gondola for the best views.

DON'T MISS: Possibly the oldest town in West Virginia, and said to have changed hands 56 times during the Civil War, Romney includes historic homes and buildings.

GETTING THERE: Romney is in the northeast corner of the state. It is about 25 miles from Cumberland, Md. Hwy. 28 takes you to the station, which is 1.5 miles north of Romney.

DISCOUNT: Take $1 off each adult ticket for up to four adults.

WISCONSIN

Brodhead
Museum, Depot
Brodhead Historical Society Depot Museum

This restored Chicago, Milwaukee & St. Paul depot, built in 1881, houses a permanent railroad display with rotating historical displays. Milwaukee Road switch engine no. 781 and caboose no. 1900 stand alongside the depot. It is open Wednesdays, Saturdays, and Sundays during summer.

ADDRESS: 1108 First Center Ave., Brodhead, WI 53520
TELEPHONE: 608-897-8411

Colfax
Museum
Colfax Railroad Museum

The museum includes a large collection of railroad memorabilia and an outdoor display of locomotives and rolling stock that features a Soo Line GP30 diesel engine, several wooden Soo cabooses, and a Soo coach car as well as a Milwaukee Road Flanger and caboose.

ADDRESS: 500 Railroad Ave., Colfax, WI 54730
TELEPHONE: 715-962-2076
E-MAIL: colfaxrr@wwt.net

East Troy

East Troy Electric Railroad

ADDRESS: 2002 Church St., East Troy, WI 53120
TELEPHONE: 262-642-3263
WEB SITE: www.easttroyrr.org

Interurban railroads once plied much of the Midwest, moving passengers easily from farm to city and vice versa. Today, a sprig of that heritage remains at the East Troy Electric Railroad, where electric trains run through the countryside.

CHOICES: On a 10-mile round trip, the railroad offers a variety of cars to ride, depending on the day, from trolleys to electric freight motors pulling a caboose and to electrically powered traditional coaches from the famous South Shore Line. Trains depart from both East Troy and Mukwonago. The railroad also offers dinner trains that run to Phantom Lake and back. Look over the exhibits in the depot and then walk two blocks to the shops and look at the equipment being restored.

WHEN TO GO: Regular weekend excursions run mid-May through October. From mid-June through August, trains also operate on Wednesdays, Thursdays, and Fridays. There are many special events during the year, including Railroad Days and Fall Fun Days.

GOOD TO KNOW: Sheboygan car no. 26 is a 1908 interurban built by the Cincinnati Car Company for Sheboygan Light, Power and Railway. These cars ran in daily service for 30 years connecting the towns of Sheboygan, Kohler, Sheboygan Falls, Plymouth, Crystal Lake, and Elkhart Lake. No 26 later became a summer cottage until it was restored and now runs at East Troy.

WORTH DOING: Be sure to explore the substation in East Troy, which is the heart of the operating gear for the electric railroad.

DON'T MISS: Regular excursions operate from East Troy to the Elegant Farmer near Mukwonago. What's an Elegant Farmer? It makes a great destination as the Farmer provides a deli, green house, and market all in one. Be sure and try the baked apple pie in a bag.

GETTING THERE: East Troy is located in southeastern Wisconsin, about 35 miles from Milwaukee and 15 miles from Lake Geneva. From Milwaukee, take I-43 south to Exit 38. Take Hwy. 20 to Main Street. Follow Main Street to Church Street and turn right to museum.

Green Bay

Museum, Train ride

National Railroad Museum

ADDRESS: 2285 S. Broadway St., Green Bay, WI 54304
TELEPHONE: 920-437-7623
E-MAIL: staff@nationalrrmuseum.org
WEB SITE: www.natonalrrmuseum.org

Begun in 1956 by a group wishing to preserve a steam locomotive, the museum has grown to encompass more than 70 pieces of rolling stock, a seasonal train ride, and an unmatched collection of drumheads, the illuminated signs seen on the rear of many passenger trains.

CHOICES: You can explore the museum on your own, or between Memorial Day and Labor Day, 45-minute guided tours are available twice a day. During the 25-minute train ride, the conductor provides information about railroad history and museum exhibits. Highlights include a Union Pacific Big Boy, a 1950s Aerotrain, and a Pennsylvania Railroad GG1 electric locomotive. The command train for General Dwight D. Eisenhower is also located at the museum in the company of a British Railways Pacific type locomotive named for the World War II general.

WHEN TO GO: The museum is open daily year-round, except for several holidays. Train rides operate May through September, and numerous special events are scheduled during the year.

GOOD TO KNOW: The museum contains 40 drumheads from a variety of famous trains including the *20th Century Limited*, *Super Chief*, and *Empire Builder*.

WORTH DOING: Climb to the top of the 85-foot-tall observation tower for a bird's-eye view of the museum.

DON'T MISS: Take the kids to Bay Beach Amusement Park for some old-fashioned fun on classic midway rides. Football fans can visit the Green Bay Packers Hall of Fame and tour historic Lambeau Field.

GETTING THERE: Green Bay is two hours north of Milwaukee. From Milwaukee, take I-43 to Exit 180. Take Hwy. 172 west and exit at Ashland Avenue. Bear right on Pilgrim Way and then turn left on Broadway.

WISCONSIN

Laona

Train ride, Museum

Camp Five

ADDRESS: 5480 Connor Farm Rd., Laona, WI 54541
TELEPHONE: 800-774-3414 or 715-674-3414
E-MAIL: info@lumberjacksteamtrain.com
WEB SITE: www.camp5museum.org

Camp Five offers a steam train powered by a vintage 2-6-2 type logging locomotive to the site of a 1914 farm camp for a timber firm, where you can tour a logging museum.

CHOICES: After boarding at an 1880s Soo Line depot, you ride the steam train 2.5 miles to the museum. You can sit in a passenger coach or ride in one of the cupola cabooses.

WHEN TO GO: Camp Five has a short season. It is open Monday through Saturday mid-June through mid-August. It is also open several days in fall.

GOOD TO KNOW: The railroad crosses the Rat River on a bridge. Lumber men who worked this river, floating giant rafts of logs together, became known as river rats. At the farm camp, the lumber company raised meat, produce, and horses to supply other camps as they set up in the forest.

WORTH DOING: At Laona, climb the set of steps to inspect the cab of the engine.

DON'T MISS: There is plenty to do at Camp Five. You can explore historical exhibits about forestry, examine logging equipment, and ride a pontoon boat down the river.

GETTING THERE: Camp Five is off Hwy. 8 west of Laona, about two hours north of Green Bay. From Green Bay, take Hwy. 141 north to Hwy. 64. Follow Hwy. 64 west to Hwy. 32. Continue on Hwy. 32 and turn left on Hwy 8 past Laona to Connor Farm Road.

DISCOUNT: Receive $2 off each adult ticket.

North Freedom   *Museum, Train ride*

Mid-Continent Railway Museum

ADDRESS: E8948 Diamond Hill Rd., North Freedom, WI 53951
TELEPHONE: 800-930-1385 or 608-522-4261
E-MAIL: inquiries@midcontinent.org
WEB SITE: www.midcontinent.org

One of the best museums for the preservation of wooden railroad cars, Mid-Continent features a large collection of rolling stock, much of it kept indoors, and numerous exhibits. The museum also offers a train ride. It's all aimed at re-creating the experience of a branch or short line between 1885 and 1915.

CHOICES: Leaving from a restored 1894 C&NW depot, the seven-mile, 50-minute ride takes you through the rolling countryside. You can ride the coaches, but you can also get a ticket for the locomotive cab or the caboose.

WHEN TO GO: The railway operates daily mid-May through the beginning of September. It is also open a few weekends prior to and after those dates and for special events such as the annual snow train in February.

GOOD TO KNOW: On display are more than 100 other pieces of equipment including an office car of Great Northern Railway founder James J. Hill's son that included space for hauling an automobile. Structures include a water tower, a crossing shanty, a section shed, a crossing tower, and a freight house.

WORTH DOING: Make sure you go into the coach shed to see some of the finest wood craftsmanship around when it comes to railroad cars and also check out the engine house, where craftsmen are restoring a steam locomotive for operation.

DON'T MISS: Explore Devil's Lake State Park near Baraboo. This large park features 500-foot cliffs, hiking trails, and camping.

GETTING THERE: The scenic route from Madison is along Hwy. 12 going north. Turn left on Hwy. 36 and then left again on Hwy. PF to North Freedom. In North Freedom, follow Walnut Street west to the museum.

DISCOUNT: Buy one coach ticket and get one of equal or lesser value free.

Osceola   *Train ride*

Osceola & St. Croix Valley Railway

ADDRESS: 114 Depot Rd., Osceola, WI 54020
TELEPHONE: 715-755-3570
E-MAIL: oscvrlwy@centurytel.net
WEB SITE: www.mtmuseum.org

The Osceola & St. Croix Valley Railway offers rides through the scenic St. Croix River Valley along the Wisconsin-Minnesota border on former Soo Line tracks now owned by Canadian National. Operated by the Minnesota Transportation Museum, the trains are diesel powered, with a former Rock Island GP7 repainted in Soo Line's classic maroon and gold colors pulling most trains.

CHOICES: Two routes leave from Osceola. One heads west 10 miles to Marine on St. Croix, Minn. This highly recommended trip follows the beautiful St. Croix Valley for its entire length. The other trip goes east to Dresser, Wis., a former Soo Line junction town that still has its original wooden depot. The railway also offers a variety of special trips including brunch trains, pizza trains, fireworks trains, and fall color trains. Another option is a guided tour through Minnesota's William O'Brien State Park with the train as your transportation.

WHEN TO GO: There's nothing like a crisp, blue-sky autumn day in the open window coaches rolling through the St. Croix Valley. The first weeks of October offer the chance to view the autumn colors before the long northern winter begins. For the best views of the St. Croix River, May is the time to ride before the leaves obstruct the river.

GOOD TO KNOW: Osceola is a small town of around 2,000. There are several good local hotels, restaurants and B&Bs, but those who desire all the amenities may wish to drive south to the larger communities of Stillwater, Minn., or Hudson, Wis.

WORTH DOING: Watch the mail being picked up on the fly with ex-Northern Pacific Railway post office-baggage-coach combine 1102 from a mail crane at Osceola's restored depot, one of the few places where this once common occurrence can be seen.

DON'T MISS: Take the train to Marine and ride over the Cedar Bend swing bridge across the St. Croix River. While the bridge doesn't swing open any more, it's a classic steel structure complete with "tell tales" on each end to warn brakemen of close clearances.

GETTING THERE: Osceola is about an hour's drive from Minneapolis. For a scenic drive, follow Hwy. 95 along the east bank of the St. Croix from Stillwater north to Osceola. Once in Osceola, you'll come to Hwy. 35. Turn right and proceed under the railroad bridge and immediately turn right again onto Depot Road.

DISCOUNT: Receive $3 off a regular-schedule adult fare.

New London   *Museum*
Historical Village

The village features a restored C&NW depot and several other historical structures, including an octagon house. Built in 1923, the depot is authentically furnished and contains railroad artifacts. It also displays a 1941 diesel engine, a Soo caboose, and a C&NW caboose. The museum is open during summer.

ADDRESS: Montgomery St., New London, WI 54961
TELEPHONE: 920-982-8557
WEB SITE: www.newlondonwi.org/historical.htm

Spooner   *Museum*
Railroad Memories Museum

This museum contains 12 rooms filled with railroad memories. Artifacts include tools, equipment, station signs, lanterns, and uniforms as well as bells and whistles. Housed in a former C&NW depot, it is located next to the Wisconsin Great Northern Railroad and open Memorial Day through Labor Day.

ADDRESS: 424 Front St., Spooner, WI 54801
TELEPHONE: 715-635-3325
WEB SITE: www.spoonerwi.com/railroadmuseum

Spooner   *Train ride, Dinner train*
Wisconsin Great Northern Railroad

The Wisconsin Great Northern Railroad offers special train rides and casual dining excursions in the North Woods along the picturesque Namekagon River. The 30-mile round trip between Spooner and Springbrook takes you over former Chicago & North Western track. There are fall foliage, pizza, picnic, and buffet trains.

ADDRESS: 426 N. Front St., Spooner, WI 54801
TELEPHONE: 715-635-3200
E-MAIL: office@spoonertrainride.com
WEB SITE: www.spoonertrainride.com

WYOMING

Cheyenne
Cheyenne Depot Museum

Cheyenne's historic depot stands as a monument to railroading history in the area. Built in 1886, the Union Pacific depot is now a museum that showcases the history of this beautifully restored building as well as the railroad and city.

ADDRESS: 121 W. 15th St., Cheyenne, WY 82001
TELEPHONE: 307-632-3905
WEB SITE: www.cheyennedepotmuseum.org

Douglas   Depot
Douglas Railroad Interpretive Center

The Douglas Railroad Interpretive Center is housed in a restored 1886 passenger depot belonging to the Fremont, Elkhorn & Missouri Valley Railroad. It displays a 1940 Chicago, Burlington & Quincy steam locomotive and seven rail cars. The building is listed on the National Register of Historic Places, and the cars, in various stages of restoration, are available for tours.

ADDRESS: 121 Brownfield Rd., Douglas, WY 82633
TELEPHONE: 877-937-4996, 307-358-2950
E-MAIL: chamber@jackalope.org
WEB SITE: www.douglaschamber.com

Evanston   Museum
Union Pacific Roundhouse

This complex includes a 28-bay roundhouse, working turntable, and renovated machine shop. Each year, Roundhouse Restoration, the group restoring the facility, holds a weekend festival in the roundhouse and gives yard tours. It is open other times during the year as well. Nearby Depot Square includes a restored 1900 depot and other historic buildings.

ADDRESS: 1440 Main St., Evanston, WY 82930
TELEPHONE: 307-783-6320

Cheyenne

Union Pacific Railroad

ADDRESS: UP Steam Shop, Cheyenne, WY 82001
TELEPHONE: 307-778-3214
WEB SITE: www.uprr.com/aboutup/excurs/index.shtml

This Class I mainline railroad maintains the only steam locomotive never retired, no. 844, a 4-8-4 built in 1944. Rebuilt between 1999 and 2004, it is used on occasional excursions and display tours.

CHOICES: Home for the locomotive is a nonpublic shop in Cheyenne, where Union Pacific also maintains its other display/excursion steam engine, 4-6-6-4 no. 3985, believed to be the largest operating steam locomotive today. Departures occur from the UP rail yards as well as from the Cheyenne Depot Museum.

WHEN TO GO: Schedules and routes vary from year to year. One annual outing is the Denver Post Frontier Days excursion train from Denver to Cheyenne for the big rodeo event.

GOOD TO KNOW: The Union Pacific provides a GPS trace system for its steam train at www.uprr.com/aboutup/excurs/trace.cfm

WORTH DOING: Visit the Cheyenne Depot Museum in the restored UP depot. Two historic engines are displayed in Cheyenne parks, a Big Boy engine in Holliday Park and the state's oldest steam locomotive, no. 1242, in Lions Park.

DON'T MISS: In July, celebrate the West during Frontier Days, a 10-day rodeo event with entertainment and other activities.

GETTING THERE: Cheyenne is in southwest Wyoming, about 90 minutes from Denver on I-25.

ALBERTA

Edmonton
Alberta Railway Museum
Museum, Train ride

The museum's collection of railway equipment and buildings focuses on the Canadian National Railway and the Northern Alberta Railway. It includes more than 50 locomotives and cars, three stations, and a water tank. On select holiday weekends, passenger excursions are available, and speeders run daily during the summer.

ADDRESS: 24215 34th St., Edmonton, AB T5C 3R6
TELEPHONE: 780-472-6229
WEB SITE: www.railwaymuseum.ab.ca

Edmonton
Edmonton Radial Railway
Trolley ride

The Edmonton Radial Railway operates streetcars in Fort Edmonton Park and in Old Strathcona. Once you are admitted to the park, the one-mile streetcar rides are free. In Old Strathcona, the trolley crosses High Level Bridge over the North Saskatchewan River.

ADDRESS: 700 143rd St., Edmonton, AB T6H 5Y1
TELEPHONE: 780-496-1464
E-MAIL: info@edmonton-radial-railway.ab.ca
WEB SITE: www.edmonton-radial-railway.ab.ca

Edmonton
Fort Edmonton Park
Museum, Train ride

Nestled in Edmonton's river valley, Fort Edmonton Park is a living history museum that represents four historical periods between 1840 and 1920. It contains more than 75 buildings. A 1919 steam train takes you through the park, and caboose rides are available. A streetcar also travels along the historic streets.

ADDRESS: Fox Dr. and Whitemud Dr., Edmonton, AB T5J 2R7
TELEPHONE: 780-496-8787
WEB SITE: www.edmonton.ca/fort

Calgary

Museum, Train ride

Heritage Park Historical Village

ADDRESS: 1900 Heritage Dr. SW, Calgary, AB T2V 2X3
TELEPHONE: 403-268-8500
E-MAIL: info@heritagepark.ab.ca
WEB SITE: www.heritagepark.ca

Discover what life was like in the Canadian West between 1864 and 1914 by visiting this 66-acre re-created village framed by the Rockies. More than 150 exhibits, including many buildings transplanted from Calgary and other locations throughout Alberta, bring the past to the present.

CHOICES: The park includes a roundhouse and turntable along with more than 20 locomotives and cars. A train ride is an excellent way to see the park. You have a variety of admission options to choose from, depending on your time and level of interest. Make a day of your visit and wander from building to building, paying particular attention to the transplanted railway stations, rolling stock, and re-created carbarn. If it's too hot, take a cruise on the water aboard the replica sternwheeler SS *Moyie*.

WHEN TO GO: Heritage Park is open daily from the end of May to Labour Day and then only on weekends from Labour Day until Canadian Thanksgiving. Avoiding the crowds found throughout the city during Stampede in early July makes for a more leisurely visit.

GOOD TO KNOW: A short streetcar line connects the outer parking area to the main entrance. It's well worth it to park out there, view ex-CPR 2-10-4 5931 and S-2 7019, and then ride over to the gate in a replica Calgary or Winnipeg trolley. A multitude of photographic opportunities are available about the park's railway loop.

WORTH DOING: During Railway Days, held toward the end of June, the park celebrates Canadian railways and rolls out much of its collection. Steam doubleheaders often operate for this event, and ex-CP Car 76 present at the driving of the last spike on the CPR in Craigellachie in 1885 is usually rolled out.

DON'T MISS: Calgary's 10-day annual Stampede, which can draw more than one million people, is the world's largest rodeo. The event also features chuckwagon racing, agricultural exhibits, entertainment, and a parade.

GETTING THERE: Heritage Park is approximately a 20-minute drive southwest from downtown Calgary. A shuttle service operates during park hours from the Heritage light rail stop. Calgary is serviced by scheduled bus and air service.

ALBERTA

Calgary
Dinner train, Train ride

Royal Canadian Pacific

ADDRESS: 133 Ninth Ave. SW, Calgary, AB T2P 2M3
TELEPHONE: 877-665-3044 or 403-508-1400
E-MAIL: info@royalcanadianpacific.com
WEB SITE: www.royalcanadianpacific.com

The Royal Canadian Pacific, an arm of the passenger department of Canadian Pacific Railway, offers periodically scheduled all-inclusive luxury-train ride packages on CPR's route through the spectacularly scenic Canadian Rockies. The operation is often called Canada's *Orient Express*. Restored vintage diesel locomotives haul a consist of about eight cars – all vintage, heavyweight CPR sleeping, observation, and dining cars with lavishly restored interiors. Cuisine in the dining room equals the finest on the continent.

CHOICES: The RCP's signature six-day, five-night Royal Canadian Rockies Experience tour circles from Calgary to the west into British Columbia, traversing some Alberta prairie lines and then two mountain summits, Crowsnest and Kicking Horse Passes, at the Continental Divide. It passes through the railway's famous twin Spiral Tunnels and follows the headwaters of the Columbia River. Other themed experiences include golf, fly-fishing, and culinary excursions. A special tour is the Ski and Snowboard Tour at Lake Louise.

WHEN TO GO: The Canadian Rockies and the prairies have unpredictable weather with temperatures that can fall or rise quickly. The mountains offer spectacular scenery during every season.

GOOD TO KNOW: Calgary, Canada's largest city between Toronto and Vancouver, is a cosmopolitan city that still retains its western flavor and offers many cultural and entertainment opportunities.

WORTH DOING: Railway enthusiasts and historians should be sure to visit Calgary's Heritage Park Historical Village, open mid-May through Labor Day and autumn weekends. The park offers a one-mile steam train ride around a living historical village with restored and replicated buildings.

DON'T MISS: Calgary's C-Train light-rail system, with three routes radiating from downtown, is an efficient and fun way to see much of the city.

GETTING THERE: Calgary is served by many major airlines, and one section of the *Rocky Mountaineer* tourist train from Vancouver, but it is not on the VIA Rail Canada national passenger rail system.

Canadian Pacific Railway Steam Train

ADDRESS: 401 Ninth Ave. SW, Calgary, AB T2P 4Z4
TELEPHONE: 403-837-1324
WEB SITE: www.cpr.ca

Based in Calgary, the CPR hosts Canada's only mainline, railway-operated steam train. Trips have operated across the CPR and Soo system from Delson, Quebec, to Vancouver and from Chicago to Portal, N.D. Often, passenger trips run in conjunction with a charity or special event.

CHOICES: The *Empress* steamed back into service in 2001 as a roving ambassador for the CPR. Built by Montreal Locomotive Works in 1930, it is the only surviving H1b Hudson. After a complete rebuild, the *Empress* was restored to original specifications with external details from the 1940s and '50s. It pulls passengers in former intercity coaches that feature reclining seats.

WHEN TO GO: Trips are not regularly scheduled, so check the CPR Web site often.

GOOD TO KNOW: Make reservations early as seating capacity on the excursions is limited. While most departure and arrival locations are accessible via some form of public transportation, not all one-way trips include return transportation to the point of origin.

WORTH DOING: Many runs are made west of Calgary through the mountains, giving the engine a good workout.

DON'T MISS: Runs through Crowsnest Pass, which straddles the Alberta-British Columbia border, offer a good mix of engine noise and scenic highlights.

GETTING THERE: Departure and arrival locations vary by trip.

Jasper

Train ride

Skeena

ADDRESS: 607 Connaught Dr., Jasper, AB T0E 1E0
TELEPHONE: 888-842-7245
WEB SITE: www.viarail.ca

The *Skeena*, operated by VIA Rail Canada between Jasper and Prince Rupert, British Columbia, is one of the scenic highlights of any trip to western Canada. Work-horse F40s haul this vest-pocket, largely stainless-steel domeliner over what was originally the Grand Trunk Pacific, making an overnight stop in both directions in Prince George. The 725-mile trip takes you from the Rocky Mountains in Jasper National Park to the Pacific coast.

CHOICES: Travelers can opt for one of three on-board accommodation classes when departing from either Jasper or Prince Rupert. Budget-minded vacationers can relax in the leg-rest seats found in comfort (coach) class. Those with a voracious appetite for scenery may want to spend a little more for totem class (glass-roofed, low-level coach). Those with even deeper pockets and a desire to experience vintage deluxe travel will enjoy totem deluxe class (day space in Park series dome observation car).

WHEN TO GO: The *Skeena* operates tri-weekly year-round, with extra trips often added in both directions during the high-tourist summer weeks. The shorter days and deep snows of winter give way to a plethora of spring flowers in May. Long, hot summer days morph into the colorful, cool fall days by October.

GOOD TO KNOW: Jasper is a typical tourist town, with a variety of hotels and services catering to the traveler who likes pampering as well as serving those who enjoy being more in touch with nature. Prince Rupert has a broad choice of accommodations. The area immediately across from the VIA station in Prince George may be considered rough by some standards. Taking a taxi from the station to accommodations a few blocks away upon the evening's arrival may be comforting for those who don't travel light.

WORTH DOING: Splurging for space in the Park observation car will provide all the scenic views available to those in the totem car ahead, with the added bonuses of forward visibility and a place to escape the rays of the hot summer sun.

DON'T MISS: Mount Robson, the highest peak in the Canadian Provinces, is visible from the train just west of Jasper for only a few cloudless days a year.

GETTING THERE: VIA Rail operates the Vancouver-Toronto Canadian tri-weekly through Jasper in each direction. Jasper is also served by inter-city bus service from Edmonton and other points. Scheduled air service operates in and out of Prince Rupert.

Stettler

Train ride, Dinner train

Alberta Prairie Railway Excursions

ADDRESS: 4611 47th Ave., Stettler, AB T0C 2L0
TELEPHONE: 800-282-3994 or 403-742-2811
E-MAIL: info@absteamtrain.com
WEB SITE: www.absteamtrain.com

A trip aboard the Alberta Prairie conjures up visions of what a central Alberta wheat line must have been like 100 years ago. Traveling from the well-developed community of Stettler, it passes through forests and fields before reaching Big Valley, where the ruins of a roundhouse and a well-kept depot remain.

CHOICES: The railroad offers an extensive schedule, including numerous specials such as murder mystery, Christmas, dinner theater, family, and teddy bear trains. The most popular excursion is the A Train, which includes a full-course buffet meal and an occasional train robbery. The winter fine-dining trains provide a five-course meal and entertainment. The trains are pulled by steam engines Baldwin 2-8-0 no. 41 and Montreal 4-8-2 no. 6060 and General Motors diesel no. 1259.

WHEN TO GO: Summer excursions begin in May and continue until mid-October each year. Dinner trains are offered November through April.

GOOD TO KNOW: The railway was once part of a vast grain railroad network belonging to the Canadian Northern. Be sure to chat with the train crew. Many of the veteran railroaders on this line have great stories. And if you get the right conductor, he might just sing you a song or recite a poem for you en route.

WORTH DOING: For steam fans, there is a no-frills special aboard one of the steam trains without any of the extras.

DON'T MISS: For an added prairie experience, the railway offers a three-and-a-half-day package that includes a train ride and a 20-mile covered wagon trip along historic rail rights-of-way.

GETTING THERE: Stettler is about three hours northeast of Calgary on Hwy. 12.

BRITISH COLUMBIA

Fort Steele   *Train ride*
Fort Steele Steam Railway

Fort Steele Heritage Town is a restored 1890s pioneer town complete with railway. The railway is located outside the historic park, so you ride the rails separately or as part of an all-inclusive ticket. A Montreal Locomotive Works 2-6-2 prairie-type locomotive takes you around a 2.5-mile loop. Along the way, you'll learn about local rail history.

ADDRESS: 9851 Hwy. 93/95, Fort Steele, BC V0B 1N0
TELEPHONE: 250-417-6000
E-MAIL: info@fortsteele.bc.ca
WEB SITE: www.fortsteele.bc.ca

Prince George   *Museum*
Prince George Railway & Forestry Museum

The museum displays historic railway and forestry in a park-like setting. The extensive rail collection dates to 1899 and includes two stations and a turntable. It also contains both steam and diesel locomotives and more than 40 pieces of rolling stock.

ADDRESS: 850 River Rd., Prince George, BC V2L 5S8
TELEPHONE: 250-563-7351
E-MAIL: trains@pgrfm.bc.ca
WEB SITE: www.pgrfm.bc.ca

Prince Rupert   *Museum*
Kwinitsa Railway Station Museum

Now located in Prince Rupert's waterfront park, this restored station house is an excellent example of the small stations once found along Canada's northern railway line. Photographs, videos, and detailed restorations depict the life of station agents and linemen who worked for the Grand Trunk Railway at the turn of the 20th century. It is open daily June through August.

ADDRESS: Bill Murray Way and First Ave., Prince Rupert, BC V8J 1A8
TELEPHONE: 250-624-3207
E-MAIL: mnbc@citytel.net
WEB SITE: www.museumofnorthernbc.com

Canadian Museum of Rail Travel

ADDRESS: 57 Van Horne St. S, Cranbrook, BC V1C 1Y7
TELEPHONE: 250-489-3918
E-MAIL: mail@trainsdeluxe.com
WEB SITE: www.trainsdeluxe.com

The Canadian Museum of Rail Travel is a magnet for anyone interested in Canadian passenger rail travel as it once was. It is home to the only surviving train set of equipment from the 1929 *Trans-Canada Limited* as well as the beautifully reconstructed Royal Alexandra Hall.

CHOICES: Visitors can elect to examine the collection at their own pace or join an informative tour that examines the interiors of various cars of the *Soo-Spokane Train Deluxe* as well as business cars and cars of state. The museum's collection contains equipment from the consists of the *Pacific Express* and the *Chinook*. It also includes historic structures.

WHEN TO GO: The collection is open to the public daily from mid-April to Canadian Thanksgiving in October. The remainder of the year, it is open Tuesday through Saturday.

GOOD TO KNOW: Cranbrook is a full-service mountain city. It is a major gateway to the Canadian Rockies, which are 15 miles away. With a wide range of accommodations and eateries, something will likely be suitable to most tastes.

WORTH DOING: Take the museum's guided tour. Guides not only explain the history of the equipment, but they bring to life the detailed work of the restoration process.

DON'T MISS: Tour the exquisitely recreated Royal Alexandra Hall from the Canadian Pacific Railway's Royal Alexandra Hotel that once stood near that road's Winnipeg station. The hall was the grand café of the hotel and features Edwardian architectural style.

GETTING THERE: Both Pacific Coastal Airlines and Air Canada operate scheduled air service to Cranbrook. Greyhound also operates daily scheduled motor coach service to the city. Many Royal Canadian Pacific trains spend the night right outside the facility's trackside entrance and include the museum on their itinerary.

Kamloops

Train ride

Kamloops Heritage Railway

ADDRESS: 6-510 Lorne St., Kamloops, BC V2C 1W3
TELEPHONE: 250-374-2141
E-MAIL: info@kamrail.com
WEB SITE: www.kamrail.com

This steam-powered tourist line's regular seven-mile round trip travels over the CN Okanagan Subdivision. In spring and fall, history-evoking excursions operate over the Kelowna Pacific line on a 115-mile round trip from Kamloops to Armstrong.

CHOICES: On the *Spirit of Kamloops'* 70-minute excursion, you can ride in a restored 1930s air-conditioned coach or in an open-air car to take in the sounds of the railway's former CN 2-8-0 and the sights of the mountain and lakeside scenery. The train departs from a restored 1927 CN station and crosses the South Thompson River on a 1927 steel trestle bridge. The *Armstrong Explorer* takes you back in time on an all-day excursion between Kamloops and Armstrong. The 115-mile round trip features spectacular scenery as you climb the 2 percent grade out of Campbell Creek and travel through a 493-foot tunnel, and around a horseshoe curve. The railway also runs ghost trains, a dinner train, and other specials.

WHEN TO GO: The *Spirit of Kamloops* operates Friday to Monday during July and August and on a limited schedule during June and September. The *Armstrong Explorer* runs on select dates in May, June, September, and October. Illuminated with hundreds of lights, the *Spirit of Christmas* is a one-hour special, complete with candy canes, hot chocolate, and caroling.

GOOD TO KNOW: Kamloops is a regional center that has a wide range of accommodations to choose from, as well as all the services you would expect in a small-sized city including city bus service. The former courthouse, where train robber Bill Miner was tried and convicted, is now a popular hostel.

WORTH DOING: Bring your camera as the *Spirit of Kamloops* stops on the trestle bridge to allow passengers to photograph the scenic vistas.

DON'T MISS: On the *Spirit of Kamloops*, masked riders reenact the famous 1906 train robbery by the Bill Miner gang. Following the robbery, listen to Bill Miner's ghost tell his story.

GETTING THERE: Horizon, West Jet, and Air Canada operate scheduled air service into and out of Kelowna, two hours to the south of Kamloops. Daily bus service operates through the city, and VIA Rail Canada's *Canadian* calls at Kamloops Junction thrice weekly in each direction.

Alberni Pacific Railway

ADDRESS: 3100 Kingsway Ave., Port Alberni, BC V9Y 3B1
TELEPHONE: 250-723-1376
E-MAIL: info@alberniheritage.com
WEB SITE: www.alberniheritage.com/rail.shtml

The Alberni Pacific offers passengers a chance to visit the former McClean Paper Mill, six miles east of Port Alberni over the former CPR Port Alberni Subdivision. The mill is a national historic site that now commemorates the history of logging and milling in British Columbia.

CHOICES: Trains to the mill are pulled by a 1929 Baldwin 2-8-2T, and passengers ride in converted former CN transfer cabooses, three of which are open and two are covered. Trips leave from a restored 1912 CPR station.

WHEN TO GO: Runs are made over this scenic trackage twice daily from Thursday to Monday between the end of June and September.

GOOD TO KNOW: The McLean Mill is the only steam-operated sawmill in Canada. This historic site and the railway are part of the Alberni Valley Heritage Network that celebrates the area's history and culture. Also included are the Alberni Valley Museum and Maritime Discovery Centre.

WORTH DOING: Visit Port Alberni's quaint harbor, which offers a mix of restaurants, galleries, tours, and shops. The Western Vancouver Island Industrial Heritage Society also operates a train ride along the waterfront.

DON'T MISS: Include a stop at the Chase & Warren Estate Winery, either as part of your train trip or separately. This offers wine connoisseurs the opportunity to sample the wares of the small Vancouver Island winery. The Alberni Pacific Railway makes daily stops at the winery.

GETTING THERE: Intercity bus service is available from Vancouver Island to and from Port Alberni. Scheduled air service is available from Victoria to the south. Scheduled ferry service operates between the mainland and various points on Vancouver Island including Port Alberni.

Revelstoke *Museum*

Revelstoke Railway Museum

This railway museum focuses on the history of the Canadian Pacific Railway in western Canada. You can take a walk through Official Car no. 4 and view other CP cars, locomotives, and artifacts. The museum also operates a small facility at Craigellachie, 28 miles west of Revelstoke, where the last spike of the Canadian Pacific Railway was driven. The museum is open year-round.

ADDRESS: 719 Track St. W, Revelstoke, BC V0E 2S0
TELEPHONE: 877-837-6060 or 250-837-6060
E-MAIL: railway@telus.net
WEB SITE: www.railwaymuseum.com

Vancouver *Trolley ride*

Downtown Historic Railway

The railway takes you on a ride between Science World Station and Granville Island Station in downtown Vancouver. Restored interurban cars 1207 and 1231 are two of the last 10 B.C. Electric's cars in existence. The railway runs weekends and holidays Victoria Day weekend through Canadian Thanksgiving. It is near the SkyTrain's Main Street station.

ADDRESS: Quebec St. and Terminal Ave., Vancouver, BC V6A 3Z7
TELEPHONE: 604-873-7623
E-MAIL: engineering@vancouver.ca
WEB SITE: www.city.vancouver.bc.ca/engsvcs/transport/railway

Victoria *Train ride*

Malahat

VIA's *Malahat* runs across scenic Vancouver Island. The excursion runs between Victoria, at the southern tip of the island, and Courtenay, at the northern end. Beside seeing the island's beautiful countryside, with a comfort-class ticket, you can get off at other stops along the way and experience Duncan's totem poles, Nanaimo's harbor, and Courtenay's downtown.

ADDRESS: 450 Pandora Ave., Victoria, BC V8W 3L5
TELEPHONE: 888-842-7245
WEB SITE: www.viarail.ca/malahat

West Coast Railway Heritage Park

ADDRESS: 39645 Government Rd., Squamish, BC
TELEPHONE: 604-898-9336
E-MAIL: manager@wcra.org
WEB SITE: www.wcra.org/heritage

Opened in 1994, the West Coast Heritage Park provides a home to the West Coast Railway Association's large collection of locomotives and rolling stock. Located in a beautiful 12-acre mountain valley setting, the museum offers visitors a chance to learn about railway history in Canada's westernmost province.

CHOICES: The park exhibits a typical railway facility of the mid-20th century, complete with stations and other buildings. You are also able to see railway equipment in various stages of restoration. The collection of more than 50 vintage railway cars and locomotives includes cabooses, snowplows, a restored 1890 business car, and the only surviving Pacific Great Western steam engine. A mini train ride circles the park.

WHEN TO GO: The park is open year-round, except for Christmas and New Year's Day. Summer months provide the least likelihood for an encounter with the area's famous "wet sunshine."

GOOD TO KNOW: Many good restaurants and chain eateries can be found in Squamish. Shannon Falls Provincial Park contains the province's third-highest waterfall, which falls more than 1,000 feet.

WORTH DOING: Incorporate a visit to the museum with a scenic drive along the Sea to Sky Highway for a nice day-long family outing. The Sea to Sky Highway travels through five different biogeoclimatic zones, from coastal rain forest to mountain forest. This predominantly two-lane road goes from Vancouver to Whistler.

DON'T MISS: Royal Hudson no. 2860 now calls the park home. It was one of the last Royal Hudson locomotives built for the CPR, in June 1940, by Montreal Locomotive Works.

GETTING THERE: From Vancouver, it is about an hour's drive north on Hwy. 99 along spectacular Howe Sound, North America's southernmost fjord, to Squamish. Turn left on Industrial Way and go to the stop sign at Queens Way. Then turn right and follow the signs.

Summerland

Kettle Valley Steam Railway

Train ride

ADDRESS: 18404 Bathville Rd., Summerland, BC V0H 1Z0
TELEPHONE: 877-494-8424 or 250-494-8422
E-MAIL: information@kettlevalleyrail.org
WEB SITE: www.kettlevalleyrail.org

The Kettle Valley Steam Railway operates over a preserved portion of the famed Kettle Valley Railway between Faulder and Trout Creek Trestle. Between May and October, passengers can enjoy the view across the Okanagan Lake and the surrounding hills from a steam-powered train traveling over the remaining portion of the CPR's famed southern route through British Columbia.

CHOICES: The KVR offers conventional excursions over its 10-mile right-of-way. The two-hour trip winds through Prairie Valley and its scenic vistas. Former BC 2-8-0 3716 has returned to service on the KVR, on an extended loan from the provincial government. You can ride in two 1950s passenger coaches or several open-air cars. Special events include an Easter train, wine trains, a trick-or-treat train, Christmas trains, and the Great Train Robbery and BBQ. One-way trips may be arranged for cyclists or hikers from either terminus, Canyon View Siding at Trout Creek Bridge or Prairie Valley Station.

WHEN TO GO: The KVR operates from late May through Canadian Thanksgiving in October on a varied schedule. It runs Saturday through Monday as well as running some excursions on Thursdays and Fridays.

GOOD TO KNOW: Summerland is situated in the Okanagan Valley amid lush orchards and vineyards, and the valley is home to more than 50 wineries.

WORTH DOING: Take a side trip into nearby Penticton to tour the former CP ship SS *Sicamous*. This steel-hulled sternwheeler was built in 1914 as a multi-purpose vessel that provided first-class passenger service as well as delivering cargo and daily mail.

DON'T MISS: The Trout Creek Trestle, at the current turnaround point south of Summerland, sits 238 feet above the canyon floor and provides spectacular views.

GETTING THERE: Horizon, West Jet, and Air Canada operate scheduled air service into and out of Kelowna, less than an hour's drive to the east.

Vancouver *Train ride*

Rocky Mountaineer Vacations

ADDRESS: 100-1150 Station St., Vancouver, BC V6A 2X7
TELEPHONE: 877-460-3200 or 604-606-7245
WEB SITE: www.rockymountaineer.com

What many consider to be Canada's premier rail tour company recently expanded its selection of rail outings. In addition to its signature Vancouver to Jasper route and Vancouver to Banff or Calgary route, there are also trips from Vancouver to Whistler and from Whistler to Jasper.

CHOICES: The Rocky Mountaineer offers two-day trips over three routes: Kicking Horse, Yellowhead, and Fraser Discovery. Kicking Horse takes you over the Rockies from Vancouver to either Banff or Calgary in Alberta. On the Yellowhead route, you travel through the Rockies to Jasper, Alberta. The Fraser Discovery route follows the Fraser River from Whistler to Jasper. The *Whistler Mountaineer* is a three-hour journey between Vancouver and Whistler, British Columbia, following the Sea to Sky corridor, which provides scenic views of waterfalls, forests, and mountains. All routes offer a choice between GoldLeaf or RedLeaf service. GoldLeaf service features bi-level dome coaches with full-length windows and RedLeaf service includes reclining seats, extended legroom, and at-seat food service.

WHEN TO GO: Although trains operate on select dates on some routes April through October and around the holiday season, aim for the longer days of the year if possible. While passengers are accommodated in hotels during overnight stops, the longer days of the year provide more hours during which to view the spectacular scenery.

GOOD TO KNOW: The Jasper and Banff/Calgary trains operate combined between Vancouver and Kamloops. Trains operating on the former British Columbia Railway north of greater Vancouver arrive and depart from the vicinity of the former BCR station in North Vancouver. You can also begin your trip in Jasper, Banff, or Calgary.

WORTH DOING: Go for the gold. You may as well take advantage of the fancy digs and pampering with GoldLeaf service. After all, it is a cruise train.

DON'T MISS: Scenic highlights include Fraser and Thompson Canyons on the Yellowhead run and spiral tunnels on the Kicking Horse route.

GETTING THERE: Air service is available to Vancouver and Calgary. Scheduled motor coach service connects Jasper, Banff, and Whistler to the outside world. VIA Rail Canada provides tri-weekly service to Jasper and Vancouver.

MANITOBA

Winnipeg Railway Museum

Located in the VIA rail station, this railroad museum is dedicated to preserving Manitoba's rail heritage. Various locomotives are on display including the *Countess of Dufferin*, the first steam locomotive to operate in western Canada. It also displays baggage cars, freight cars, and a CN caboose. The museum is open year-round.

ADDRESS: 123 Main St., Winnipeg, MB R3C 1A3
TELEPHONE: 204-942-4632
E-MAIL: wpgrail@res1.mts.net
WEB SITE: www.wpgrailwaymuseum.com

Winnipeg
Prairie Dog Central Railway

ADDRESS: Prairie Dog Trail, Winnipeg, MB
TELEPHONE: 204-832-5259
E-MAIL: info@pdcrailway.com
WEB SITE: www.pdcrailway.com

This 36-mile round trip over the former CN Oak Point Sub from the north side of the Manitoba capital to the town of Warren offers a glimpse into prairie railroading of the past.

CHOICES: You can choose to travel in either open-vestibule or closed-vestibule coaches. All the wooden coaches, built between 1901-1913, are fully restored and air-conditioned – when the windows are open. Power is provided by diesel locomotive 4138, which was built in 1958 for the Grand Trunk Western Railroad. The train makes a stop in Grosse Isle on the way to Warren. Special excursions include Halloween, Santa, and family trains. Others feature dining or dancing options.

WHEN TO GO: Trains operate regularly on weekends from mid-May through September. Special runs also operate on select holidays such as Victoria Day, Canada Day, and Labour Day.

GOOD TO KNOW: Ex-Winnipeg Hydro 4-4-0 no. 3, nearing completion of an extensive rebuild, is expected to return shortly to the head-end. Built in 1882 by Dubs in Scotland, it would be among the oldest operable engines in North America. The railway's station, a Canadian Heritage Railway station, was constructed in 1910 by the Canadian Northern Railway. It was moved from St. James Street to its present location in 2000 and renamed Inkster Junction Station.

WORTH DOING: Secure a ticket in either combine 104 (built in 1906) or coach 105 (built in 1901). These beautifully maintained relics are rolling time machines to another century.

DON'T MISS: When stopped in Grosse Isle and Warren, explore the towns' public markets. Grosse Isle is home to the 72-mile Prime Meridian Trail, a recreation and conservation trail built on an abandoned CN rail line.

GETTING THERE: The railway is located north of Winnipeg on Prairie Dog Trail. It is on the north side of Inkster Boulevard between Hwy. 90 and Sturgeon Boulevard. Air, motor coach, and rail service is available to Winnipeg. The railway offers a complimentary shuttle bus to several Winnipeg hotels.

NEW FOUNDLAND

Museum

Railway Society of Newfoundland

The society maintains a collection of narrow gauge rolling stock from the Newfoundland Railway. Several trains are displayed including the *Newfie Bullet*, once Newfoundland's fastest passenger train. Steam locomotive no. 593 now is displayed with a representative selection of cars. A snow plow train is also featured. You can walk through all the railcars. The museum is open daily during the summer.

ADDRESS: Marine Dr. and Station Rd., Corner Brook, NF A2H 6G1
TELEPHONE: 709-634-2720
WEB SITE: www.cornet.nf.ca/web/rsn

NOVA SCOTIA

Orangedale   *Museum, Depot*
Orangedale Railway Museum

The museum was originally built in 1886 as a Queen Anne-style station. The ground floor includes a replica of the original office and waiting rooms. The second floor has been restored as the station agent's living quarters. The museum also displays a small diesel locomotive and several rail cars. It is open Wednesday through Sunday late June to the end of August.

ADDRESS: 1428 Main St., Orangedale, NS B0E 2K0
TELEPHONE: 902-756-3384
WEB SITE: www.fortress.uccb.ns.ca/historic/oranstat.html

ONTARIO

Brighton   *Museum*
Memory Junction Museum

Memory Junction features several structures including the original Grand Trunk station, a baggage shed, and an unloading depot. A rare N-4-a locomotive is on display along with a wooden, outside-braced 1913 boxcar and other railcars. The museum includes local as historical as well as railway artifacts. It is open May through October.

ADDRESS: 60 Maplewood St., Brighton, ON K0K 1H0
TELEPHONE: 613-475-0379
E-MAIL: re.bangay@sympatico.ca
WEB SITE: www.memoryjunction.netfirms.com

Capreol   *Museum*
Northern Ontario Railroad Museum & Heritage Centre

This museum emphasizes railroading history in northern Ontario and includes additional exhibits on mining and lumbering. Artifacts are displayed in the Museum House, which was used by the Canadian National as a superintendent's residence. In nearby Prescott Park, it displays a U-1-f bullet-nosed steam locomotive, a wooden CNR caboose, and other equipment.

ADDRESS: 26 Bloor St., Capreol, ON P0M 1H0
TELEPHONE: 705-858-5050
E-MAIL: normhc@vianet.ca
WEB SITE: www.northernontariorailroadmuseum.ca

Chatham   *Museum*
Chatham Railroad Museum

Housed in a retired 1955 CN baggage car, the Chatham Railroad Museum includes interactive exhibits and photos on local as well as national and international railroad history. Open May to September, it is located across from the VIA rail station.

ADDRESS: Queen St., Chatham, ON N7M 2H6
TELEPHONE: 519-352-3097
E-MAIL: cktourism@chatham-kent.ca
WEB SITE: www.chatham-kent.ca

Cochrane

Train ride

Polar Bear Express

ADDRESS: 200 Railway St., Cochrane, ON P0L 1C0
TELEPHONE: 800-268-9281
E-MAIL: choochoo@polarbearexpress.ca
WEB SITE: www.polarbearexpress.ca

Ontario Northland's *Polar Bear Express* takes you on a summer excursion to the shores of James Bay and the edge of the Arctic. Its *Dream Catcher Express* takes you on a brilliant fall foliage trip out of North Bay.

CHOICES: The summer-only *Polar Bear Express* is a day trip that operates between Cochrane and Moosonee on James Bay. After arriving mid-day, you have five hours to explore the area before returning. To get to Cochrane from Toronto, you can take the *Northlander* passenger train. Its daily daylight run operates over the CN south of North Bay. One of Canada's two mixed-train services, the *Little Bear*, operates over the same route. In the fall, you may want to consider riding the *Dream Catcher Express* between North Bay and Temagami to view the brilliant colors.

WHEN TO GO: A long summer weekend allows you to make the journey all the way from Toronto to James Bay and back in daylight.

GOOD TO KNOW: In Cochrane, the Station Inn provides handy overnight accommodation on the upper floors of the train station.

WORTH DOING: Riding to Moosonee and back on the *Little Bear* offers you a chance to see how one of Canada's two remaining mixed-service trains provides a lifeline to people along the line.

DON'T MISS: On the *Polar Bear Express* layover, be sure to take one of the side trips to the island of Moose Factory, a former Hudson's Bay Company fur-trading settlement. If you want to see polar bears close up, you can visit the Polar Bear Conservation and Education Habitat, a polar bear rehabilitation facility, in Cochrane, where you can see the bears in natural habitat and even swim alongside them (with a window in between).

GETTING THERE: Cochrane, North Bay, and Toronto are connected by bus and train service. VIA and Amtrak service connects Toronto with southwest Ontario and New York. Scheduled air service is available to Toronto and to Moosonee.

ONTARIO

Clinton   *Museum*
CNR School Car

Back in the good old days, you didn't have to walk miles through the snow to get to this school. Instead, it came to you. This car was one of seven railway schools that served children and adults along northern Ontario railways. Tour the car and see how teachers brought learning to isolated students. It is open Thursday through Sunday Victoria Day weekend through September.

ADDRESS: 76 Victoria Terrace, Clinton, ON N0M 1L0
TELEPHONE: 519-482-3997
WEB SITE: www.schoolcar.ca

Cochrane   *Museum*
Cochrane Railway and Pioneer Museum

Looking as if it could still ride the rails, Temiskaming and Northern Ontario Railway locomotive no. 137 provides the perfect introduction to the museum housed in the coaches and cabooses behind it. The preserved cars contain railway photographs and artifacts. A replica of a trapper's cabin and exhibits display pioneer life in Cochrane.

ADDRESS: 210 Railway St., Cochrane, ON P0L 1C0
TELEPHONE: 705-272-4361
WEB SITE: www.museumsnorth.org/cochrane

Fort Erie   *Museum*
Fort Erie Railroad Museum

This museum site features the restored Grand Trunk's Ridgeway station, which houses historic furnishings, telegraph equipment, tools, and other artifacts. Canadian National Railway steam engine 6218, a 4-8-4 Northern type, is the museum's centerpiece. Also on display are a fireless engine, a CN caboose and other equipment. The CN's B-1 station that monitored traffic over the International Railway Bridge is also on site.

ADDRESS: 400 Central Ave., Fort Erie, ON L2A 3T6
TELEPHONE: 905-871-1412
E-MAIL: museum@forterie.on.ca
WEB SITE: www.museum.forterie.ca/railroad.html

Ottawa

Canada Science and Technology Museum

Museum

ONTARIO

ADDRESS: 1867 St. Laurent Blvd., Ottawa, ON K1G 5A3

TELEPHONE: 866-442-4416 or 613-991-3044

E-MAIL: cts@technomuses.ca

WEB SITE: www.sciencetech.technomuses.ca

The Canada Science and Technology Museum's rail collection contains 1,000 artifacts that range from photos to locomotives and dates back to the early days of Canadian railway history. Locomotive Hall showcases four locomotives, but other rail equipment is displayed throughout the museum as well as outside in Technology Park. The museum also operates a demonstration train ride.

CHOICES: In Locomotive Hall, you'll find four unique engines. Canada's oldest mainline steam locomotive, CNR no. 40, was built for the Grand Trunk Railway in 1872 and is the only surviving standard gauge engine built by the Portland Company. Canadian Pacific no. 926, built in 1911, spent 50 years hauling freight and passenger trains between Winnipeg and Calgary. CNR no. 6400 has a distinctive semi-streamlined design and is painted in CN olive green to match the passenger cars. Another semi-streamlined locomotive is CP no. 2858, one of five CP Hudsons preserved. Two early passenger coaches are also displayed in the museum. One was constructed in 1854 and the other in 1859.

WHEN TO GO: The museum is open year-round but is closed on some Mondays during its winter schedule. It also closes down for about four days for its annual cleaning.

GOOD TO KNOW: Canadian National no. 6200 is displayed outside the museum in Technology Park. The steam locomotive was built in 1942 and operated in eastern Canada. The 4-8-4 was one of 200 such locomotives operating on the CN during the 1940s. Technology Park also includes a lighthouse, windmill, and Atlas rocket.

WORTH DOING: With a great deal of help from the Bytown Railway Society, the museum operates a two-truck Shay on Wednesdays and Sundays in July and August on a few hundred feet of track bordering the parking lot. A century-old business car and caboose form the usual consist.

DON'T MISS: For an extra fee, try a virtual space trip on the Virtual Voyages simulator.

GETTING THERE: Scheduled air, bus, and rail service operate to Ottawa. The museum is located approximately 10 minutes southeast of downtown Ottawa. Exit Hwy. 417 at St. Laurent south and turn left on Lancaster Road. You can also reach the Museum by the no. 85 or no. 86 city bus.

259

Sault Ste. Marie

Train ride

Algoma Central Railway

ADDRESS: 129 Bay St., Sault Ste. Marie, ON P6A 6Y2
TELEPHONE: 800-242-9287 or 705-946-7300
WEB SITE: www.algomacentralrailway.com

The Algoma Central Railway offers the chance to ride into unspoiled Canadian wilderness from Sault Ste. Marie north into Ontario as far as the spectacular Agawa Canyon or to the end of the railroad at Hearst. Either way, you will not go away disappointed.

CHOICES: You can ride the tour train to Agawa Canyon and back, or you can ride the entire railroad – almost 300 miles one way – to the end of the line at Hearst. Or best of all, you can do both: ride the canyon train out, then catch the regular train to Hearst and back. Going to the canyon, you'll see mixed forests, mountain lakes, and streams and past the canyon, boreal forests, muskegs and moose. The railway also offers winter snow trains and wilderness adventure trains.

WHEN TO GO: The railroad runs year-round. Fall bookings can be intense so plan ahead. The average daily temperature stays below freezing during December, January, and February.

GOOD TO KNOW: The tour train is usually packed, but the regular passenger train is more relaxed. You'll stop at only the canyon on the tour train, but the regular train pauses to let fishermen, hunters, and other outdoor types get off at just about any point. It's a lot of fun to see what people will load or unload onto the baggage car.

WORTH DOING: For scenery viewing, ride one of the railroad's two domes, and for a wilderness experience, camp out overnight in a caboose at Agawa Canyon.

DON'T MISS: For a spectacular view, find a good vantage point at mile post 19, where the railroad crosses the Montreal River on a huge curving trestle perched atop a dam. Boat tours of the Sault Locks are available in Sault Ste. Marie.

GETTING THERE: Sault Ste. Marie is located on I-75 and Hwy. 17. Signs show the way to the depot, which is located downtown.

Huntsville   *Museum, Train ride*
Muskoka Heritage Place

Muskoka Heritage Place contains Pioneer Village and the *Portage Flyer,* a restored 1902 steam train that takes you on a short trip to the past. After boarding at the station museum, you travel along the Muskoka River to Fairy Lake, where you can watch a turntable in action. At the museum, you can view exhibits on the Portage Railway and send a telegraph to yourself. You can combine a Pioneer Village tour and train ride or just ride the *Portage Flyer.*

ADDRESS: 88 Brunel Rd., Huntsville, ON P1H 1R1
TELEPHONE: 705-789-7576
E-MAIL: village@muskokaheritageplace.org
WEB SITE: www.muskokaheritageplace.org

Komoka   *Museum*
Komoka Railway Museum

Komoka's restored Canadian National station houses a collection of artifacts and photos dedicated to rail history in the area. It includes tools, lanterns, and a tiny flagstop station. Also on display are a 1913 Shay locomotive and a steel-sided baggage car. The museum is open Friday through Monday during summer and on Saturdays the rest of the year.

ADDRESS: 133 Queen St., Komoka, ON N0L 1R0
TELEPHONE: 519-657-1912
E-MAIL: komokarailmuseum@aol.com
WEB SITE: www.komokarailmuseum.ca

Milton   *Trolley ride, Museum*
Halton County Radial Railway

The railway offers rides on a variety of restored street cars, dating back to the 1890s, through three miles of scenic woodlands. A museum exhibiting various railway items is housed inside a 1912 station that was built for the Grand Trunk Railway. Streetcars run May through October. You can enjoy lunch in one of three picnic sites.

ADDRESS: 13629 Guelph Line, Milton, ON L9T 5A2
TELEPHONE: 519-856-9802
E-MAIL: streetcar@hcry.org
WEB SITE: www.hcry.org

ONTARIO

Orangeville
Credit Valley Explorer
Train ride, Dinner train

The *Explorer* offers three different excursion options on the ride between Orangeville and Brampton. Scenic half-day tours operate year-round, dinner trains run May to October, and Sunday brunch trains run September through April. The ride aboard 1950s rail coaches takes you over rolling hills, the forks of the Credit River, and a 1,146-foot-long trestle bridge.

ADDRESS: Townline Rd., Orangeville, ON L9W 2Z7
TELEPHONE: 866-860-3371
E-MAIL: info@creditvalleyexplorer.com
WEB SITE: www.creditvalleyexplorer.com

Port Stanley
Port Stanley Terminal Rail
Train ride

Excursion trains depart from a historic station next to the King George lift bridge. Early diesel locomotives pull open and closed coaches that have been converted from cabooses. There are three different destinations: a 1920 flagstop station, Whytes Park, where you can view some rolling stock, and scenic Parkside.

ADDRESS: 309 Bridge St., Port Stanley, ON N5L 1C5
TELEPHONE: 1-877-244-4478 or 519-782-3730
E-MAIL: info@pstr.on.ca
WEB SITE: www.pstr.on.ca

Smiths Falls
Smiths Falls Railway Museum of Eastern Ontario
Museum

This museum is housed in a restored 1914 Canadian Northern Railway station that contains thousands of artifacts relating to the Canadian Pacific, Grand Trunk, Canadian National, and other railways. The national historic site displays a 1912 steam locomotive, a CP diesel, a dental car, and passenger cars.

ADDRESS: 90 William St., Smiths Falls, ON K7A 5A5
TELEPHONE: 613-283-5696
E-MAIL: sfrmchin@superaje.com
WEB SITE: www.sfrmeo.ca

Stouffville
York-Durham Heritage Railway
Train ride

The York-Durham Heritage Railway operates excursions between Stouffville and Uxbridge. Diesel locomotives pull passenger coaches built between the 1920s and the 1950s. The Uxbridge station, which was built in 1904, contains displays of artifacts.

ADDRESS: Main St., Stouffville, ON L4A 7Z7
TELEPHONE: 905-852-3696
E-MAIL: info@ydhr.on.ca
WEB SITE: www.ydhr.on.ca

St. Thomas
Elgin County Railway Museum

Museum

ADDRESS: 225 Wellington St., St. Thomas, ON N5P 4H4
TELEPHONE: 519-637-6284
E-MAIL: thedispatcher@ecrm5700.org
WEB SITE: www.ecrm5700.org

The Elgin County Railway Museum is located in the former Michigan Central locomotive shops. This working museum helps preserve and display the railway heritage of St. Thomas and the surrounding area.

CHOICES: Equipment restoration is ongoing at the museum, and it displays a variety of equipment including a CNR Hudson, a Grand Trunk Western caboose, a Pullman sleeper, and an electric-powered car that transported children to school in the 1920s. Also on hand is the *Spirit of Elgin*, the St. Thomas Central Railway no. 9. In St. Thomas, the BX interlocking tower is available for touring by appointment.

WHEN TO GO: The museum operates daily between the Victoria Day weekend and the end of September. During the remainder of the year, it is open on Monday, Wednesday, and Saturday mornings when its winter schedule is in effect.

GOOD TO KNOW: The railroad has been a part of life in St. Thomas since 1856. Over the years, a total of 26 railways have passed through town helping it garner the moniker of the Railway Capital of Canada. A short drive from the regional center of London, St. Thomas is a small town with all services.

WORTH DOING: Combining a visit to the museum along with a ride on Port Stanley Terminal Rail a few miles to the south makes for an interesting day of exploring the preserved rails of southern Ontario.

DON'T MISS: The museum celebrates Canadian railways on Railway Heritage weekend, which is usually held in August. During the celebration, short train trips often operate within town.

GETTING THERE: VIA Rail Canada offers scheduled passenger service through London to the north. In addition, scheduled air service is available to that city's airport. If you're tied to the rubber tire, the museum is two hours from Toronto, two hours from the U.S. border at Detroit, Buffalo, or Niagara Falls, and one hour from Sarnia and Port Huron. Once in St. Thomas, you will find the museum on Wellington Street between Ross Street and First Avenue.

Tottenham

Museum, Train ride

South Simcoe Railway

ADDRESS: Mill St. W, Tottenham, ON L0G 1W0
TELEPHONE: 905-936-5815
E-MAIL: info@steamtrain.com
WEB SITE: www.steamtrain.com

The South Simcoe Railway operates over 4.4 miles of former CN trackage through rolling countryside approximately an hour north of Toronto. The operating roster includes a former CP 4-4-0 and a 4-6-0 made famous by 1970s Ontario Rail Association excursions about southern Ontario.

CHOICES: Regular excursions from Tottenham to Beeton and back take about an hour. As the train rolls through Beeton Creek Valley, the conductor provides an informative commentary. The railway also operates fall foliage, Halloween, and Santa Claus specials. Passengers are carried in open-air, steel heavyweights dating from the halcyon days of Canada's railway industry.

WHEN TO GO: The railway operates multiple trips on Sundays as well as on holiday Mondays between Victoria Day weekend and Canadian Thanksgiving.

GOOD TO KNOW: The town of Tottenham has a variety of quaint shops and eateries. Across the road from the railway is Tottenham Conservation Park, which offers camping, fishing, and nature trails.

WORTH DOING: Take one rail trip and then follow one of the others for some great photos. The engine faces south into the sun and the relatively slow pace makes it easy to get from one location to another.

DON'T MISS: For a combination rail-water excursion, the RMS *Segwun*, one of the oldest operating steamships in North America, sails June through October on the Muskoka lakes, about a two-hour drive north to Gravenhurst.

GETTING THERE: No public transit is available to this neck of the woods. From Hwy. 400, take Hwy. 9 west nine miles to Tottenham Road and turn right. Continue into downtown Tottenham and turn left onto Mill Street.

PRINCE EDWARD ISLAND

Elmira

Elmira Railway Museum

Museum

The museum offers a look at railroading on the island in the early 1900s. It features re-created buildings representing the original wooden station house, platform, freight shed, and master's office. The station building contains two rooms of displays and artifacts. A miniature train operates around the museum, and a variety of special events take place on the outdoor stage, which was built from the base of a flatcar. The museum is open June through September.

ADDRESS: 457 Elmira Rd., Elmira, PE C0A 1K0
TELEPHONE: 902-357-7234
E-MAIL: elmira@gov.pe.ca
WEB SITE: www.elmirastation.com

QUEBEC

Gatineau *Train ride, Dinner train*

Hull-Chelsea-Wakefield Steam Train

Hop aboard this train and you'll climb the Gatineau Hills as the pioneers did 100 years ago. The 1907 steam locomotive takes you on a half-day excursion. Along the way, guides and musicians offer entertaining commentary. In Wakefield, you can watch the train turn on a manually operated turntable and explore the town. Other options include the Sunset Dinner Train and Sunday brunch trains.

ADDRESS: 165 Deveault St., Gatineau, QC J8Z 1S7
TELEPHONE: 800-871-7246 or 819-778-7246
E-MAIL: info@steamtrain.ca
WEB SITE: www.steamtrain.ca

Vallée-Jonction *Museum*

Railway Interpretation Center

Housed in a 1917 station, this museum (Centre d'interprétation ferroviaire de Vallée-Jonction) relates the history of the Quebec Central Railway. On display are a CN 4-6-4T steam locomotive, a caboose, a tank car and a boxcar. In August, the museum holds a railway festival.

ADDRESS: 397 Rousseau Blvd., Vallee-Jonction, QC G0S 3J0
TELEPHONE: 418-253-6449
E-MAIL: garevalleejonction@globetrotter.net
WEB SITE: www.garevalleejonction.ca

Canadian Railway Museum

ADDRESS: 110 St. Pierre St., St. Constant, QC J5A 1G7
TELEPHONE: 450-632-2410
E-MAIL: mfcd@exporail.org
WEB SITE: www.exporail.org

The largest collection of railway equipment in the country is well worth a stop for anyone interested in Canadian railways and rail transit. Locomotives, rolling stock, and streetcars from many parts of the country tell of the evolution of both industries from a uniquely Canadian perspective.

CHOICES: The museum's collection boasts 140 railway vehicles including unique locomotives and streetcars, such as the former CPR 4-6-4 2850 that pulled the 1939 Royal Train; MTC 350, the first electric streetcar in Montreal; former CNR 6711, which pulled the first conventional train through the Mount Royal tunnel in 1918 as well as the last in 1995; and former CPR 4744, the test-bed for the now-popular AC traction motor. A number of special events and exhibits scheduled throughout the year are geared toward the modeler, the transit enthusiast, or those with a love of railways. In addition, there are daily streetcar and miniature train rides.

WHEN TO GO: The Canadian Railway Museum is open daily between May and September. During September and October, it is open Wednesday through Sunday. The remainder of the year, the museum is open only on weekends and holidays.

GOOD TO KNOW: Wear good walking shoes and dress for the weather. The main building contains only a portion of the collection, and you can explore the rest of the site from stops along the streetcar loop and demonstration railway main line.

WORTH DOING: Experience a means of communication that predates the telephone by sending a telegram between two buildings.

DON'T MISS: A Sunday or holiday visit gives you the chance to ride the demonstration passenger train.

GETTING THERE: Montreal has extensive air, bus, and rail service. Amtrak's *Adirondack* connects the city with the rest of its network in Albany, N.Y. The museum is located 12 miles from downtown Montreal. CIT Roussillon provides bus service near the museum from the regional bus terminal across from VIA's Central Station downtown. AMT operates rush-hour commuter rail services between the Lucien L'Allier station and St. Constant, stopping adjacent to the property, and occasionally runs a *Museum Express* on select Sundays.

SASKATCHEWAN

Carlyle   *Museum*
Rusty Relics Museum

Rusty Relics Museum portrays pioneer life in Saskatchewan. Housed in Carlyle's 1910 CNR station, its collection features several buildings, machinery, and artifacts. Railway items include a caboose, a jigger, a tool shed, and a working telegraph. It is open Monday through Saturday June to September.

ADDRESS: 306 Railway Ave. W, Carlyle, SK S0C 0R0
TELEPHONE: 306-453-2266
WEB SITE: www.sesaskmuseumsnetwork.ca

Saskatoon   *Museum*
Saskatchewan Railway Museum

This seven-acre museum contains more than 10 buildings, including a station, express shed, interlocking tower, and tool sheds, from the Canadian National, Canadian Pacific, Canadian Northern, and Grand Trunk Railways. On display are a variety of freight cars, passenger coaches, streetcars, cabooses, and a CPR S-3 diesel locomotive. You can take a guided tour or explore the museum on your own. The museum also offers short motorcar rides.

ADDRESS: Hwy. 60, Saskatoon, SK S7K 3J6
TELEPHONE: 306-382-9855
E-MAIL: srha@saskrailmuseum.org
WEB SITE: www.saskrailmuseum.org

Index

D

E

S

T